The Flirt Interpreter
Flirting Signs from Around the World

Jean Smith

Lucidus Publishing
London

Published in Great Britain by Lucidus Publishing
A catalogue record for this book is available from the British Library.
Copyright@Jean Smith 2012.

Find out more about the author and any future books at www.flirtology.
co.uk
ISBN 978-0-9574288-0-5

To Nic, my favourite flirting partner

TABLE OF CONTENTS

FOREWORD

I've written a book about flirting – the art of it. I am, after all, uniquely qualified. As an anthropologist, I have been researching flirting, leading Flirting and Walking Tours™ all over the world, conducting interviews and seminars, and making scientific observations on the subject for over a decade.

Flirting is not a universal language. The well-worn chat up line, 'Nice shoes, but I bet they'd look better under my bed,' can either lead those shoes to that bed, or to a painful kick in the proverbial. It depends on who's wearing the shoes, and where they come from. A New Yorker may be willing to slip off her Manolo Blahnik heels; a Parisian may think you're pulling her leg while a Londoner might be inspired to do the Lambeth lurch toward one-night-stand land.

Much has been written about flirting by other authors, but such works usually take the form of 'how to' books that offer a 'one-size-fits all cultures' set of guidelines. The problem with this is that what will work in one country, won't necessarily work in the next. Thus, this book isn't merely a collection of universal 'Flirting for Dummies' tips. Granted, you will come across some tips in here, perhaps recognise some of them as your own, but this is not your sure-fire guide to 'gettin' some'. This is The Flirt Interpreter: Flirting Signs from Around the World.

This is a light-hearted anthropological study of flirting rituals across the different urban cultures of New York, Paris, London, and Stockholm. At first glance, this selection of cities may appear an odd one for a comparative cross-cultural study, when they are similar in so many ways. While these cities are becoming increasingly homogenous with the same global brands, bars and restaurants, a closer inspection reveals that their citizens vary greatly in how they perceive themselves and others, and how they interact with each other. While a comparison between Quebec and Singapore might sport more obvious cultural differences, a juxtaposition of superficially similar Western cities teases out complexities which are all the more remarkable for their subtlety. Each is a popular tourist destination, cultural hub and cosmopolitan capital whose permanent populations alone are a maze of culturally promiscuous flirters. New York, Paris and London are at the forefront of all that is related to the media, fashion trends and social life, and in Stockholm, women have the highest standard of living in the world.

In each city, I interviewed 50 single professionals, (25 male, 25 female) between the ages of 28 and 40. If they weren't native to the city, they had lived there for at least five years. Primary research took the form of an interview based on 35 questions regarding the interviewees' definitions, motivations, techniques and locations for flirting. I also included some more general questions on social interaction in the city in question as well as some questions relating to how the participant perceived their friends when flirting. I should add that the names of the interviewers have been changed to protect their identities. If you think you recognise a character in the book, you don't. Great lengths have been taken to protect identities. And, I can't thank them enough for their participation. Without them, there would be no book.

The book is intended to be a talking point, generous with its practical insights. Although I seek to probe further into the flirting phenomenon than any universal theory can do, I have necessarily categorised entire cities and cultures for the sake of simplification; I don't for a minute assume that all people in a city fit in with a city's majority. It is unlikely that all of the cultural traits I cite will accord with all of your experience of the cultures under discussion.

The book is intended as an entertaining rumination on the subject of flirtation, wherever the reader they may be. According to UN projections, by 2050, over 70% of the world will be urban dwellers. Not only do more of us live in cities than ever before, but more of us travel between them. And not only do we travel, but it has become fairly usual for individuals to live in more than one or two cities in their lifetime – hence, the decision to focus on urban environments. As we are more likely to interact with other cultures we need to appreciate that the meanings of winks and blinks differ from one culture to another. And yet, city dwellers are both physically close and socially distant. On the eve of this unstoppable urbanisation we deserve to be reminded of those simple things we once did, back in ye olde village—smiled, chatted, touched…

The Flirt Interpreter offers an insight into why people flirt the way they do, and how they flirt, paying special attention to the ways in which men and women approach this unisex sport. The book affords flirting its rightful place as an essential tool, to be employed in contexts more far-reaching than the local pub, as you're about to discover.

Chapter 1: What is Flirting?
A LITTLE WORD WITH A LOT OF BAGGAGE

Picture the scene…Boy makes eye contact with Girl across a crowded bar. He makes his move, buys her a drink and the ritual begins…

'So, what do you do?'

'I'm writing a book about flirting.'

And there you have it, one of the best pick-up lines in the book – a surefire way to get a conversation going, and a flirtatious one at that.

So, is flirting an activity, a behaviour, or a way of life? Most people can't quite put their finger on exactly what flirting is but many think that their lives would improve if only they were better at it. Flirting is an essential component of social and cultural behaviour, not merely a trick in need of polishing for Friday night.

According to the Oxford English Dictionary, the origins of the word 'flirt' date all the way back to 1583. The word was onomatopoeic – the sound of the word imitated its meaning. Thus, 'flirt' sounds like 'flick', 'flip' or 'throw' and this is what it initially meant: 'To propel or throw with a jerk or sudden movement.' While this meaning may seem obscure to us now, what is flirting but throwing yourself at someone? And when we initiate a flirtatious conversation, we employ pick-up lines. I throw myself at you so you might pick me up. The flirt is little more than a reincarnation of the salesman – or woman.

Flirting is a little word with a lot of baggage. For some it can mean just being friendly; others may regard flirting as sexual harassment. The end result could be a simple ego trip, a memorable or forgettable roll in the hay or the wedding march. The end goal of flirting defines how, when, and where the flirting happens. The desired outcome also dictates whether people flirt in packs or fly solo. When there's a goal in sight there's always the chance you'll miss it no matter how skilled you are. So, without the pressure of being expected to get the ball in the net, the game is just fun, isn't it? But even in a fun setting there's the underlying question of whether a flirt is a flirt or a friend, or a fake.

Flirting is not a universal language. What may work for one culture may not have the same effect elsewhere. While some aspects of flirting such as fluttering eyelashes, hair-twirling and head-tossing laughs may seem generic, there are many other facets of flirting that do not translate quite so directly. Even body language has its cultural variations. For example, touching a Londoner's knee will almost certainly get you off on the wrong foot while touching a New Yorker's knee might well get you a foot in the door. Opinions about what flirting is and what it is used for vary according to culture and gender. Playful', 'light-hearted', 'fun', 'game'…these are some of the words used by interviewees in New York, Paris, London and Stockholm to define flirting.

NEW YORK

New Yorkers find flirting a 'Playful, harmless, simple interaction.' 'Cute, light-hearted displays of interest' are part of 'having fun and being spontaneous.'

New York women say it best. They describe flirting as:

• 'A kind of interpersonal dance.'
• 'A way to engage someone through charm, guile, attractiveness and personality.'

Like their male counterparts, the women of New York also see flirting as an ego boost. 'I flirt if I see someone I am attracted to and as a way to build confidence,' Dana, a pretty brunette business analyst, said. Some women even admitted flirting for sex. Sarah, a smart and sassy fashion buyer, admitted, '…at my age, I flirt because I have more interest in men and sex.' Belying the frivolous descriptions, flirting is a serious business and the end goal, for many women, is a family and a house in the Hamptons. The men are looking for sex, if they can get it, but expect girls who want a wedding to hold out for at least three to five dates. The men also wanted to start relationships: Flirting '… could lead from hooking up to getting married,' said curly-haired Chris, a 30-year-old environmental engineer. However, there were divergent views on whether you could have an emotional and sexual connection with the same person, especially when it came to one-night stands. Take it from Doug the dentist, with the perfect teeth, who surmised that no 'functional' relationships could ever come out of a one-night stand.

PARIS

Flirting, in Paris, is a national sport. Martine is a logistics coordinator for an event company. Her black-rimmed glasses highlight her obvious intelligence. She said, 'The French learn poetry at school - poésie courtoise – 13th century flirting and philosophising is a French sport.' In Paris, as in New York and London, the most common definition of flirting was that it was 'a game' between two competitors. The men made it clear that flirting was not about physical rewards: 'It's when you try to seduce someone but not necessarily to have sex. It's trying to provoke a sexual desire, the game.'

Isabelle, clad in black and with a complexion like vanilla nougat, looks nothing like a librarian, despite her day job in a library. To her flirting is, '…the tension of expectation, the prey-hunter thing.' Both men and women provoke each other to see how the other will handle it and to catch them off guard. They might disagree with something they believe in, just to provoke. And, for Parisians, voila, this is flirting.

The men never miss an opening. Take 30-year-old Mathieu, for instance. An artistic director with chiselled jaw and a twinkle in his eye, he cheekily responded to a rhetorical question about deciphering when someone was flirting with you thus: 'If I had your number I would call you to let you know, but I don't.' Dancing is an integral part of the handbook. Men woo the ladies with their twinkle toes. Greg is a student in communication with a dapper taste in hats and a way with words. He went so far as to say, 'If I'm not dancing, then I don't have what it takes to impress a woman.'

When asked if they had any goals when flirting, most said things like a kiss, a phone number, or just the fun of the flirt. However, Alexandre, who works in business tourism, seemed to have swallowed an anthology of Victor Hugo quotes. He said, 'At the minimum to create a unique universe. When we see each other again, we know more than our public image.' The Parisian men were particularly lyrical about the aim of flirting. Guilliame, a bookseller, with a romantic disposition and beautiful eyelashes that just didn't seem fair, said, 'To create a universe for just the two of us... to create a world of desire. To keep her when she tries to escape.'

The Parisian men seemed not only to like women, but to like all women.

Eccentric Olivier, a lightly tanned, recently unemployed graphic designer declared, 'I fall in love with girls I see on the street every five minutes.' And then added, with a dreamy expression, ' ... I have always been distracted by women. It's a passion of mine.' Like golf, one assumes. Alexandre summed it up, 'Flirting,' he said, 'gives you one reason to exist on this earth.' Ergo, flirting is the meaning of life.

The concept of flirting as a game was mentioned less frequently by the women. For them, flirting was mostly about attracting, talking to, and paying attention to someone they liked. However, some women admitted testing their one's own attractiveness. Francine is 35, petite and works in publishing. She said, 'It's a game of seduction which plays with words, feelings and attitudes. It's a selfish game to see if one still has it.' Geraldine is a jewellery maker with style and earrings to match. 'Sometimes you just want to know more about your ability to attract. Flirting is playing a game. Seduction you don't need to talk. It's the way you hold a glass.'

The English word 'flirting', in French, is sortir avec quelqu'un' or 'to go out with some-one'. The Parisians' version of 'flirting' translates more accurately into 'seducing'. Seduc-ing in Paris is apparently as common as a stroll along the Seine.

Frederique, a 28-year-old sales manager in a large supermarket chain, explained, 'Real flirting means you want to learn more about the other person. Supermarket checkout flirt-ing is not real because of the short amount of time; you can't discover the other person. That might be called 'seduction'. Light seduction I do all the time, it's more for you than for the other person. A flirt is for both people.' To Parisians flirting is 'what happens after two people have kissed.'

Time plays an important role in determining if the relationship is a 'game of seduction' or something more. Shy Laurent, a 30-year-old architect explained, 'Flirting is to see some-one on many occasions and still not know if you will have a stronger relationship.' Never quite knowing where you stand seemed to be part of the fun. So, if flirting is seen as a game, then it's easy to be philosophical about a flirtation that doesn't go quite the way you wanted. 'That's the nature of the flirt,' said Lorraine, a 40-year-old Parisian author resident in London. 'Sometimes it works and sometimes it doesn't. Flirting is light, fun and pleas-ant. It's like champagne.' Martine, the logistics coordinator, summed up the characteristics of a good flirt in three evocative words, 'improvisation', 'inspiration', and 'intuition'.

LONDON
Like the New Yorkers, 'playful' is the word that Londoners use most often when describing flirting. Flirting is thought of as 'playful banter' and 'sending signals to communicate inter-

est'. James the optician is sweet, charming, and obviously sporting a killer pair of specs. He said 'Flirting is a nice way to put myself and the person I am speaking to at ease'. Max is a 39-year-old music publisher, with regulation rock-n-roll collar-length hair. He looked like he was familiar with a good whiskey. 'It's fun. It makes both people feel attractive,' he said. The chorus went on. 'It's not just a desire to sleep with someone. It's the company. It's nice to make people feel good,' said Samuel, a 38 year-old furniture maker, whose self-deprecating charm is clearly modelled on Hugh Grant. Adrian, a real estate agent in his thirties, with shiny shoes and a quick wit echoed this sentiment, 'Everyone likes to make someone feel good. Fundamentally, it's a sexual thing but you want her to think, "He's a nice guy."'

The American journalist and humorist Helen Rowland said, 'Flirting is the gentle art of making a man feel pleased with himself.' It seems these London ladies share her view. 32-year-old, genial Gemma is a television producer for a morning breakfast show. She said, 'Flirting makes me feel alive, happy, and attractive. I like making people feel the same. I like watching someone blossom'. The Londoners often mentioned flirting in relation to others, pointing out that flirting happened between two people. Jennifer is a down-to-earth business analyst, originally from Devon, with pale skin and light blue eyes. She said, 'It makes both you and the other person feel good'. London seemed to be full of Mary Poppins. The London ladies use flirting to fill the grey and drizzly city with sunshine. Rachel is long and lanky with blonde hair to match. She is a 29-year-old illustrator of children's books. She said 'Flirting makes it easier to get along with people.' Catherine has a strong, roman nose, a calm demeanour, and is in IT, but is far from what you'd call geeky. She described flirting as, '…fun and funny and it's nice if it's reciprocated. It makes you feel good.' Rachel agreed, 'It's healthy, I get a kick out of it; it makes you and the other person feel good.' Londoners use flirting as a social tool at work and play. Anoushka is a petite, 32-year-old solicitor, with gorgeous red curls that would distract any judge. Her take on flirting is that 'It helps social situations by lightening the mood and fun.' 'I flirt to get my own way or appreciation; it's a powerful tool. You can make friends more quickly,' said soft-spoken Anthony, who has wavy brown hair and is in IT. Liz is a 32-year-old account manager for an advertising agency. 'It's a good way of building relationships and getting things done. It's quite useful and good for meeting people.'

London men viewed flirting as a means to an end, often using phrases like 'could possibly lead to something more'. This could explain why the women tended to distinguish their brand of flirting – 'being nice and polite' – from 'having sexual intent.' Anoushka the solicitor explained the two types of flirting. 'There are two categories: being charming and flirting. Flirting is being sexual.'

Yet flirting with the aim of having sex was a much higher motivation for New York and Parisian men than for the Londoners. The London males seemed less inclined to want to 'seal the deal'. Charlie is a 30-year-old, floppy haired, entrepreneur with a cheeky smile. He said 'I prefer the anticipation of something that never happens.' Max, the music publisher, agreed 'It's enjoyable and an intellectual pastime in its own right.' London was the only city where the women admitted to being flirtier than the men! However, this isn't the kind of 'flirting' done in the dark corners of New York clubs. Instead, think Princess Diana. London females associate flirting with 'being charming'. In the case of some of the cities studied, women made a distinction between their style of flirting and the men's, most often by creating categories which removed sexual connotations. In New York, one of the most 'sexually charged cities' this was especially true, as the women said they were 'very friendly', while the London ladies created their own category of 'being charming'.

London women use flirting as a way to attract someone. The men, on the other hand, seemed more inclined to flirt with women to whom they were already attracted. In the opinion of Anna, a feisty, 36-year-old voiceover artist with tight brown curls, 'English men take flirting too seriously. They look at it more as a chore than a fun thing.' They're not comfortable with initiating contact. They save their best moves for when they are already in an interaction with a woman in whom they are interested. Some men used the phrase 'chatting up'. Samuel, the 38-year-old furniture maker, put it this way: 'There is a difference between flirting and chatting up. You would flirt at a dinner party and chat someone up at a nightclub. Flirting is easy and pleasant. Chatting up is putting on the moves.'

STOCKHOLM
In Stockholm, flirting does not require speech. It's all about the eyes, as Eva, a well-spoken, 33-year-old press officer explained, 'It starts with the looks; flirting is communication without words.' Eva was not the only Stockholmer who spoke about flirting in non-verbal terms. Anders, the sales rep with the blue eyes and blonde locks of a Viking god, pithily described flirting as '...somewhere between a handshake and a hug.' Henrik, a 34-year-old banker, with equally Nordic good looks, compared flirting to performing, 'It's an act, open the curtain and start to play a certain role, either fake or yourself.' Whichever approach he went with, let's hope he got a standing ovation! To the women of Stockholm, flirting is about 'making contact and getting it back'. It's how this contact is made that differentiates the Swedes from other cultures. Because it is socially acceptable for women to be assertive in flirting, it is no surprise if they initiate the contact with men. Reciprocation means it's officially flirting.

CONCLUSION
Parisians view flirting as 'natural'. To New York men and women, flirting is 'harmless' and simple fun, with serious intent. In London, there's flirting, which is light and pleasant and then there's chatting up. Flirtation, for those Londoners who admit to engaging in it, is a social grace. They flirt for fun, to make others feel good, and to smooth relations at work or play. What flirting is to the Yanks and Brits, is seduction to the French. Flirting

Paris-style involves testing one's powers of attraction, and finding out where one stands in the shaggability stakes. To the Swedes, 'Flirting is what is between first meeting someone and totally hitting on them'. But the last word on the subject belongs to Londoner Christopher, a 32-year-old ex-military man, who described flirting thus: 'It's like an arms race. Start small and with any luck it goes nuclear.'

FLIRT FILE

- Flirting is about starting conversations, about meeting people, about brightening up someone's day. We are social beings. We thrive on interaction – sometimes it's an exchange of opinions; sometimes of ideas; sometimes of smiles.
- However you define it, effective flirting techniques have a number of elements in common:
- An air of the unknown
- Communication that both people understand
- Communication that makes both participants feel special, understood, unique
- Both people acting as a mirror for the other, reflecting the image of one's best self.
- Focus on the other person and fine-tune your flirting style accordingly. You will be able to pick up important cues about them and develop rapport more quickly. You'll also be attuned to when your charm is having the desired effect. Are they becoming more comfortable? Holding your gaze longer? Touching your arm, perhaps?
- By not focusing on yourself, you won't feel self conscious, because your attention is on the other person – an important feat in any culture!
- Some people view flirting as a fun way to pass the time, others take it very seriously! Make sure you know how the other person in your interaction views flirting.

THE CITY THAT NEVER SLEEPS – ALONE.

'It is an ugly city, a dirty city. Its climate is a scandal. Its politics are used to frighten children. Its traffic is madness. Its competition is murderous. But there is one thing about it – once you have lived in New York and it has become your home, no other place is good enough.'

~ John Steinbeck

New Yorkers flirt the way New Yorkers do just about everything else: brusquely, boldly, brashly. Straight up, no nonsense, they flirt to get laid and admit it.

As Carrie Bradshaw from the popular TV programme Sex and the City said:

'New York City is all about sex. People getting it, people trying to get it, people who can't get it. No wonder the city never sleeps. It's too busy trying to get laid.'

While Sex and the City is not necessarily what the most rigorous of scholars might consider a valuable source of reference, the fictional sitcom was derived from the questions and conundrums that real New Yorkers face. The women interviewed continually made reference to the show, with some condemning and others praising it. A number of women related so strongly to the dilemmas faced by the four characters they almost 'inserted themselves' into the scenarios being played out.

Sex and the City simply had to be New York-based. Imagine, had the locale been London, by the second season we'd find the ladies still talking about the weather, while debating which goes in first, the milk or the teabag. Had the setting been Paris, the ladies would be chain-smoking in a dark, mirror-filled café philosophising over Sartre.
Does everyone, everywhere, flirt to get laid or is this a particular New York proclivity? Or are the New Yorkers simply more willing to admit it?

New York has long endured an association with erotic or sexual culture. As the critic Holden writes,

'Despite Mayor Giuliani's effort to sanitise New York's erotic culture, there more than ever, remains a sexual supermarket in which anything one can dream of is right out there in the media display case. Service is just a click of a button or a phone call away.' [1] .

Even though New York's inhabitants like to think of it as a sexual city, it is more complicated than that. On the surface, things between New York women and men may seem straightforward: She needs to be beautiful, he needs to be rich. One of them needs to propose sex, and the other to accept it. They go home together, get a standing ovation from the envious onlookers, and it's on with the show. But, at what point does she stop being 'beautiful' and start being a 'slut'? And at what point does he realise that he probably ain't

---

1   Holden, cited in RSATC.

that special after all?

The rigmarole of New York flirting, dating, and sex is entangled in countless cultural co-nundrums. Beneath the brash attitudes of the New Yorkers lie a hundred other traits as delicate as eggs. So it's a case of treading carefully.

WHAT IS A NEW YORKER?

New York compels you to ask questions to which there are no answers like: 'Why would someone need dry cleaning at three in the morning?' This is a city that embraces excess and eccentricities, unlike London, where everyone follows the same unwritten rules. In London, if someone acts outside of these strict boundaries, it means they are either a tourist or someone best avoided. Not in New York. People seem to be free to do their own thing. You can whistle a happy tune on the subway, start up a random conversation with the person next to you, and even yell at arboreal rodents. A hefty Caucasian man, wearing baggy shorts and a T-shirt that was once white, yells at a squirrel that he is going to cut out its eyes and eat it for dinner. The squirrel seems to be listening up to that point, and then has enough sense to scurry away. A homeless, middle-aged, African American woman, when asked for directions, embarks on a conversation about literalism, poetry, music and butterflies, while escorting you to your destination. A Wall Street banker, brags to his friend over double-whipped, low-fat, macchiatos how last night he 'banged a super-hot model'.

New Yorkers are a breed so famously eclectic and cosmopolitan, so seemingly miscellane-ous, that to define them is not an easy task. People have tried. The city's occupants have been characterised to infinity and beyond, by both themselves and others. New York is a nation in itself, complete with its very own cultural identity, making it all too easy to get caught up in the countless stereotypes associated with it.

Thomas Wolfe wrote, 'One belongs to New York instantly. One belongs to it as much in five minutes as in five years.' So, how to define a category to which it seems everyone can, or does, belong? What exactly is that Empire state of mind?

NATIVES AND MIGRANTS

Except for the indigenous Native Americans, the United States is a continent of immigra-tion and relocation. Each region of the States could be its own country, with different dialects, customs, traditions and, sometimes, even laws. The huge geographical landmass of the United States offers countless opportunities and choices for the average American. Where to live? Mountain? Sea? Desert? Often job availability governs the decisions peo-ple make and they end up starting new lives in cities they never thought they'd live in. American culture tends to be socially fluid, making it easy for newcomers to mesh into new groups and make friends.

While parts of England might have different accents, her people aren't nearly as diverse. It makes sense when you consider driving from the west coast to the east coast of England would take six hours and in the States, six days. It's going to take more energy, money, and motivation to make your way all the way to New York, then the average, one-hour trip to London. New Yorkers have to work hard to get there and, therefore, the city attracts motivated, go-getters.

Since 2006, New York City has ranked number one for seven consecutive years as the city most US residents would most like to live in or near. The reputation and allure of a city like New York make it highly desirable. People who've moved to New York rarely got there by chance. Many of the people who live there have put a lot of time, money, and energy into getting there. Some will have travelled thousands of miles, led only by their dreams and the promise of being able to crash on a friend's sofa. It's a very specific type of person who'll try their luck in the Big Apple. Joel is a successful entrepreneur, who left his Midwest life for the city ten years ago and has never looked back. He said, 'The definition of a New Yorker is a cosmopolitan city person. They could be from any country. As long as they have the right mindset, they are a New Yorker.'

For those migrants who have left their families and past behind and moved to New York alone, to pursue a dream or career, New York is not simply a city they happen to live in; it is the stage on which they have purposely put themselves. They aspire to 'making it'. They want to see their names in lights, whether that be on Broadway, Wall Street or in the by-lines of the New York Times. They are ambitious, competitive, intelligent, aggressive, and have, or will do, whatever it takes. For them, New York is not the backyard of their childhood dreams; it is the battleground of their grown-up ones.

The New Yorkers interviewed were single professionals between the ages of 27 and 40. Some were at least third-generation immigrants to New York while others had lived in New York for at least five years. The native New Yorkers tend to inhabit the boroughs of Brooklyn, the Bronx and Queens, while the migrants settle in Manhattan. For them, New York City is Manhattan, and they might be caught echoing the Sex in the City girls' dictum, 'I don't do Brooklyn.' The various religions associated with the boroughs or ethnicities means that there are predominant Catholic, Jewish or Orthodox mentalities that underlie the way native New Yorkers interact and flirt. Gina, a 33-year-old occupational therapist of Chinese descent, is from Brooklyn. She went so far as to point out a distinction between the Manhattanites and the rest by saying, 'Guys from Brooklyn and Queens want a steady relationship, whereas men in the city are commitment-phobes or prefer to play the field.'

The native New Yorkers interviewed were mostly of Eastern European, Irish, Italian, Asian and Hispanic descent. On the whole, they tended to be more traditional or conservative than the 'new' New Yorkers, perhaps because, unlike the migrants, they continue to maintain strong relationships with their families and upbringing, as they live in the same city. These interviewees often referred to their upbringing and how it shaped or formed their attitudes towards society and culture. Furthermore, they strongly depended on, or emphasised rigid distinctions in traditional gender roles. There are men; there are women, and there are things each should and shouldn't do. These strict codes became most obvious on questions regarding sex and promiscuity, for it was on these topics that they made a point of declaring, 'I'm not that kind of New Yorker.' The migrants were much more assertive in their careers and in their love lives. More noticeable too in New York than in any of the other cities studied, was the difference in the answers given by different generations. The 27- to 28-year-old women were much more assertive and willing to approach guys, than the 30-plus crowd.

Regardless of where they have come from and how long they have lived in New York, they all live in the same city, walk the same streets, sleep – or not – beneath the same infamously bright night sky. And more importantly, they all compete for their share of the American Dream.

COMPETITION

New Jersey's most famous son, Frank Sinatra sang, 'I want to wake up on the city that never sleeps, and find I'm king of the hill, top of the heap.' New York was the most fast-paced and money-obsessed city of those researched. In the commercial capital of America, it is the mix of consumerism and individualism, which makes New Yorkers so competitive. The ideology of winners and losers was an ingrained mantra with both the men and the women interviewed. Alesha is a striking broadcast journalist with the poise and confidence to take on Christiane Amanpour. She pointed out, 'We have more access to more things in New York. It makes it more competitive.'

New York women are as competitive as the men. 28-year-old Susan is from Ohio, one of the new 'migrants' to New York, in search of fame and fortune as a journalist. She under-stands the rules. 'We compete for everything, boys, friends, jobs; you're going to lose out if you don't go for it. It's so heavily populated you either win or you lose.'

Auburn-haired Rebecca is 35 and works is in recruitment. She admitted, 'Some women are socialised to want the trappings of success. They first compete as singles, then it's competi-tive parenting. The urge to compete makes women want the nicest house. They play the roles. Then there is the 'perfect couple role', then 'super mom'.'

They even compete with themselves! New Yorkers, it seems, are always setting themselves personal tests. Both men and women seem to regard approaching people as a personal test. 'I like to challenge myself to approach people', said Jason, a high school science teacher, who is so full of fun, that he is bound to be popular with his students. 'Sometimes it's to challenge myself and make myself talk to people' Walking up to someone is something New Yorkers dare themselves to do. If they do it, then they pass – the outcome less relevant than honouring their inner voice.

PERSONAL SPACE

Trying to find your own peaceful park bench in New York City, where you can just be alone with your thoughts, your caramel, non-fat, double-whip macchiato, and your Vogue magazine, is not easy, and it's not because there's a shortage of benches. In half-empty cafes, people seem to want to sit at the table right next to yours. You could be forgiven for thinking a New Yorker is sitting next to you because he or she wants to chat you up. While it wouldn't seem unreasonable, it's not necessarily the case. These sociable New Yorkers just don't seem to understand the concept of giving someone some space. Their attitude is 'Why would you want to sit by yourself on the other side of the room?'

EXTROVERTS

New Yorkers are extroverts. Extroverts get their energy from other people, which might explain why New Yorkers always seem to want to be where the action is. Granted, most people don't move to a city of 8 million so they can stay holed up in their room reading. New Yorkers are 'quicker, talk faster, move faster, have more energy, and aren't laid- back,' said Justin, a literary agent originally from Santa Barbara , who therefore, knows about laid-back. This is not a city where people stop and smell the roses. Andrew is a 34-year-old attorney with hair to match his slick manner and perfectly pressed suit. He explained, 'You have to be quick in New York. You have to keep talking and fill in the conversation.'

Being social, friendly, and a good conversationalist is very important for New Yorkers. Ironically, if women don't feel like speaking with particular men, the men's responses are 'You're such a New Yorker'.

Because of the ease in which New Yorkers mix and mingle with strangers, you have to hold your own immediately. It's so important for men and women to be talkative, sociable and extroverted, that the very fact that you are out, and not at home, means you are fair game.

BODY LANGUAGE

And there's no chance of getting mixed signals. There was a clear correlation between how extroverted a culture was and how well those within it were able interpret each other's actions. New Yorkers' direct approach means that you don't have to read between the lines. Both men and women cited physical contact as one of their main flirting indicators. 'She'll use physical contact; she puts her hand on top of yours and leaves it there,' said Chris, a 30-year-old environmental engineer with a mop of curly brown hair.

'He'll be touching me if he's really interested,' said Marie, a sassy 28-year-old sales assistant whose tell-it-like-it-is approach got her fired. Another migrant, she is originally from the West Coast.

It's usually up to the woman to break the 'touch barrier'. As Bjorn, a 31-year-old doctoral student from Stockholm said, 'I wouldn't touch her first. Girls would be most likely to start that.'

New York males were the only group researched that showed their interest by touching. More importantly, they were the only group of males that initiated touch first.

NEXT BEST THING

New York City is all about the new, about the next best thing, about Tomorrow! Which, as the famous theme song from the musical Annie tells us, is only a day away. New Yorkers are confident that tomorrow will always bring something better, or at least, something new.

In this trendsetting fashion capital, it isn't even a question of the latest trend, for the latest trend has always already happened; it's about the next one. Pink is the new black, Jay-Z is the new Sinatra, and something is, or always will be, the new something else. Sarah is a smart and sassy fashion buyer, who oozes style with her short, trendy haircut. 'In New York, it's all about the next best thing, how much better can I do? Is he the best that I can possibly do? Is he in my league? There are only winners and losers.'

'The next best thing' were four words that came up time and again. Both the men and the women of New York are constantly asking themselves, 'Can I do better than this?' Knowing that they can indeed do better, they are actively looking for 'better' to come along.

FLIRTING PACE

New York is a city of short attention spans, and you've got to be quick, for in a New York minute... everything can change. When it comes to flirting, New Yorkers move faster than a cabbie who has just been offered an extra $20 to get you there in ten. With their preoccupation with not wasting time, the city should be called Now York.

Doug, a 34-year-old dentist whose pearly whites admirably advertise his services, said, 'Here today, gone tomorrow is the mentality. Because you will never see the person again, it's much easier to be bold than smaller cities.'

Alexis, a willowy, sharp-witted research assistant, who could have easily passed for a J Crew model, described the typical New York man's approach. 'Guys here ask for your name, and without wasting any time, follow that up with, "Are you married?" I like this though, because I don't like to waste time either.'

Mike, a tall, handsome banker with expensive taste in watches, chose to circumvent the name and marital status altogether and said he liked a woman to cut to the chase. 'Grab me, take me into the closet and say "Seven minutes in heaven, baby!" Be clear, be direct, don't play games.' In fast-moving, quick-thinking, walk-don't-walk New York, even seven minutes might be too long, but hey, we're not counting.

Because of the New York obsession with the new and the next best thing, time is money in the city that never sleeps. The saying, 'You snooze, you lose' carries more weight here than it does anywhere else. Joel, the entrepreneur from the mid-West, described the popular approach. 'You see if she's interested, if not, you move on.' To the next best thing, of course – or to the next best friend. Joel admitted, 'I'll see if her friend is interested.' So, it's full speed ahead! Corey is a part-time actor and fire-fighter whose good looks and sculpted body serve him well in both his jobs. 'As a male you pursue without thinking. There's no time for that. Move now, think later.' New York women have a similar peremptory approach. Such directness offended Charlotte's ladylike sensibilities. A soft-spoken, 32-year-old Parisian editor, she shared her experiences of being in New York. 'Americans are maladroit – badly skilled. I was at a party in New York with a friend and she looked around and said, 'Yes, No, Yes, No." I couldn't believe it! I was the hit of the party because I didn't judge the men like that, I talked to everyone.' To the outsider, these approaches may come off as rushed or rude, but to New Yorkers they're merely efficient.

WANDERING EYES

You don't need wait until tomorrow, for something better could walk by in a minute. So not only do New Yorkers flirt, but they flirt a lot, often with more than one person in a single room or evening.

New York men have wandering eyes. The women know it and accept that at any moment, the men could leave them to go and talk to someone more beautiful. Andrea, an earnest 30-year-old who works for a charity, said with resignation, 'I get the point. I am not one of those girls who is blind-sided. Maybe he was looking around for someone prettier.' The men were conscious that the women were aware of their roving eyes. But whether the women like it or not, the men do it anyway, or at least Chris's friends do. The environmental engineer, admitted, 'My scumball friends say hi to every girl who walks by.'

FEELING SPECIAL

Because it's common to flirt with many in one night, there's a risk that flirting could lose its impact. Not surprisingly, both genders mentioned that the other liked to be made to feel special. Stacey is a 28-year-old make-up artist of Puerto Rican descent. 'Guys like having women soup them up (with compliments) and pay attention to them.' Of course, the value of that flattery is dependent on how beautiful the woman who bestows it is. The more beautiful the woman, the more flattering the flattery. As Joel, the internet-start up entrepreneur said, 'To be seen talking with a gorgeous girl, is automatic cred.' The women often expressed a desire to know that a man was flirting just with them and not everyone. Despite their willingness to so readily dispose of a woman in pursuit of Miss Better, it became clear that the men, as much as the women, liked to be singled out, and made to look good in front of their friends.

CONCLUSION

Nothing is as easy as it seems here. In fact, nothing is as it seems. Much is illusion, and the emphasis is on image. The socio-economic, political and cultural attitudes that govern New York go some way to explaining why New Yorkers flirt the way they do. Time, money, power, beauty, image and competition – all of these play their respective parts in the realm of flirting. Armed with this knowledge, should you find yourself in the city that never sleeps, you'll know exactly what to do to ensure that you won't be sleeping alone. Better still, you won't be sleeping at all.

FLIRT FILE

To help make your way in New York, follow these guidelines:

When in New York ... DO:
- Ask for what you want. If you still don't get it, ask again, and if it's still a no, then move on and ask the next person.
- Wait three to six dates to 'give it up' if you really like someone. Feel free to have lots of sex with others' to take the edge off in the meantime.
- Feel free to engage in eye foreplay. I mean, stare up ... down ... and up again.
- Flirt with as many people as you like in one night. Why settle for only one when something better might come along?
- Flirt shamelessly with anyone who will buy you a drink, get you into a club or do you any sort of favour.
- Brush up on Body Language 101. New Yorkers know the handbook by heart.
- Expect to mix n' mingle. If you want to be alone, then you should stay at home!
- Touch, touch and touch. This city flirts with its fingers...
- Expect flirtatious encounters at all places or times. Your dentist's office, a church, a funeral ...

When in New York ... DON'T:
- Beat around the bush. Straight talking and upfront is the favoured style.
- Waste. Any. Time.
- Try to be subtle. Subtlety is inefficient.
- Feel affronted if approaching you also doubled as a 'personal test' for him.
- Be surprised if she's a bit guarded at first. Being inundated with male attention isn't a walk in Central Park you know.
- Be surprised if someone has just been rejected by your friend and is now trying their luck with you.
- Ever suggest going halves on the bill, unless you're doing so as a clever ploy to never have to see her again.

HAVE YOUR CAKE AND EAT IT TOO

Unlike Paris, where the traditional male/female roles are still firmly in place, New Yorkers seem, on the surface, to enjoy gender equality. After all, just as the Big Apple attracts the most ambitious, confident, assertive, persistent males, it attracts the same kind of females. Why New York hasn't moved in the direction of Stockholm, which seems to have achieved the closest thing we have seen to equality, is that traditional gender roles are still deeply ingrained in the culture. And, at the heart of these roles are the ideas of 'free sex' and marriage.

At face value, New Yorkers – the women in particular – seem to flout traditional gender roles. The New York men and women interviewed shared many similarities: Both genders had the same turn-offs; were competitive, dealt similarly with rejection, and sex with no strings attached is not the exclusive preserve of the men folk. Attractive, no-nonsense Lisa, works for a large credit card company. She explained, 'New York women are doing what the guys do. There is always a carrot dangling in front of them'. They are driven to achieve, believing that there is always something – or someone – better out there. New Yorkers, both male and female, believe in being direct and going after what you want. While New York women prefer the men to make the moves, they will step in if need be. New York men, for their part, seem quite happy to welcome women to 'the boys' club'. Alexis, the research assistant who should be a J Crew model, said of one-night stands, 'It's more acceptable for men, but in general I don't think it's looked down up on that much. It's a driven culture that stresses for both sexes to go for what you want.'

Women, too, have a great deal of financial power. And woe betide you, if as a man, you don't make as much money. Alesha, the broadcast journalist, summed up the prevalent attitude of New York women towards under-earning men: 'It's common for women to make more than their husbands and therefore we have the 'eunuchs'.' Yet, upon closer inspection, New Yorkers' deepest desires are stereotypically conventional. For women, it's to be beautiful and for men it's to be rich.

The Survivor mantra of 'Outwit, Outplay, Outlast' could well be New York's motto. New Yorkers thrive on challenge. The most satisfying achievement is that which is the hardest won. In this city of cut-throat ambition, people here want to be the best. Being rich and beautiful are the outward signs of that success. Mike the banker explained, 'Everything here stems from greed. It's the business capital of the world. Being rich and having a beautiful woman on your arm means success.'

MONEY
Money is integral to the New York flirting scene. 'New Yorkers flirt by buying drinks, showing money, or mentioning money,' said Chris, the 30-year-old environmental engineer. Money dictates where you go and the kind of people with whom you flirt. Susan, the 28-year-old journalist, said, 'Where you go is self-selecting. You don't go out wherever you want. If you are a rich guy, you go where all the beautiful girls are. Most men with

money want the model-type girls.' Rebecca, the recruitment consultant, agreed, 'In New York, it's about flaunting money, old wealthy men and younger beautiful women'. In New York City, the young and beautiful have the best shot at snagging a wealthy man to set them up financially. Conversely, older men with money have the best odds for 'bagging' a pretty young thing.

If a man is deemed successful by how attractive the woman is at his side, for New York women, success is measured by the size of their man's bank balance, and her engagement ring. One woman said, bluntly, 'I'm looking for a guy who earns over $200,000 a year.' Others said they simply wanted to be with men who earned more than they did. This is, in itself, a challenge. According to research based on US Census data, single women in their twenties in New York City earn, on average, 17% more than their male counterparts. It wasn't just the women of New York who felt that men should have more money than them. Corey, the firefighter who wants to be an actor, said, 'All the women care about is money and cars so that's all the men think they have to work on to impress.' 'Men like to have the upper hand of supporting the women,' agreed Doug the dentist, 'My guy friends try and make a lot of money so they can support the girl. They say, "How am I going to get a girl if I don't make any money?"'

However, not all men can achieve wealth, especially by New York standards. Who cares if you're a millionaire when you're surrounded by billionaires? So sometimes they have to fake it. As Jason, the high-school science teacher, said in summing up a typical New Yorker, 'Superficial, emptiness with expensive clothes, people here care a lot about image.'

People even talk about flirting in financial terms. The words 'seal the deal', 'worth', 'value', and 'assets' kept popping up in interviews like the dollar signs in a cartoon character's eyes. It shouldn't come as a surprise that money is such a focal point in New York. Manhattan has, for many a year, been home to some of America's wealthiest citizens. Ultra-high net worth individuals have assets of at least US$30 million. America is home to 57, 860 such millionaires. Of these, 13% live in New York, including Mayor Michael Bloomberg and Donald Trump. The sad truth remains that while rich men there are a-plenty, demand outstrips supply.

'Why no great, unmarried men?' Carrie Bradshaw poses this question in the first episode of Sex and the City. 'There are thousands, maybe tens of thousands of women like this in the city. We all know them, and we all agree they're great. They travel. They pay taxes. They'll spend four hundred dollars on a pair of Manolo Blahnik strappy sandals. And they're alone. It's like the riddle of the sphinx: why are there so many great, unmarried women, and no great, unmarried men?' Almost all of the women interviewed echoed this question. While there are, in fact, almost 10% more women than men in the Big Apple there are other reasons, apparently.

New York women are the victims of their own success. As their degrees and income multiply, they believe their choice of men gets smaller. There aren't necessarily less men, just not enough men to fit the narrow criteria of the successful New York women. Dana, the 38-year-old business analyst, said, 'There's a lot of pressure on the men as the women have high expectations. They have evolved faster than the men.'

If you want to be big in The Big Apple, it helps to be sleeping with the model fro₁m that billboard in Times Square. But if a 'regular' man can achieve this while a 'regular' woman can't, what is it that the men have that the women don't? Skewed population numbers are made worse by the New York females' strict financial criteria. Sarah, the sassy fashion buyer, bemoaned the fact that, 'In New York there are groups of women not meeting men. There are so many beautiful women that regular women are finding it hard to meet a regular guy… A 'regular' guy can get a beautiful woman, but a 'regular' woman can't get a great guy.' Perhaps it is the ability to make a woman his wife, something these fundamentally conservative women seem to all be searching for.

NEW YORK WOMEN

New York females are a conundrum. On the one hand, they are confident, successful bread-winners in their own right; on the other, they still follow deeply ingrained patriarchal roles.

The stereotypical New York woman is a successful career woman. She is an executive, or works in the financial industry. She puts in the long hours and wants the promotion. She can afford her Prada bags and expensive cocktails. The men interviewed shared this view, seeing New York women as 'ambitious, hard-working, financially stable and independent.' Andrew, the 34-year-old attorney, gave a historical perspective, 'Back in the day the man was the main breadwinner. Now women can earn their own money and be independent. In the office, the bosses are now 50/50 male-female.' Superficially, New York women have taken on social roles that were traditionally reserved only for men. In response to the question 'How can you tell when a woman is flirting with you?' one man responded by saying, 'They ask for your number, or buy you a drink'. New York women approach men. They ask men out. Take Lisa, the credit card executive, 'In New York, I'm used to the power structure. I can relate to the men and their attitudes. I look for the alpha male. I know where to go and what to look for. I know the game and what it's about.' Nonetheless, they expect the men to lead from the front in the flirting game.

During daylight hours, the women are happy to compete with men for financial reward. When night falls, they prefer to pretend that they don't. Even though the New York women interviewed can usually afford to buy their own drinks, they thought it was the man's responsibility – nay, duty – to foot the bill. Their reasons ranged from: 'He makes more money', to 'It's a compliment,' to good ol' fashioned chivalry. As Stacey, the Puerto Rican make-up artist, said, 'Guys have more money, power and stature. If they want to keep that they should earn it by paying for everything. It's chivalry.' Thus, a pick-up line guaranteed to work on New York women is, 'Hey what's up, do you need a drink? Let me take care of you.' This sentence encompasses three values that are very important to New York women: sociability, show of resources, and willingness to share those resources.

---

2. She works hard for the money …and pays for the date.' by Carrie Seim, New York Post, 23 Feb 2011; http://www.nypost.com/p/entertainment/date_works_hard_for_the_money_and_rW7bKzX 7mR5zMDvNRk8fOJ#ixzz1x6UtAy3Q

3 'Where the "one percent" live', CNBC
http://www.cnbc.com/id/46369591/Where_the_One_Percent_Live?slide=1

Lisa, the credit card executive explained, 'It's a treat when someone pays f$_2$or you, regardless of how much money you make.' A man who doesn't think twice about buying a woman, who is a complete stranger, a $20 martini and, of course, one for her friend as well, obviously has more money (and hence more sex appeal) than a man who only stumps up for a $4 beer. Marie from the West Coast, whose temporary loss of earning potential, may explain her perspective, said, 'Guys make more money so they should pay. It's a compliment'. Sarah, the fashion buyer, agreed, 'Guys should buy more drinks. I expect the guy to buy drinks, if he doesn't then I don't want to talk to him. It's a compliment if the guy buys and besides they make more money so they should give more'. However, As Miranda told Carrie, 'Once you start letting a man pay, he has power over you.' It was Alesha, the broadcast journalist, who recognised the paradox: 'To be asked out on the date is to be hosted on the date. New York women have a funny schism between her power and money yet undying need for a man.'

BALANCE OF POWER
When it comes to gender dynamics in New York, who has more power? Most men said that the women did. 'Women have more power because she can get sex anytime she wants,' said Mike, the handsome banker.

Corey, the actor/fire-fighter, agreed, however, with a caveat, 'Overall women, but it depends on how attractive they are'. The men saw the women, particularly the good-looking ones, as being spoilt for choice. Justin is a tall, well-read, 38-year-old literary agent with dimples to make Brad Pitt jealous. He said, 'A good-looking girl in the city can be approached so many times in an evening'. Joel, the entrepreneur, said, 'Good-looking girls get drinks bought for them all the time. It's typical to see old wealthy men and younger beautiful women'. The men seemed to realise this 'power' was only for short-term advantages. The men also knew that the women didn't like passive men. Russell, a 28-year-old graphic designer who looked like he was 12, said, 'Women don't have time for weaklings like me. New York women are strong and confident and much more likely to initiate. Compared to Japan, New York girls are upfront and not afraid to be strong'.

The men thought New York women were formidable. David, a cool and affable, 28-year-old architect, with an air of confidence said, 'Women rule the world. Women are hunters'. Chris, the 30-year-old environmental engineer, summed it up, 'Men think they have control, but if it's going to be a good flirt, it has to be the woman'.
Some women agreed it was they who had the power because they could accept or reject those who approached them. Gina, a 33-year-old occupational therapist of Chinese descent, answered the power question by saying, 'Women – they can be choosy, they have the power to say "No" or "Yes".' Dana, the pretty brunette analyst said, 'Women – if you flirt with a guy, there is a .001% chance that he will reject you'. However, it depends on what the goal is. If it's sex, women definitely are in control. Alexis, the research assistant, spelled it out, 'A woman in New York can get sex anytime she wants.' But they also recognised this depended on if they were 'good-looking' or not. Andrea, who works for a charity, said, 'Overall women, but it depends on how attractive they are.'

In contrast, a few of the men thought they had the upper hand.

---

4 According to the US Census Bureau, there are 77 227 more females than males in New York; in percentage terms, that means there are 9,61% more females than males.

Bryan, 34, a tall, lanky aspiring musician, said, 'Women are more hard up because there are less men than women'. This was most likely the case if an older woman was trying to find a partner. As Rebecca in recruitment said 'Men after a certain age have more power as there are more available women and women lower their standards.' Lisa, the high-powered credit card exec agreed that as they get older, men in their 30s and 40s have more pulling power. Dana, the pretty business analyst, told this story. 'I was once in a gallery and was introduced to someone by a friend. He looked me up and down and said "Nah" and walked away. And I was looking cute that night!'

This anecdote tells us three things:
1. New Yorkers are direct and don't waste any time.
2. The older a woman gets, the less power she has because her power rests in her looks and beauty.
3. Men, most notably wealthy ones, have the power and the choice, if the woman is looking for a partner.

So, when you are not looking for a husband, and prefer being single, you have the power. When you are looking for a husband, and the men know it, they have the power. In either case, the 'power' depends on your point of reference. Both men and women agree that in a short-term relationship such as one-night stands, then it's the woman who calls the shots. But, if 'power' is finding a good mate, than it's the men who have the advantage.

GENDER ROLES
Several women expressed the view that these traditional roles were immutable. Even though they intellectually understood the dichotomy, they didn't seem to want change. Susan, the journalist, knew the background but was still confused, 'New York culture is so career-focused. You have the Bill Clinton syndrome. Any dorky guy who is rich and powerful can get the girl he wants because girls want someone to take care of them. Women fought so hard for the feminist movement and our generation takes it for granted. We are still wired for the traditional male/female roles. I know I am confused about it.'

Diana, 30-year-old events planner, with short, bleached blonde hair, blamed feminism. 'Deep down, gender roles are ingrained. I have a friend who just wants a degree so she can hang it on her wall. Women's lib has messed us up. We are forced to do too much and to do it perfectly.' It was a common observation that being independent and trying to 'keep up with the guys' was 'exhausting'. And perhaps, herein lies the reason that women seek a provider. Even Lisa, who 'knows the game and what it's about' admitted, 'It takes a lot to make it here, so survival of the fittest prevails. But that can be quite exhausting so it's nice to take a back seat sometimes. New York women like to be independent. Sometimes it's nice to let the man take care of you.'

Like the women, New York men are also struggling to come to terms with changing gender roles. And the women know it. Stacey, the make-up artist, sympathised, 'Men are confused about female power like who pays'. The men weren't quite sure of the line between manly and sensitive, as Russell, the graphic designer said, 'You don't want to be considered weak or a meathead. I still want to feel I am hard because I live in New York, but also sensitive, because being in touch with feelings is a good way to connect with women.'

The American author,   Joan Didion, wrote, 'The secret point of money and power in America is neither the things that money can buy nor power for power's sake… but absolute personal freedom, mobility, and privacy.' While their spending power affords many New York women freedom, they often choose to exercise that freedom by allowing themselves to be bought. 'Have your cake and eat it' was an expression often used by both the women and the men. Mike, the banker, admitted, 'If I knew I could be independent and still have people chase after me, I would do it too.' But regardless of who made more money, most women expressed a wish for the man to pay, or, as they put it, to be 'taken care of.' Rebecca spoke for the maidenly masses, saying, 'We don't want to be independent. There is a deep need to be taken care of.' But 'being taken care of' had nothing to do with TLC or chicken soup. In the New York flirting context 'take care of' is a euphemism for 'pick up the tab.' The women work hard to present themselves as attractive, interesting and charming in the hopes that they'll hit the jackpot. Thus do New York women translate emotions into economics.

The constant refrain of 'Get him to pay for drinks and dinner,' was joined by a chorus of:
- get him to approach
- get him to chase
- get him to make the first move
- get him to ask for my number.

It would seem that the way to 'get him' is to get him to do it all. While such tactics may seem passive, beneath the surface you'll find a laborious and meticulous construction of subtle manipulations and invitations, ones that will put him in the role of 'aggressor.'

Andrea, who works for a charity, said, 'Men will come up to groups of girls,' She continued, 'They like being the pursuer and should be the pursuer.' In the view of Gina, the Chinese occupational therapist, 'The most successful interaction is when the man closes the deal by doing something.' Rebecca, who works in recruitment, was of the same opinion, 'I expect him to seal the deal. I am used to it and it makes things more clear. There is nothing to figure out. It's black and white.'

The men wholeheartedly concur with this approach. Andrew, the 34-year-old attorney, said, 'Guys like to be the aggressor and don't want to be perceived in the feminine role.' Although some don't mind a little nudge. Jason, the science teacher, admitted, 'But it's hard for guys to make that first step, so anything the woman can do to help is great.' The women played along. They admitted to resorting to the textbook tactics of the femme fatale, 'I'll lower my eyes, twirl my hair, giggle, and act coy and feminine.' Defending this traditional approach, Alesha, the broadcast journalist, pointed out, 'Everyone is flattered by sexual attention, coyness, demureness.' 'However,' she said, in the same breath, 'I think someone is bullshit if they can't hold eye contact'. And there you have the conflicting personas of New York women – assertive, confident, but not shy to employ their womanly wiles. In New York, appearances are everything. So while it has to seem like it's the man who has the power; the man who's making the moves; the man who's getting the woman, truth be told, it's the woman who has made it all happen. It is the woman who has 'got' the guy; got him by the billfold and by the balls.

MARRIAGE

In this city where women seem liberated on the glossy surface, they are still holding on tightly to traditional and patriarchal ideals. These are, unknowingly, holding them back. Diana, the events planner, points out how closely held these ideals of the patriarchal family are when she says, 'It's very strongly embedded in the culture. I am 30 and three people in one night asked me why I didn't have a kid; my mom, the cab driver and a guy at a party'. So, while on the surface, the women adopt similar attitudes and behaviour to the men, deep down, they still expect to be rescued by Prince Charming. Drawing on the language of fairytale, Gina, the 33-year-old occupational therapist, expressed it thus, 'The New York lifestyle forces you to be strong and independent but all women are really looking for is a knight in shining armour. New York women were all too eager, it seemed, to give up their financial independence. Gina continued, 'Many women work on their career in their 20s and when they hit 30, they want to find a man to put them up in a house in Connecticut. Some women say, "I don't really want a promotion, I'm just waiting for a guy to put me up".'

If it's all about how things seem in New York – then even that name is just a façade. New York women may seem liberated, and they seem modern, but at their core, they want the announcement on page 6 of the New York Times followed by a by-the-book wedding. And after the wedding there's the china and cappuccino makers, the monogrammed towels and eight-slice chrome toasters. And from there, once the inevitable (or obligatory) offspring have been produced, it goes from cribs to strollers to tuition bills with alacrity. Sarah, the fashion buyer, summed up the New York woman's American Dream, 'New York women have an ideal of what a perfect guy should be. Investment banker, down-to-earth, American, handsome, house in the Hamptons, never cheat on you, adores you. It's all about the gloss on the outside, but not about what's underneath. The fact that you are in an unhappy, loveless marriage and your husband is gay, isn't as important.'

But before you write off the women of New York as gold-digging, husband-hunting hussies, consider what Alexis, the research assistant, said, 'If I am going to stay home and raise the children, I need the security of knowing someone can support me. Family is very important to us. We want it all.' Thus, it should come as no surprise that, although some of the men did raise the subject, it was mostly the women who had weddings in mind.

ONE NIGHT STANDS
While many New York females (and some males) paid lip service to the belief that a woman can have sex with whomever she wants, because many of the women are looking for Mr Right and a house in the Hamptons, they can't risk casual sex. They are aware that New York men have different criteria for one-night-stands and the long walk down the aisle. Over half of the men interviewed say they wouldn't think of a woman they had a one-night-stand with as marriage material. Similarly, many women said that if they liked a guy, they wouldn't have sex with him straight away. It's safe to say that generally, New York women are looking for husbands. This means that they have less space to behave as they would like as they are forced to play the game by male rules. However, many women now have access to things which used to be incentives for marriage, such as financial and sexual freedom, and even sperm banks. As the playing field levels, it will be interesting to see how this gender dynamic plays out.

CONCLUSION
While traditional gender roles seemed to have been turned on their heads in New York, at

least on the surface, both men and women still cling to tradition. In New York, he is supposed to approach. She is supposed to bat her eyelids like crazy to get him there. He is supposed to ask for her number. She is supposed to make it as easy as possible for him to ask.
He is supposed to initiate the kiss, and she will part her lips suggestively. He is supposed
to pay for the date, and she will make a 'fake grab' to pretend that she is willing to pay
as well. However, if he fails to do any of these things, at any stage, she will do it for him,
although admittedly they would prefer him to do it. But if he doesn't 'step up', she will!
As a group, New York women fall somewhere in between their liberated, do-it-ourselves
Stockholm sisters and the decorous Parisian mademoiselles. New York women are strong,
assertive and often financially independent. Anything guys can do, they can do better, but
they still hanker after traditional gender roles. In this city where women seem liberated
on the glossy surface, they are still holding on tightly to traditional and patriarchal ideals.
These are, unknowingly, holding them back.

When gender roles become less restrictive, confusion is bound to arise. However, as the
New Yorkers negotiate the new terms and conditions, it seems a small price to pay. The end
result for both sexes is more freedom to be who they really are and perhaps find a partner
that best suits them, a happy state of affairs that can only bode well for a happier society.

SO THIS IS PARIS

'Paris, a city of gaieties and pleasures, where four-fifths of the inhabitants die of grief.'
~ Nicolas Chamfort

The City of Love. Its flirting habits were bound to be as pleasing as uncorking a bottle of vin de maison. However, Paris, with its diverse cultural layers, proved as nuanced as a vintage Veuve Clicquot!

Paris is synonymous with romance; dreamy views over the Seine enhanced by champagne mousse and soft jazz played by a trio of Maurice Chevalier look-alikes; Robert Doisneau's 1950 photograph of lovers kissing, oblivious to the busy Parisian street; Charles Boyer whispering declarations of love to Greta Garbo, Marlene Dietrich and Ingrid Bergman in Hollywood romances of the 1930s. The French actor once confessed, 'That love at first sight should happen to me was life's most delicious revenge on a self-opinionated fool.' Boyer was married to his wife for 44 years and committed suicide two days after she died. So, if romance equals love, and love equals long-lasting fulfilment, then surely this must be the most fulfilled city in the world, right? Wrong!

Parisians, both men and women, seem to feel that it's as natural to flirt as it is to draw breath. When asked about their flirting habits, a common response was, 'I have no techniques, it's just natural.' Looking and acting natural are all important. And yet the mating dance is intricately choreographed. In Paris, the men are men, and the women are women and, if they want to get lucky, they'll play their respective parts. The Parisians are conflicted in the face of this cultural pressure.

THE BIG BAD CITY
In both the United States and England the capital cities aren't perceived as greatly different from other areas. They are seen as representative of their respective nations, whereas Paris is viewed by the French as very much its own beast. And not everyone judges it favourably. Parisian practices are not necessarily the same as in the rest of France. The French people interviewed, even Parisians themselves, seemed to regard people living in Paris as colder, less friendly, and untrustworthy. Although people were quick to point out that other parts of France still had a joie de vivre, Paris was repeatedly described as a 'stressful' place to look for love. 'It's very intense,' said Sandrine, a 30-year-old IT director's assistant with a sleek brown bob that matched her trim figure. Laurent is also 30. A shy architect, with an attitude and a style that belongs to the past, he described the temperament of the city's inhabitants, 'People in Paris are always sad and complaining.'

There is also the belief that Paris is potentially less moral than other areas of the country. Paris was often held up as the 'big, bad, city', a place where people often flirted only for amusement. Antoine, a trim, 35-year-old banker, with impeccable dress sense, said, 'People in Paris are here just for fun. They can lie about their intentions.' Francine who works in publishing, was obviously well aware of this, 'You have to protect your time and yourself.' Jean –Luc, a chain-smoking, bespectacled man, who was native to Paris, explained,

'In Paris, the relationships between men and women are more complicated than in other parts of France. Women in Paris aren't as easily seduced, because they are constantly approached.'

Why were people so quick to point out the difference between Paris and the rest of France? A village mentality still prevails throughout this largely rural country. As many as 82% percent of the towns in France are home to less than 100,000 people. With a population of around 2.2 million, Paris isn't a very big city. It is a mere speck of dust, in the eye of megatropolises like Seoul or Mexico City. However, it is the only French city that houses over a million people, and is almost three times the size of France's second biggest city, Marseille. Densely populated, Paris offers a lot of choice and even more cover. 'For me, it's either a one-night stand or a long-term relationship, nothing in between. There are so many people in Paris, that you don't want to waste your time,' said Mathieu, a 30 year-old artistic director with a chiselled jaw and a twinkle in his eye. The anonymity of the big city also provides the perfect excuse for promiscuous behaviour. Nicolas, a 32-year-old project manager for a software company, put it this way, 'In one-night stands you will most likely never see the woman again. Paris with her suburbs is very big.'

With the exception of the native Parisians, the majority of French people who come to Paris have come from small towns where everyone knows everyone else's business. In a smaller community people are obliged to fit in, and thus there is greater emphasis placed on socially acceptable conduct. Behave in an unacceptable way, and everyone will know about it. In larger cities, people feel less connected to each other and this lack of community brings with it a degree of anonymity. And anonymity affords people the freedom to act in certain ways and to do things they might not if they were always held accountable by their communities.

In New York, there's no nosy matriarch watching your every move. The Big Apple's big enough to conceal many a misdemeanour. When you don't personally know your neighbours, you don't feel as much pressure to keep your stereo's volume at an acceptable level. Nor do you concern yourself with what others might think about the number of people slipping out of your front door in the wee hours. Likewise, if you know you will probably never see someone again, you might flirt with him or her all night long, take a phone number, and never call. This is, after all, big city life, not life in rural France.

GENDER STEREOTYPES
So do French men live up to their romantic reputation? Many of the men interviewed were not aware of their renown – or so they said. When asked which country produced the best flirts, the men compared themselves to Italian men, but not always favourably. Frederique (28), with his dark hair and warm laugh, is the sales manager of a large supermarket chain. He was unequivocal, 'Italians are full of shit. They have no imagination. They sound like they only want to get a woman into their bed.' While Parisian men are no different in this regard, they know women want romance and try to provide it. The more well-travelled men were aware of their romantic reputation, and certainly used it to their advantage. Olivier, a recently unemployed graphic designer, and thus lightly tanned, never responded as one would expect. He said, 'Our reputation helps us. Every French guy outside of France knows that he can get a woman.'

Parisian men and women have very distinct job descriptions, and part of a man's job is to make romantic overtures to women. Antoine the banker said. 'If a man sees flowers on the street he will buy one for her, we do very romantic stuff.' Laurent the architect had spent some time living in London. He remarked, 'I get so embarrassed in the UK when women say "Thank you" when I open the door; like it's some big thing. This is a man's job. It's a man's job to open the door and a woman's job to walk through it.' Intriguingly, it was only the men who talked about romance, and only the men who ostensibly exhibited romantic behaviour. The theory is that '…women want a 'romantic commando' sometimes romantic, sometimes tough.' explained Mathieu, the artistic director. Jean-Luc put it another way, 'Men are the bosses, and women work under them.' Enter 32-year-old Claire, of the big teeth and small smile. She is the assistant to the Chief Financial Officer of a large bank. Claire also listed the stereotypes of Parisian flirting, 'Being romantic, taking you to dinner, champagne and candles, although I hardly ever meet one of these guys. In Paris we say 'no smoke with out fire', so they must be out there.'

HISTORY

Book seller Guilliame observed that 'In a city like Paris, a woman's flirting is the same as a man's. Men and women are becoming more similar.' This was not a common sentiment. The mindset that seems to have prevailed in France over the centuries is the Napoléonic Code of 1804. It dictated that 'a husband owes protection to his wife; a wife owes obedience to her husband.' Interviewees pointed out that before 1978, French women couldn't get a credit card in their own name. Francine is originally from the south of France but has lived in Paris for ten years. She is the commissioning editor for a publishing company. She pointed out, 'It has only been since 1983 that women could declare their own income to the government, which means they are not dependent on their husband or father anymore.' No, that's not a misprint; you read it right, 1983. In that same year American astronaut, Sally Ride, became the first woman in space on the Space Shuttle Challenger and Margaret Thatcher won a landslide victory in the General Elections in the UK. While in other countries, sisters were doin' it for themselves, in France women were just emerging from the Napoleonic era.

It was only as recently as 1944 that French women were granted the right to vote. Their first bids in 1919, then again in 1922, and yet again in 1925, all failed. No wonder when they were up against politicians like Senator Pierre Marraud who said, 'The woman of the Latin race does not feel, has not developed in the same way as the woman of the Anglo-Saxon or Germanic races. As a person, she is generally more involved in her church, whose dogmatism she does not dispute. It is perfectly reasonable, then, that her legal status should be different.'

This, despite the litany of female icons like nationalist heroine (and Catholic saint) Joan of Arc, the writer Anaïs Nin and feminist theorist Simone De Beauvoir. Lorraine, with her smart glasses, and glossy brown hair swept up into a sophisticated bun, has mastered the sexy author look. She said, 'The women's movement and Simone De Beauvoir's 1949 treatise Second Sex challenged the social place of males. We were revolutionaries. We don't want to be passive servants. We are people in our own rights and the power can be shared.' It took the Second World War to liberate France's women.

While they have all shared a similar, male-dominated history, Parisians seemed to be much more tied to their history than the New Yorkers, Londoners, or Stockholmers. The Parisians often made reference to France's history.

The French use the excuse of being 'old-fashioned' and 'conservative' to justify why out-moded sexist attitudes are prevalent. Alexandre is a slim, sensitive Parisian who works in business tourism. He explained, 'In French culture you get your rules from history.' Laurent, (30) is a shy architect, with an attitude and a style that belonged to the past. He said, 'France is a conservative country. Quite old-style.' This influence of the past came up repeatedly in the Parisian women's narrative, usually with mixed feelings about whether women had a better life back then or not. Isabelle is a tall, slim, 32-year-old librarian, who had just returned from a stint in London. She lamented, 'A girl is a 'bitch' and a guy a 'Don Juan', we had big revolutions and then we stopped.' Claire, the assistant to the CFO, who uses her smile sparingly, agreed, 'We are not very liberated. A woman's position in life is not recognised.'

French women collude to keep the patriarchal dynamic in place. Juliette (29), is a social worker with a warm smile and brown eyes that could have been the inspiration for Bob Marley's song. She believes it's the man's prerogative to make the first move. 'I wouldn't want to lead the man into something, it stems from their choice. It's very French, an old-fashioned value.'

Francine, who works in publishing, admitted there was an inequality between the genders, but defended it by saying, 'We are more romantic and less pragmatic.' This is one of many examples of how French women are willing collaborators in the gendered distinctions that govern Parisian relationships

So, a male-dominated history colours France's present attitudes, as does religion, another traditionally male-dominated domain. Certain behaviours and attitudes in modern-day Parisian flirting were frequently put down to Catholicism – but this certainly didn't seem to help the woman's cause. Anthropologist Dani Cavallaro said that France's Catholic heritage kept women in a dominated state since, according to the Catholic view of marriage, the woman's primary responsibility is to her husband as a wife and mother. This helps to explain the emphasis that Parisian women place on relationships – without one, you have no value or esteem. Sophisticated Stefanie is a business analyst. She has the air of a woman who knows what she is doing, as her perfect make-up attests. She said, 'The single French woman feels sorry for herself because of the social pressure to be in a relationship.'

THE STIGMA OF BEING SINGLE

In the French language, you are either married, or if you are an unmarried woman, you are célibataire. Yes, that's right, ladies, in French, 'single', means celibate. This could explain why few Parisians are 'officially' single. In keeping with the Parisian trend for taking things slow, people date each other for years. It's not uncommon for young people to date the same person for eight years or more. Isabelle the librarian had just returned from a stint in London. She explained, 'In Paris we go on two dates and then we are boyfriend and girlfriend. We don't have the 'dating' culture.' While New Yorkers don't waste a moment speaking to someone who doesn't meet the criteria, the Parisians seem to have nothing but time. If all it takes is two dates to be in relationship, it's easy to see why a lot of people would technically be in one. Yet, in describing their 'relationship status', many of the participants were 'not single' but also 'not in love'. 'It's complicated,' was a phrase much bandied about. Many of the interviewees were in long-term relationships – but didn't want to be. In response to the question, 'Are you single', these were typical responses:

- 'We've only been dating a few months.'
- 'I'm trying to find a way to break up.'
- 'In my mind I am single.'

A new union often starts while the old relationship is still in its dying throes. While it was usually only the men who felt the need to redefine what 'single' means, some women admitted to dating guys while he decided if there was 'still something there with his girlfriend'. It was so common to be 'just coming out' of a relationship, that one woman told me, 'It's also an excuse guys use if they don't want to see you anymore.' The relaxed attitude the Parisians seem to have towards affairs makes these actions appear less hazardous to their emotional health than they would seem in other cultures. After all, the longer it takes for two people to make a monogamous commitment dramatically reduces the chances of making it to that stage. It takes more than two dates to realise that he still sleeps with his one-eared teddy bear or that she is a kleptomaniac with a penchant for collecting used ashtrays.

CONCLUSION
The Parisians' default setting is 'flirt'. Their methods are as stylised and formulaic as a Gavotte, the 17th century kissing dance. However, they don't follow the prescribed moves to the (French) letter, because that wouldn't be mysterious enough, would it? Flirting in Paris isn't only about dancing, romance and demure, intelligent, beautiful – yet natural – women you can take home to Mama. Parisian men are always on the prowl and romantic gestures often hide predatory intent. Sexually assertive women threaten their territory and even though sex is what they're after, if a woman plays by his rules, she'll earn herself an unsavoury reputation. Thus, Parisian women aren't easily seduced. And Parisian men are not easily put off. You have been warned!

FLIRT FILE

To help make your way in Paris, follow these guidelines:

When in Paris ... DO:
- Speak about Sartre. Those Parisians love a good, philosophical discussion.
- Think back to when you were a teenager. If she is ignoring you, she really likes you!
- Start a heated debate. Provocation is a Parisian passion.
- Act coy and mysterious.
- Make sure that both parties are at the same skill level:
- Imitate Justin Trousersnake. Here, dancing is the business.

When in Paris ... DON'T:
- Get too drawn in. Never get too serious about the other person, or forget that it's all just for fun.
- Think that men and women in Paris can be 'just friends'. They can't.
- Drink more than two glasses du vin, ladies, or you'll never see him again! Flirt with someone in whom you really have interest.
- Ever admit you're genuinely interested in someone or you'll lose the game and the girl.
- Go out in single-sex groups or you'll look like you're trying to pull.
- Look like you're gussied up – beauty should be au naturel.
- Be obvious!
- Ever give in too easily.

BOYS WILL BE BOYS AND GIRLS WILL BE GIRLS

Choose carefully when you take your seat on the Paris metro. Here be dragueurs! In Paris, there is a particular type of man. If you are a woman you will see him leering at you on the metro, feel his eyes burning into you as you pretend not to notice. When exasperation and anger sets in, you'll yell at him, 'What are you looking at?' He'll give you a brief glare, turn red, and finally look away. Or, he might appear on the street. You won't dare make eye contact with him as he passes, lest you pique his interest. You definitely won't wear a short skirt or show any part of your body, for fear of being swallowed whole.

GENDER ROLES
The Parisians' answer to the question, 'What do you think men/women like when it comes to flirting?' was revealing. Both men and women answered, 'Act like their respective sexes'. The more so, the better! And, if you can help emphasise those attributes in the other gender, then you score even more brownie points. This is flirting Parisian style.

In Paris, gender roles are firmly instilled. France is predominantly a patriarchal society heavily influenced by history and religion. The culture has stringent views on women and men, and their 'inherent' behaviours. Laurent, the 30-year-old architect, said, 'It's playing on the fact that you're a boy and she is a girl.' And that both of you know what it means to be a boy or a girl. The divide and the difference between the genders in Paris is obvious. The doors are clearly marked Femme and Homme and when it comes to doors, it's the man's duty to open them and a woman's to walk through them. Mademoiselle, when she's not walking through those opened doors, must sit demurely in high heels awaiting Monsieur's attentions. But she's not just a showpiece. While she's sitting there she could be pondering the significance of the early pseudonymous works of Kierkegaard.

Most Parisian interviewees believed that men and women had different duties, roles, and desires. The men preferred women to stick to their traditional roles, and interestingly, the women claimed they were happy to stay there. Perhaps because, as Charlotte, the 32-year-old editor said, 'The French men like to believe they have power, so we let them think they have it while we are the ones who really have it.'

One thing Parisian women have in common with their ostensibly more emancipated New York sisters is that they are not shy to employ their womanly wiles to advance their agenda.

Watching a Parisian flirt is a bit like watching an old movie. The men are the relentless pursuers, who are always sexually ready. 'I love life so when I see a woman I like, I have to talk to her. ' explained handsome Mathieu, the artistic director. Parisian men see themselves as inherently flirtatious. Several of the male interviewees described their flirting style as 'natural,' '… part of my character'. It seems that Parisian men don't try to flirt; they were just born that way. And just as a lion enjoys the hunt as much as the feast, Parisian men confess to losing interest if the game is too easily won. Sandrine, the IT director's assistant, explained, 'There is still the concept here that a man and woman aren't equal and a woman needs to be taken care of.' Women are expected to be modest and discreet in their dress, speech and conduct. 'At parties she can wear her sexy tops and clothes but not in the streets. It's like a person showing their jewels on the street – this will attract thieves,' explained Jean-Luc, with an echo of the hijab.

The Parisian women understand their role well. The women said that men like them to accentuate their femininity. This in turn emphasises his masculinity. They admit to 'acting coy' and 'looking just a little, not a lot'. They are aware of their bodies' curves, yet act feminine and look naturally and effortlessly glamorous. Likewise, most of the female interviewees believed that men liked women to make them feel manly. 'The man has to feel like he is the man and can protect the girl.' 'They are not sure of their masculinity these days,' explained Lorraine, the Parisian author, living in London. 'They want to make sure the woman won't emasculate them; they want to make sure they can still be a guy with this girl.' One Parisian woman relayed the story of going to her local department store, where they were offering free pole-dancing classes. She came away with the all-important knowledge that women must look and act like strippers, and wear high heels at all times. This, as you can imagine, goes down a treat with the Parisian men. Guilliame was an unwitting spokesman for his gender, 'I like when she is trying to behave like a woman, very feminine.' Similarly, most of the men interviewed thought that women like a man to look and behave like a man. 'This means he should carry her bags and open the door,' said Mathieu, the artistic director. Being manly also involved 'making the decisions'.

The guys weren't too far off the mark. The women did like it when men took the initiative, or at least they thought they did, since that was what they believed was permissible. Monique, the 28-year-old sales rep, was forthright, 'I don't want a man who acts like a woman!' Geraldine, the jewellery maker, put it this way, 'You want him to take the initiative in the beginning. You want to know that he is able to lead.' Is this simply an excuse for women not to act on their flirtatious impulses? Perhaps some of the women really do prefer to let the man make that never-ending journey across the room because then they hold the balance of power. If they're the sort of women who have bought into the 'high heels at all times' illusion they're probably wise to stay seated, even if they do want to take the initiative.

PARTNERS IN CRIME
But do the Parisian women actually want to be freed from the restrictions of high heels, real or metaphorical? Not surprisingly, given the strictures of their society, some of the women saw what many might call 'liberation' as just hard work, and preferred to stick with the traditional roles assigned them. In response to the question, 'Do you approach men?' one reasoned, 'It's more socially acceptable for men to do the approaching.' Women do not approach men because are encouraged not to. In Paris, men and women are not supposed to step out of their gender roles and, instigating flirting, is the role of the man. Sophie is a 28-year-old primary school teacher with boundless energy and a very pink cardigan. She seemed to have given up without even trying, influenced by what her male friends think. 'My guy friends say it's too difficult and complicated if the woman approaches.' And if a woman wanted to do the choosing? 'Women who flirt are like hunters. Men are supposed to drive the relationship.'

In their responses, some of the women interviewed would step out of their assigned role and then jump quickly back into their boxes. 'It's not that we don't want to talk to men, we're just not brave enough to do it,' admitted one but hastily countered her statement by saying, with perhaps a hint of defiance, 'Besides, some women like the tradition of guys coming to them.' As if enacting a highly skilled collaboration, the women made excuses for the men. Isabelle, the lithesome librarian, complained, 'I can't sit down on my own for a half hour without someone coming up to me…we speak so easily because we are Latin.' See what happened there? No? Let's do an action replay. She started out with a complaint about not being left in peace but quickly neutralised this with what seems like a defensive statement. Yes, she confesses to getting annoyed with men coming up to her, but then she rushes to their defence. It's not their fault they come over and chat, they can't help it, they're Latin. It's natural. More revealing than her defence of the men is her willingness to take part of the blame. Notice she says 'we' are Latin. So it's not all the guys fault… she's equally responsible for somehow encouraging men to invade her privacy. Thus the women collude with the men.

BALANCE OF POWER

It is often noted by anthropologists that women uphold cultural boundaries, a position which is always riddled with responsibility. It seems in France women carry this burden on behalf of the men. They are responsible for provoking and then controlling a man's desire. A Parisian man doesn't like a woman to give in at the snap of his fingers, but where is the line? Parisian girls learn the boundaries from a young age. Martine, the logistics coordinator, said, 'You have to put a limit on the Parisian boys.' And, although the woman might want to say, 'Oui,' she knows that her responsibility is to keep the situation under control. Why? 'Because the boys would prefer for you to say 'Non!'

The women see any overstepping of the mark as their fault, never mind that it takes two to tango. The female's role as regulator seems a fruitless one. She's in trouble if she takes things too far; she's in trouble if she draws a halt to the interaction. Carefree Geraldine the jewellery maker said 'The men are not happy when they want to take it further and you stop it. The game is to play with their masculine expectations, but not to take it too far.'

Parisian flirting operates on a balance system. The Parisian male's flirtation technique is more aggressive than the female's and this in turn has to be balanced by the levity of her response. Women need to keep it all as light as soufflé. 'Women are more subtle, they flirt differently from guys. When a guy flirts it's obvious; a girl will mask it,' said Claire, the assistant to the CFO of a large bank. Sandrine, the IT director's assistant, agreed, 'Guys are heavier. They might just come out and say, "Do you want to have sex?"'

Alexandre, who works in business tourism, confirmed this stereotype. 'The guy is always ready so it's up to the woman to decide.' However, since there's little room to question male virility in Paris, this decision equates to a woman 'holding back' – disguising her sexual appetite so that a man's readiness (or lack of it!) is never put to the test.

PLAYING HARD TO GET

Parisians call the continuous process of testing and checking during flirting chat et la souris, 'cat and mouse'. Parisian women feel that the key to success with men is to carefully ignore them! Being nonchalant, to a Parisian woman, is as much hard work as achieving that au naturel look – it's artifice disguised as indifference. The golden rule is: 'Women ignore men. To show interest, you show disinterest. You look a tiny bit, but only just a little. If a girl looks at a guy a lot, especially with a smile, she might appear easy,' Charlotte, the 32-year-old editor, explained. It's her sophisticated ability to keep things within these boundaries that explains why Parisian women give only a hint of eye contact during flirtation. Too direct a flirtatious glance and there's a chance the recipient will pounce or the woman may be deemed 'easy'. If a woman catches a guy's eye he'll take that to 'lock down' if he can, by fixing the gaze. Juliette, the social worker, observed, 'If you give a guy even a bit of eye contact, you can't get rid of him.'

Veronique is a 28-year-old PhD student in French literature. She has the effortlessly natural look down pat and has obviously also attended classes on what men want. 'French women are hard to get and part of being classy is being hard to get. It's refinement'. While some men might be frustrated by this reserve, this is exactly the men said they wanted: a classy, refined, woman. Religion plays a part here too. Monique, the sales rep, said of Parisian women, 'They want the boy to do many things to get them; they think they deserve the best, maybe due to Catholicism.' Stefanie, the business analyst, made reference to France's history. 'This stems from the 18th century,' she said, 'French women gained power by using sexual favours. They would trade their bodies to get what they wanted. It seems to have survived. The body is a prize.'

Whatever the explanation, Parisian women admit to holding back. And there doesn't seem to be space for them to do any differently. Guilliame conceded that, 'Parisian women are constantly approached by men.' In a country where the men are driven by their desire for women – and I mean all women – how can anyone be sure that she is special unless she makes him work hard to prove it?

Parisian women play hard to get because men make unrealistic assumptions if they don't. For example, they assume that when a woman says yes to getting down on the dance floor she's also saying yes to getting down in the bedroom. But, by placing the burden of controlling the pace on the women's shoulders, men have also given away their ability to negotiate what both parties want: an opportunity to get to know someone and see if they are worth getting to know.

Parisian women walk a tricky tightrope. In a culture that believes straightforward and obvious is gauche, especially if you are a woman, it wouldn't work if Parisian men and women were both too pushy, a la New York. Likewise if both parties were overly coy, nothing would ever happen. They would both be too busy being aloof in the corner, throwing an occasional nonchalant look over their shoulders, and leaving without so much as exchanging names. Therefore the women are obliged to control the dynamic, but discreetly, without the men noticing their power and therefore feeling emasculated. They must arouse, allure, and seduce, but make sure the men's egos are never hurt, and make sure not to actually have sex if they don't want to be stigmatised.

Geraldine, the jewellery maker, is aware that she falls short of this mark. 'I don't impose limits, I always take the flirt too far.'

However, what's almost as bad as being too easy to get? Being too hard to get! Sophisticated Stefanie, a business analyst, added, 'Guys like to know you are not too easy to get, so you give a bit of resistance, but not too much because then they get bored and leave.' The see-saw effect, in turn, strongly reinforces the flirting rules: women, as prey, are obliged to simultaneously conceal and reveal themselves; they both set the flirting boundaries and make sure the men continue to come on strong. It's the Parisian woman's responsibility to control the pace of the flirtation. Sophie, the primary school teacher, said, 'I force myself to slow down.' She must, in her subtle way, be the enforcer of the limits. Geraldine, the jewellery maker, agreed, 'You have to put a limit on the Parisian boys.' Quite a few of the women confessed to finding this difficult. 'It is not so easy to do,' said Juliette the social worker with the big, brown eyes. Martine, the logistics coordinator, also found the balancing act tricky. 'If he texts or emails, you have to make him wait, but it's hard!' Although the woman might want to say, "Oui," she knows that her responsibility is to keep the situation under control. Why? Because as Stefanie the business analyst said, 'The boys would prefer for you to say "Non"!'

One reason Parisian men subscribe so confidently to the myth that they are all walking sex machines, is due to the modest behaviour of the women. After all, the women keep the men at arms length, so they never have to prove their prowess. So, is it fair to say that girls play the classic 'hard to get' line while the guys overcompensate? You have to wonder what would happen if one day all the Parisian women made a pact to respond to the leery dragueurs by boldly saying, 'You, me, behind the bush, now!'

The female's role as regulator seems a fruitless one. She's in trouble if she takes things too far; in trouble if she draws a halt to the interaction. 'The men are not happy when they want to take it further and you stop it. The game is to play with their masculine expectations, but not to take it too far.' Is this a game that can't be won? Perhaps it's advisable to follow the lead of one woman interviewee and let what will be, be. Martine, a logistics co-ordinator said, 'It's hard to control the rhythm of a good flirt. It's beyond the sum of the parties.'

Women too have natural wants, needs, and urges. But, for Parisian women, it seems being human isn't an option! The cat and mouse scenario, the constant see-sawing of the balance of power that takes place in Parisian flirting unfairly gets women the reputation for being hard work. But in reality, this narrative glosses over the care and control they have to put into their every interaction with a potential mate.

SUSPICION
In Paris, flirting was reported as a common occurrence; which made it less likely to be taken seriously. Think about it. If a man flirts with a myriad other women, as well as you, it's hard to believe in his sincerity. Speaking for the fairer sex, Stefanie, the business analyst, said, 'You have to make sure the other person is flirting at the same level as you. I am careful if I feel they want more.' There is a need to play the game on a level playing field, with someone who has similar expectations. The suspicion that someone wants more than you want to give, makes women, in particular, more cautious when playing 'the game'. Sharks lurk in these murky waters. Geraldine the jeweller pointed the finger at Parisian men, 'They can lie about their intentions.'

While Parisian men are expected to lead the charge, Parisian women ultimately hold the reins of power, if things look like they're 'going too far'. Thus, fear that the flirtation may be getting out of hand is a particular concern for Parisian women. It's not just the women, however, who are suspicious of others' motives. Antoine, the 35-year-old banker voiced the male perspective, 'We wait because we want to be sure it's for real. It's difficult to know because girls like to play.' Thus, the Parisians take their time before embarking on a relationship.

And a relationship, is what Parisian women are after, it seems.
They will do everything they can to get a guy in a relationship, whether they think they will improve their chances by sleeping with him or not. Men seem to realise this and as they are the ones who generally decide whether or not the relationships will happen, they use this to their advantage. To their credit, the women are not mindless victims. They're aware that the men might be playing them, and that's another cause for suspicion. Charlotte, a 32-year-old editor said, 'Men don't think about it, they just try to have fun. However, they know their 'let's have fun act' won't necessarily work with the women.' 'Women like to dream and plan the future,' agreed bespectacled, chain-smoking, Jean-Luc.

So what's a poor, testosterone-driven man do? 'He tries to reassure her about what he can bring to her in the future,' according to Nicolas, the project manager. Or in the words of Alexandre, who works in business tourism, 'Make a woman dream by alluding to a relationship which might or might not ever be.' This is high-level seduction, folks, and not to be attempted by amateurs!

Some of the Parisian men thought talking about children was a good way to win a woman's heart – or another part of her anatomy! Frederique, a 28-year-old sales manager admitted, 'I say I have four nieces. I talk about kids and I have a picture of my niece on my phone. Women love it!' Some men assume the persona they think the woman will respond to. Eccentric Olivier said, 'I hate to keep using this word 'test', but all women are different, some like you to be shy and others like you to be aggressive. That is why I keep testing and seeing their reaction before moving ahead.' Jean-Luc, another adept flirter, explained, 'You adapt yourself to the girl as to what you should and shouldn't say'. Once you target, you can change your direction according to what she would like. You just understand what type of guy she likes and become that.' When asked if this wasn't a little manipulative he gave a Gallic shrug, 'I'm talking about flirting, not about being myself.'

It's no wonder women are always on guard, never fully letting themselves become naively immersed. As Nicolas, the project manager said, 'In Paris, girls think too much. They don't think the guy could be serious.'

Misunderstanding and uncertainty abound in a culture where the mating ritual dictates that women act aloof and mysterious and men are expected to be constantly on the make. The men like the women to keep a distance as gallant Guilliame said, 'French girls look discreetly and wait.' Similarly the women, according to Mathieu, the artistic director, '… like you to be honest, but not too honest because it has to be credible.' Geraldine the jeweller illustrated this thinking, 'I can tell he is flirting because the "Hello" isn't the same. He acts too nice.' So even when he's being nice, or actually is nice, the sceptical Parisian woman deems him too nice, and believes she's seeing through the act. Victor Hugo said, 'A compliment is something like a kiss through a veil.' But the Parisian women don't like being buttered up. They see compliments as false flattery. Francine, who works in publishing said, 'I don't like compliments. They're not real.' She has reason to be wary, especially if she is flirting with Antoine's friends! The banker said, 'My friends are quite good. When they say things, it sounds sincere.' While he might be impressed by his friends' acting methods, that doesn't mean the Parisian women are falling for it.

So actual truth can be difficult to believe. It seems like both the men and the women are caught in a trap. 'Girls are very special, but there are traps everywhere. I have given up trying to decipher Parisian girls,' said Frederique, the 28-year-old sales manager, throwing his hands up in the air. Greg, the communication student, who uses his dance moves to impress the ladies, was equally frustrated, 'When you ask a French woman to dance she will say "No", even though she really does want to dance with you. They liked to be desired and chased after. They are a lot of hard work for nothing!' Ahem, gentleman, but haven't you set these rules?

The frustration is not surprising. If a society stresses difference, it cannot expect its members to think alike and easily understand each other.

CONCLUSION

Flirting in Paris is a game and there are winners and losers. The game doesn't allow people to show their real feelings. So, you must put on an act. How do you ever find out who the other person really is? Both parties are on guard and, the moment you think you've won, you've probably lost. Does anyone win by playing by these rules?

Parisians play the flirting game but the rules prevent anyone from winning. The woman adopts the feminine role and if she is lucky, lures a man into a coveted relationship. In pursuit of this ambition, she should be 'naturally' gorgeous, demure and ladylike, but risk being labelled 'hard work' for such efforts. She will look at him, but not actually look at him. He will 'be the man' and take charge. He will buy the drinks, and she will not have too many of them unless she wants to be branded a lush! He will do everything that a man 'should' do and she will do everything that a woman 'should' do. They will not change or swap roles, nor would the other expect, or even want them to. Oh no, the Parisians, despite the French Revolution, are quite happy with everyone in their natural places.

While the sexual frisson is always guaranteed to be high in a society in which both genders play their roles to the hilt, they seem to be, ultimately unsatisfied. Because the men and women are in a constant game, the two genders regard each other with suspicion. The man is wary of the woman, thinking she is using her womanly wiles to seduce him, even though, she is simply doing her 'job'. If a woman wasn't waiting for a guy to make up his mind about whether to be in a relationship with her, or trying to herd him into a relationship, she felt herself doomed to be 'chronically single'. One disheartened woman said, 'It's difficult to meet people. We just pass in life.

Nonetheless, the women help the men keep up this charade by making excuses for them.

IT'S A LONDON THING

'An Englishman, even if he is alone, forms an orderly queue of one.'
~ George Mikes

The flirtiest people in London are the Pedi cab drivers, little old ladies in the supermarket and homeless men. Granted the bicycle-cab rider wants your business; the septuagenarian with the blue hair a jar of marmalade from a high shelf, and the homeless guy, well, he'd like you to take him home. While their motives might be different, they all see flirting as harmless fun, and they all do it with a bit of pizzazz. Unfortunately, if you are not flirting with the Mr Rick Shaw, Mrs Blue Rinse or He-of-No-Fixed-Abode, flirting in London can be tricky.

In New York, any woman with a modicum of common sense and an interest in bagging a bond guy can easily decipher the flirting etiquette. It's not surprising that the New Yorkers read each other with such comparative ease. After all, they pride themselves on their straightforwardness, and it pays off. Even Parisian behaviour is pretty clear-cut if the basics are adhered to; le homme act like le homme, les femmes act like les femmes and neither reveal their 'real feelings'. You would be excused for thinking that London doesn't have a flirting culture. Here, there are no finite rules, as in New York, and no fixed gender roles, as in Paris. In London, there are only the unwritten rules, which to those unversed, can be the most complicated of all!

GENDER ROLES
In London, both men and women are pretty confused when it comes to figuring out what the opposite sex is thinking. This wasn't just a case of not being on the same page; they seemed to be reading entirely different books! Both genders either misunderstood, or didn't deliver, what the other one wanted. Each gender, although asked the same questions, gave very different answers. The men often mentioned standard protocol and unwritten rules as major influences on how they behaved. This wasn't an issue with the women. The women brought up things such as it was important to make men feel manly and to 'act like a lady'. The men, on the other hand, went out of their way to avoid emphasising male/female differences. London men do not care for superficial attempts at femininity. Thus, it appears that the women don't understand the men's needs and desires. The men seem to understand what women want, but don't have the courage or interest to act in the way the women expect. It's little wonder Londoners end up feeling bewildered and dissatisfied. At the root of the misunderstanding is the time-honoured British tradition of the stiff upper lip.

UNWRITTEN RULES
The American satirist Ambrose Bierce described politeness as 'the most acceptable hypocrisy'. He could have been talking about London. Max, the music publisher, made the point, 'There is always an unwritten code and this can very often be misinterpreted.' There are many unknowns. London culture is riddled with subtlety, understatements, and unwritten rules. These can be so ingrained that they're not consciously considered, but are rather just a way of 'being'. Take the English and queuing, for example.

First and foremost, the English queuing system operates on a 'first come, first served' basis. Even if you have only one item in your shopping basket and the harried mum in front of you has a laden trolley, never ask to move to the front of the queue. Also, you are responsible for finding the end of the queue. It's not good enough to stand at what you think is the end of the queue. If there is any doubt, it's of utmost importance to check with everyone present if they are 'in the queue'. 'Is this the end of the queue?' is a commonly asked question in Britain. Incidentally, it's also one of the few times that it's socially acceptable to talk to strangers. Transportation breakdowns and delays is another. Thirdly, you must physically stand in the queue. Oh no, there's no relaxing in the comfy chairs and eyeballing your place. You must be in your exact spot, even if you have to stand sideways, and restrict exhalation, due to lack of space. And last, but not least, if a person doesn't follow any of the above rules, others are entitled to mutter derogatory remarks under their breath, glare, or even put the offender in their place, both literally and figuratively. All this, just to cash a cheque at the bank! Now imagine the minefield of manners that you have to negotiate when it comes to flirting with Londoners!

English ideals of politeness are at the core of these unwritten rules. Three main areas of convention both infuse and inhibit flirting culture here: a dislike of over-familiarity, an emphasis on personal space, and a general lack of social fluidity. The ability to easily interact with others in the city is the biggest obstacle to successful flirting.

OVER-FAMILIARITY
Being polite doesn't necessarily mean being friendly. For example, if you call to make a doctor's appointment, polite is good, friendly a bit too much. Keep it simple. The standard 'Yes, please' 'No, thank you' 'That's ever so kind' is all that is required. Anything outside of these expected exchanges is not appreciated. After all, this is London. It's a fast-paced city of eight million people, and there is probably a mile-long queue – a very orderly one, of course – waiting to talk to that same receptionist. There's no time for 'What have you been up to lately?' or 'Did you catch the X-Factor last night?' This situation would be completely different in smaller towns in England, as it would be in smaller towns in any country. Part of this behaviour is simply due to big city life. However, rules such as not being over-familiar, a cornerstone in English culture, make interacting with someone you don't know on a personal level a real no-no.

For those of you who are under familiar with the meaning of 'over-familiar', it means not getting too close too quickly. Avoid being friendly with people you don't know, be polite, and keep a distance. Relationships, even casual acquaintances, take time. Rachel, the book illustrator, warned, 'You shouldn't be over-familiar when you first meet people. I hate it when people call you "Darling" or "Mate" and they don't know you.' Another Londoner put it this way: 'My mother would be Mrs Barnes until she said, "Please call me Elizabeth." You wouldn't shorten it to Betty or Liz.'

Soft spoken Anthony, has wavy brown hair, and works in IT. He said, 'On the train you don't talk to the person next to you unless something has gone wrong, then you are quite happy to talk about it, but you won't make the first approach. We don't like to intrude on people. We just don't like to butt in. Nobody speaks on the tube, speaks to strangers or smiles at strangers, not even their neighbours.' This is a classic example of how extreme the reserve can be – you are not over-familiar even with those who live so nearby that they are probably using your Wi-Fi.

PERSONAL SPACE

Picture this: There's a woman, holding a map, looking confused on a street corner. A typical New York male would walk over and ask if she needed help. A typical London male, on the other hand, wouldn't want to encroach on her space. He might also assume that she would not welcome a stranger's help, perceiving it as interference, and prefer to work things out for herself. Claire, a red-haired accountant from Devon, acknowledged the cultural divide. 'What the Brits see as courteous, those from overseas see as reservedness.'

Londoners continually referred to respecting people's private space.
'Flirting is an invasion of personal space, you either mind it or you don't,' said Anoushka, the petite, 32-year-old solicitor, with the head of red curls. Alistair is a smart and likeable 32-year-old. He is a broadcast journalist with the voice for radio and the face for TV. He said, 'I'd prefer flirting one-on-one, if she was with a friend, I wouldn't want to intrude or interrupt. Being mindful of others' space is more than just physical proximity. Even 'noise' can pollute the space of others – Londoners definitely have a different volume-o-meter than New Yorkers! Baby-faced Sam is an erudite 30-year-old website designer. His advice was, 'Don't talk on the bus or train. We don't like our space to be invaded.'

Yet, understanding the English version of personal space, can help you tell if someone is interested in you. Samuel, the charming, 38-year-old furniture maker read the situation this way: 'If you just met someone they're not going to be overly friendly, so the more attention someone gives you, the more they sexually desire you.'
The slavish adherence to personal space inhibits flirting. In London a woman can enjoy her space without being pounced on by every Tom, Dick and Harry – a state of grace that her Parisian and New York sisters would envy. However being mindful of other people's space can stop people from approaching each other.

SOCIAL FLUIDITY

In London, it takes time to get up close and personal. You know how your mummy told you not to talk to strangers? Well, the Londoners are still minding their mums. Sam, the website designer, compared English culture to America. 'In US culture you flirt like crazy the first night if you are interested. In the UK it happens over a period of time.' In New York a 'stranger is a friend you haven't met yet'. In London, a stranger is viewed with suspicion. While in New York it might be commonplace to sidle up to someone at the bar and start chatting, this doesn't go down very well in London.. Jane, with her long legs and self-assured air, works in the financial district. She said, 'People who come up to you in pubs or clubs don't necessarily like women. Sometimes it's just a game for them.'

This is not a socially fluid culture like New York where the very fact that you are out on the town means that you are open to interactions with others. In fact, when asked how they would begin flirting with someone, some New Yorkers said they'd be listening to someone's conversation, then put their 'two cents in'. However, across the Atlantic, the two pence would not be appreciated. Striking up a conversation with the English rose sitting next to you is not something which is often done. Londoners would take offence if someone eavesdropped on their conversation in the first place, but 'butting in' with uninvited opinions would earn a frosty reception, indeed.

Londoners don't immediately welcome people they don't know. Even though he is smokin' hot and keeps flashing his baby blues at you, he is still a stranger, after all. And, you just don't go around striking up conversations with strangers, young lady! Bubbly Georgina is a 28-year-old secretary, who is originally from Manchester. She admitted, 'I'm not good at meeting people cold at a bar. I like it when you are introduced to someone.' Catherine's calm demeanour serves her well in her IT job. She explained, 'We don't like to give too much away without knowing people. We are suspicious of strangers; it's instilled from a young age.'

The men feel the same way. Charlie, the floppy-haired entrepreneur with the cheeky smile, said, 'If I see a girl that I like, I wouldn't necessarily start flirting right away. There is certain protocol because in London, people are naturally guarded with strangers.' This inbred 'suspicion' could be why the English like to take their relationships very slowly. Jennifer, the down-to-earth business analyst, with the China doll skin and light blue eyes, said, 'I wouldn't like to be blatantly chatted up. I like them to get to know me first because then I can relax.'

Why are the English are so reluctant to bring new people into their lives? 'Out with the old, in with the new' doesn't apply to them. It's more a case of 'I don't have room amongst the old to accommodate the new.' The London attitude is since you only have so much free time, it's best to keep a few close people around you and have tight friendships with them, rather than lots of acquaintances whom you see every so often. In contrast to the United States, where you could go out for a night and end up with lifelong friends, in the UK you already have the lifelong friends and are very reluctant to add any more. Most English people meet friends and/or partners in three ways: at school or university, at work, and through friends. England is a small, island country, so one is never too far from any of these people. At least not so far away that they'd be forced to make new friends. Liz, the account manager for a big advertising agency, explained, 'English friendship takes time and everyone knows their place in that. Really good friends I talk to a couple times a week; peripheral friends I see once a month. I am always careful if I meet a new person, do I have space in my life? I don't want to cut out an existing friend.'

Friendships here are about quality rather than quantity. The English are very particular about whom they call 'friend'. You will often hear them say, 'I can count the amount of close friends I have on one hand.' They may know many more people than this select handful but these would be referred to as 'acquaintances'. The mentality is that if people have so many friends, they're obviously not capable of judging a quality relationship. This attitude explains why the English culture is not socially fluid; they don't want it to be!

HISTORY
Where does the English reputation for being reserved come from? Londoners often pointed to their history as way of explanation: the Victorians, the Church of England and even King Arthur – despite the fact that much of what we think we know of him comes from folklore and poetically embellished fiction. Emma is a pretty blonde presenter who sells gadgets on late night television. She admitted, 'It's true that history plays a part in our tendency to be reserved.'

Many of the interviewees mentioned past notions of restricted sexuality. Yasmin is a PR consultant with sharp cheekbones.

She spoke of the historical dress and dance of the late 5th century. 'They wore restrictive corsets,' she said, 'and their dancing was very reserved.' Take the legendary King Arthur and his consort Guinevere, for example, 'Their tables were streets long.' Alas, a couple heralded as one of the most romantic couples in English history didn't even sit close enough to play footsie under the table. This erudite interviewee blamed the Industrial Revolution, which spanned the 18th and 19th centuries. 'It was the juxtaposition of Victorian excess and discipline coming together, and the erecting of institutional buildings with the purpose of ruling over others for the benefit of themselves…Ornate phallic pillars were used to represent the suppressed sexuality of the culture in the architecture. In London, we don't fuck; we just go to a bank that looks like a vagina.'

The Victorians were mentioned repeatedly with regard to British restraint. Samuel, the furniture maker, claimed the reserve was, 'Based on the Victorian image of ourselves,' adding that there is, in British culture, 'More of a shift towards conservatism.' The London ladies often mentioned aristocracy, and 'good breeding' when referring to their history. Emma, the late-night gadget presenter, who still manages to look refreshed, without much sleep, said, 'This stems from the British aristocrats of the 1800s. They were prim and proper and ladies had to be ladylike and polite.' It seems that some English women are still emulating this two-hundred-year-old English ideal. Much was made of good manners and breeding and not pushing opinions onto people, although Liz, the account manager, was the lone dissenting voice. 'I don't think it still applies in our generation.' Bearing in mind the age demographic of the interviewees (27-40) it's notable that participants should express such conservative views. While none of the Londoners interviewed wore bowler hats and pinstripe suits, they are aware of the stereotypes even if they didn't actually apply them to themselves. But what keeps a culture buying into its own mythology with such dedication, and how was this reputation formed?

Duncan is a 33-year-old newspaper journalist who conducts a conversation as though someone might be listening in. He pontificated, 'The law was pragmatic and was a law of precedent rather than a law of stature. It allowed people do what they wanted and if there was a problem, then they would change it. It stems from respect, it's a historical legacy.'

This historical legacy, according to interviewees, had the following effects on modern day behaviour resulting in:

- people being more observant
- greater social civility
- a strong sense of identity
- an awareness of what has gone before, with people being aware of the backdrop against which they exist
- a more insular demeanour because we are island dwellers
- an 'implied' class system which promotes a sense of belonging –It's fine to be a butler.

There was also the view that the English were reserved because they were expected to be so. 'It's probably a self-fulfilling prophecy,' said Max the music publisher. Mary is an astute 28-year-old personal assistant with mousy brown hair and sensible shoes. She agreed, 'It's self-perpetuating because it's been a part of the culture for so long.' Alistair, the broadcast journalist, echoed this view. 'Historically, England hasn't been invaded and therefore has grown and developed as its own culture. It's an insular island.'

Thus, he seems to be saying, the English are reserved because they live on an island isolated from the rest of the world. Despite what you may think of his grasp of history, he wasn't alone in this explanation for the famous English reserve. Jane who works in the financial industry said 'We've never had to fight for our homeland. It was always away.' Adrian is a quick-witted real estate agent in his thirties. He said, 'It's the image of the colonial empire which we were brought up to believe.' This harking back to a lost era of international dominance and ideas that should have disappeared with the empire, still permeates the mindset of young Londoners, many generations later.

Yasmin, of the razor sharp cheekbones and striking good looks, said that her ancestors, '… believed they were a class above other nations, 'superior' 'civilised'.'

Charlie, the entrepreneur, said, 'After the Second World War, our great empire was all taken away so we adopted the attitude 'it's not the winning, it's the taking part that counts'. This attitude, which permeates our modern day thinking about winning, stems from our lost empire.'

So, if today it doesn't matter whether you win or lose, perhaps this is why the London males don't feel the need to challenge themselves to woo a lady. In a society that believes participating is more important than winning, you don't have to try for a woman out of your league. It's worth remembering that the ancestors of many of those people living in England sought a better life by undertaking the long and perilous voyage to the United States. Perhaps the most adventurous souls left England in the 1850s and took with them their adventurous genes.

Yes, flirting in London does happen, but it's slow, it's awkward, and no one even thinks about attempting it without a few glasses of… anything on offer! And, because it isn't goal oriented, as in, people aren't necessarily looking for sex or a wedding ring, it means it is much easier to hang out with one's friends drinking, until an opportunity falls into one's lap.

CONCLUSION
If flirting was something that could be actioned at the flip of a switch, the signals would be as apparent as the Christmas lights being switched on in Oxford Street and things would be a lot easier for Londoners. Unfortunately, it isn't. Mr London and Ms London have completely different aims and perceptions when it comes to flirting. The men say they want the women to be assertive while the women believe the men don't appreciate assertiveness. The women want the men to take more action, while the men wish the women would. London males are hesitant to make the first move, 'What! Approach someone I don't know?' Meanwhile, many women expect the men to do the traditional thing while they cling to the long-established roles of their corset-wearing ancestors. While the London males seem

more than happy to share the duties equally, some might even say they would be relieved to do so, the question is do the women want to share them?

FLIRT FILE

To help make your way in London, follow these guidelines:

When in London … DO:
- Remember to flirt. Being timid will get you nowhere.
- Use irony, sarcasm, and facetiousness. It's all about the importance of not being earnest.
- Dress to impress. The first round begins after work and they are all still in suits and ties.
- Make a few attempts at eye contact, and then follow up with an approach
- Follow the 203 unwritten rules of conduct, if you can find someone to show you the ropes.
- Know that once everyone is drunk, the rules no longer apply. (It's one of the rules)

When in London … DON'T:
- Try and get too familiar with someone too quickly.
- Be an American tourist. They will only snigger behind your back
- Wait for the men to start coming up to you. Assertive (not aggressive) ladies in London win!
- Be too obvious. You're in the land of 'it's what you don't say that matters'.
- Talk loudly, eat in public, make direct eye contact on the tube, say 'sorry' if you mean it, make a scene, queue jump…

THE SENSITIVE NEW AGE MAN

When the Spice Girls, that '90s incarnation of British 'girl power' sang, 'So tell me what you want, what you really, really want,' they could have been singing the anthem of the modern marriageable London male. There didn't seem to be a correlation between what the men wanted – or said they wanted – and what the women thought they wanted. Most London women interviewed seemed to want the men to initiate the mating dance. But the men don't want to take the lead. Unlike their Parisian brothers, London men are shy and reserved, which isn't helpful in a city where the women expect the men to make the moves. The men, for their part, would prefer women to make their intentions plain, yet the women resist assuming the traditionally male role of hunter, often because they feel the men wouldn't like being usurped. But, how obvious do the men really want the women to be? Add to the confusion, those prized elements of English culture like subtlety, a reserved nature, and unwritten rules which prevent people from mingling, and there you have it – why London men, in particular, have a reputation for not flirting.

ENGLISH MEN DON'T FLIRT

Mr Darcy from Jane Austen's Pride and Prejudice famously said, 'I am ill qualified to recommend myself to strangers.' Not much as changed it seems since 1813. London men are reluctant to recommend themselves even to those they do know. English males don't feel comfortable approaching women. This could be because of their hyperawareness of the unwritten rules and a reluctance to 'intrude'; it could be a case of simple shyness. Or, it may be due, as one guy put it, to the voices in their heads that warn, 'Don't talk to her, she won't fancy you. Don't bother her, her boyfriend's in the toilet.' Unlike New Yorkers who flirt with single-minded, thick-skinned, intent, English men have trouble expressing interest, proactively flirting, and determining when women are flirting with them. Londoners often mentioned that the American flirting style was too full-on for them. As Duncan, the journalist said, 'When I'm in the states, I feel like flirting is so in your face. It's like "Hi, my name is Duncan, and I am going to flirt with you now!"' While this may be true, the English constraint, is an impediment to meeting new people, and possibly, a long-term partner.

Foreign women are stymied by English men's lack of action. In their home countries, these ladies are used to men showing obvious interest in them. They complained that the London guys take as much notice of them as Elton John would of Angelina Jolie. Isabelle is a 32-year-old Parisian librarian, who lived in London for a few years. She said of her experience of the Brits, 'The English men didn't talk. I had to do everything. They were much more shy than French men.' In New York, on the other hand, '…, a guy came up to me straight away and we talked about everything.' Sophisticated Stefanie is a Parisian business analyst whose work often takes her to London. She was equally unimpressed with the English level of conversation. 'In London they would always ask me "Where are you from? Where did you learn English?" It's hard to tell if they related to me, or just to me as a French girl. Also, you can't play with words like you can with your mother tongue.'

GENDER ROLES

Some Parisian women, on the other hand, felt that there was less pressure in London's flirting culture. This might be because there are fewer social rules of the kind to which Parisians feel bound. Monique, the 28-year-old Parisian sales rep, who had also lived in London, was more appreciative of the British way. She said of the English, 'They are much more relaxed than the French, more open and have a good sense of humour.'

Unlike Paris, London men expect an equal playing field for flirting, the London men interviewed showed a respect for the opposite sex and an appreciation of the fact that a woman has influence beyond her looks. In different ways, the London men made it clear that a woman is more than her double-X chromosomes; she is a person in her own right. 40 year-old David, a recruitment consultant with a dry wit, and a very expensive watch, said, 'They are all individuals, you have to treat them differently.' This appreciation that a woman does not have innate characteristics because she is female, means there is more room for gender fluidity in English culture than there is Paris.

For example, a few of the London females mentioned they flirted with other women. Annette is a sultry and curvaceous jazz singer, with a silky voice. She admitted, 'Flirting is a sexual teasing. I flirt with girls too.' London men also admitted to flirting with each other in a joking, sexual way. In contrast to the New Yorkers males, who pride themselves on being seen as virile heterosexuals, English men were quite open about making overtly sexual comments to their male friends. Charlie, the 30-year-old entrepreneur, lifted the lid. 'It happens in the men's toilets with the guys, gay banter, even though you all know you're not gay.'

Simon is a tall, freckly-faced charmer, who is in PR. He mentioned joking with his friend who was going to take a shower. 'I said to my friend, 'Don't worry, I'll be right in.' Such sexy quips are exchanged in the spirit of male bonding in Ol' Blighty. In a culture that does not insist on heterosexual masculinity, there is space to make these kinds of jokes. Also, with this kind of faux-homosexual flirting, there is no risk of rejection. Both guys know they're not gay, so there is no end goal; one isn't trying to get the other into bed. Men in London are not going out with the sole attempt of having sex, as the New York males admit to doing. It would be typical for a group of male friends to go out for the sole purpose of spending time together, not concerned with whether women were present but, rather, just wanting to spend time with friends.

And, as much as the males value their time with their friends, they also seemed to genuinely value women. Max, the music publisher, said. 'London women are hard work because there's a lot of competition amongst the men for the women. There are lot of good looking and successful women in this city.' And he didn't mean hard work in the way the Parisian men did. She's not 'hard work' because she makes him chase her to prove she's valuable; she's hard work because the men already know she's valuable.

The men also stressed that flirting was a two-way street. When asked whether they liked to chose or be chosen as a flirting partner, 33% of the London men interviewed came up with their own category of 'mutual choosing' – the only men in the study to create a 'mutual' category. The men seemed to be looking for an equal partner, not someone they can put on a pedestal. 'It's about building a bond of confidence between the two of you,' said

Sam, the website designer. Christopher, the 32- year-old ex-military man, agreed, 'I would try to work out if there was a 'we' part of the conversation or just an 'I'.' Unlike their Parisian counterparts, the London males didn't put women into the two equally restrictive categories of either mistress or wife. The men did not believe that if a woman has sex with him on the first night that she is therefore ineligible to be anything other than a casual sex partner. Anthony, who works in IT, said, 'I can't remember having a one-night stand and not contacting her after.'

In comparison to the aloof Parisian women, London lasses are not shrinking violets. Here, the women often have to make the first move, if there is to be any hope of a meeting of the minds – or bodies! Many of the London females are not shy to take this step. Jane, who works in the financial district, said, 'I will open the door and if he wants to walk through… brilliant!' Gemma, the bubbly TV show producer, admitted, 'I am impatient. I have confidence. Approaching doesn't have to be a bloke's prerogative.' One Parisian woman, however, took a dim view of such assertiveness. 'In the UK the women leave their brain at their house and do want they want. If they want something, they take it,' sniffed 32-year-old Isabelle the Parisian librarian, living in London.

Despite this fluidity in gender roles, nonetheless, the Brits share some of those good old-fashioned values still in play in Paris. The majority of men and women interviewed acknowledged that in the flirting ritual, it is expected that the man makes the approach. Tradition was usually the explanation, as Max, the music publisher, made clear. 'When men do approach it's most often because that is what is traditionally known', he said.

Like the Parisian mademoiselles, many English lasses thought that 'Men want a woman who makes them feel like they are a man…They like to find a woman who is delicate and emotional so they can be the man and harness their manliness and fulfil their role,' said Rachel, the children's illustrator. She went so far as to place women in two categories: life partner or one-night-stand. 'They also like a girlfriend to be demure, sensitive and a little bit sparky. If it's just a woman he wants to go to bed with, they like them lively, but this sort of woman is not for the long-term.' This kind of thinking has a whiff of Paris, but it's definitely not Chanel!

None of the men interviewed, however, expressed this desire for the women to pander to their egos. Nor did they categorise women by their sexual assertiveness. In fact, the men wanted partners who would relate to them as equals. They were the ones pushing for females to catch up to their own feminist thinking. One broad-minded bloke said, 'I think women should have more say in things,' and another rallied to the cause with a cry of, 'Vive la feminisme.' Take Adrian, the real estate agent, for example. In the tug-of-war between the sexes, he didn't feel threatened by the equal opportunity come-on. Rather than playing to the traditional role that men pursue and women are the prey, he said, 'Women don't like it to be too easy. Women also like to hunt. They need the allure to be kept. So the string is taut and you don't know who is pulling harder.' Samuel, the 38-year-old furniture maker, dismissed the idea that women are constantly looking for ways to bag a man. 'The idea that women are looking for a relationship is wrong. They enjoy flirting and the whole dance around relationships for fun as well.'

CONCLUSION

While, Londoners are less tied to traditional gender roles than the Parisians, London women's failure to appreciate that the men want partners who relate to them as equals, threatens to put the brakes on the slow but steady progress towards gender equity. The men wish there was more fluidity with the gender roles, ideally with both sexes doing the initiating, but... the women don't want that! Is this because the women mistakenly believe that the men don't want them to be so forward? The London ladies are desperately waiting for their Mr. Darcy. They fail to appreciate how good they have it now. At least they don't have to pay dowries to the man who takes them off their fathers' hands. Once they accept the 21st century mindset, and stop getting frustrated with the men for not playing the role of the masterful lord of the manor, and take their place beside them, as the men say they want, everyone will be better off. For the London ladies, equality is there for the taking. Everything is on their side, including the men.

THE STOCKHOLM SYNDROME

'In Sweden everybody has this perfect surface. Everyone's very polite and controls their feelings.'

~ Noomi Rapace

Stockholmers are by nature, shy and reserved. You can't just walk up to people who fit your demographic on the streets of Stockholm and ask to interview them. The retiring Swedes first turn red and then turn tail. The Swedish way to arrange interviews is to be recommended by a friend, have the meeting pre-arranged, and ultimately meet in a place of their choosing. The place turned out to be Södermalm, a recently gentrified part of Stockholm, where urban grime has metamorphosed into metro chic. The other interview venue was in Stureplan, the playground of Stockholm's rich and beautiful. It has the most expensive bars and restaurants in the city, with prices that make London look like Cambodia. Unlike other cities where people would choose to meet somewhere convenient for them, or somewhere central, the places chosen by the Stockholm interviewees seemed to reflect their identity. They would say things such as, 'I am not a Stureplan guy'. Some of the more glamorous Stockholm women would rather let their roots show then meet in 'hippyville' Södermalm. 30-year-old Eva is a press officer with bright blue eyes and a smile that could get her out of a speeding ticket. She explained, 'Because people tend to stick to their areas, you don't want to make a fool of yourself in your local bar, because then you can't go back there anymore and you won't have anywhere to go.'

FLIRTING IS A SERIOUS BUSINESS
In Paris flirting is a way of life; in New York, it helps pass the time while you are waiting for someone better to come along; in London it takes time to get up close and personal and in Stockholm, flirting is as serious a pastime as football. And, like a team other than Brazil winning the world cup, flirting doesn't happen often either. Because it doesn't happen often, when it does, it is significant. Elegant and sophisticated Mia, a buyer for an art gallery, explained, 'If you are going to flirt with someone, you'd better choose carefully, because you'll be stuck with them the whole night!' Flirting in Stockholm is a big deal, which is probably why they proceed with caution. Easy-going Eric owns a café that sells the best pastries in Södermalm. He explained, 'In Sweden if someone responds or talks back, they are interested. You don't go up talking to anyone in Sweden so when you do, it means something.'

Stockholmers admit that they are a serious people who do not take flirting lightly. For some people, a short conversation is simply a way of showing humanity; for the Swedes, it's the first step towards a long-term relationship. 'If he talks to you for more than 15 minutes, then he really likes you,' observed Emelie, a small, cautious, 32-year-old accountant, who is no free spirit. Easygoing Eric said, 'In Sweden, if someone responds or talks back, they are interested. You don't go up to anyone in Sweden so when you do, it means something.' Kristina is a confident, chatty, global Human Relations manager. She summed it up, 'It's more serious to flirt in Sweden because Swedes take life very seriously,' Such diffidence could explain why the Swedes have such a need for alcohol, and lots of it!

ALCOHOL

'In Sweden you are not supposed to stick out.' But, 'When we get drunk we get social,' said Frederik, a 28-year-old law student who was as well spoken as he was well dressed. For Stockholm men, alcohol is a great aid in helping them approach women. Stefan, a tall, lean, 33-year-old bicycle store owner, said, 'The men have to be drunk and they should be the ones to approach. Although', he added hastily, 'Men and women are more equal in the flirting culture. There are no social codes about women not being able to approach guys.'

Bjorn is a black-haired, blue-eyed, 31-year-old doctoral student of Physics. He confirmed that 'Men are a bit shy, but they can approach you after a few drinks.' However, he went on to admit that, 'Maybe some aren't good at judging how many drinks it takes.' Aha, and that is the Stockholm flirting curse, not knowing when to stop! Rather than having a drink or two, paced throughout the week, they save it all up for the weekend. 'We go out Friday and Saturday and drink a lot. The flirting only happens in the last hour and very intensely. People go out at 11pm and leave at 1am,' said Clare, a hard-working, enthusiastic 30-year-old air traffic controller. Jenny wears her blonde hair in a high pony-tail. She is a PhD student in biology and is a perfectionist – except when it comes to flirting. She summed up the central mystery of Swedish sexuality, 'We get superficial confidence when we are drunk. We're not known for flirting. It's a great mystery how Swedes conceive at all.' Quite so. Take Hugo the accounts manager, for example. He's the accounts manager for an advertising agency in the city and is
a big man, in stature and in confidence. 'At the beginning of the night I decide on my intent. You can't party like I do and be successful with women.' So, Hugo has to make a decision every time he goes out, meet women, or get rat-assed. Tough choice!

SWEDISH EGALITARIANISM

Although the interviewees were initially shy and had to be reassured of confidentiality, as the interview progressed, the private Swedes opened up. The men and women often gave similar responses to the same questions. A constant refrain from both the men and women was the idea that they should all be the same. When asked, 'What do you like a man/woman to do when he/she is flirting with you?' the Stockholm respondents replied, 'The same as me.'
There is a strong emphasis in Swedish culture on conformity and uniformity. Mia, who works in a gallery said, 'We can never say "I did a great project." There is a Swedish expression 'jantelagen' – people don't want to be too much. We can't give ourselves too much credit.' Sweden is a secular, egalitarian society, which regards individual success as unworthy and inappropriate. Clare, the air-traffic controller explained, 'In Sweden we aren't supposed to take up too much space. Big personalities are not appreciated.' The roots of this desire to be the same stretch as far back as the days of the Vikings, according to friendly Mattias, the tall, striking, 28-year-old managing director of a soft drink company. 'We wish not to be different from everyone else. It comes from our history. In the small villages a stranger was a problem. You had to lock your door from the Vikings. In order to stay in a small group you had to behave like everyone else or you would be kicked out.'

This concept of egalitarianism among Scandinavian communities is known as the 'Law of Jante' after a novel published in 1933 by Aksel Sandemose. The small Danish town of

Jante in the novel was modelled on Sandemose's home town at the beginning of the 20th century where everybody knew everybody else and individuality and success was frowned upon. Although 85 years old, the ideology expressed in this novel is still deeply rooted in the Stockholmers' psyche. Hugo, the advertising accounts manager, provided a reason from more recent history. 'We had a Socialist government for 80 years, which said everyone should stick together and work towards the common goal. You shouldn't stick out or be noticed. It's changing as immigrants come in and we are travelling more. The new generation is different.'

In contrast to Paris, where the culture stresses gender difference, Sweden is a society where people are less confined by gender roles. They are much more able to see the opposite sex as equals, not opponents. Take Swedish men, for example. When asked, 'What do you think women like when it comes to flirting?' their response was, 'The same things I do.' They didn't think there was much difference between women's needs and their own. 'Women want the same things as the men,' said Eric, the café owner.

WOMEN

The women in Sweden are a force with which to be reckoned. Swedish women have an unprecedented economic independence. Maria, with the long, blonde, poker straight hair is a 33-year-old project manager. She explained, 'In Sweden it's all about economics. The women don't need the men to pay because they have their own money. If the woman made more money than the man, then she would go to work and he would stay with the kids.' Jenny, the biology student, explained how women being more financially independent affected the flirting scene, 'It's easier to say no if you aren't interested. Not many people have to marry to survive.

'Thus, the women of Stockholm aren't as interested, or as dependent on men, as they are in the other cultures researched. This is particularly evident when the women go out together for a night on the town. They go out with their girlfriends simply to have fun and are not necessarily looking for men. In fact, the men said that it was common to hear, 'Could you please leave me alone? I am out with my girlfriends.' Frederik, the law student, said, 'It's very common for women to go out with their friends and only want to talk to them. They are very picky about men. If you don't fit their criteria, forget it.' This is one of the advantages of being financially independent and not necessarily looking for a relationship. Maria the project manager said, 'Swedish women want a relationship, but on their own terms. Sometimes I think our expectations are a bit too high. People have lots of friends and often that's fulfilling enough.'

The Stockholm women know what they like. Andreas is a 34-year-old personal trainer whose rippling physique leaves you in no doubt as to his day job. He explained, 'Swedish women like to take care of themselves and like to be independent. Women approach and like to choose.' This observation was borne out by Eva, the press officer, who said, 'If I liked him, than I would like to meet again, but by him letting me choose if I want to.'

The men have to work hard. Swedish women don't like the flirting to be too obvious, to move too fast, to be too sexual or for the guy to be too full of himself. A casual New York 'How you doin', baby?' or a steamy stare from a Parisian playa', just won't cut it with these liberated ladies. Many a harassed New York or Parisian woman would agree wholeheartedly with Katarina's sentiments, 'When I pass someone, I don't like to hear comments. I don't like pushy men. I like more sophisticated men who see first from a distance if I'm interested, and then approach.'

Different rules, however, apply to foreign men. As Per, the virile Viking who works for an Internet start-up company was well aware. 'Swedish guys can't be too aggressive. On vacation the Swedish women love flirting with the foreign guys, but if a Swedish guy did that they would just think, "He wants to sleep with me".' Antoine, the Parisian banker, made this comment about Swedish women, 'In Sweden, girls are very cold at first and stay in their girly groups and don't like first part of conversation but, if you do get accepted, she will surprise you and turn around and say, "Do you want to go home with me?"' Some men liked the direct approach. Mattias, the MD of a soft drinks company, learnt his moves from women like Kristina. 'Sometimes, I see an aggressive woman and think, "Ah, that's how you do it?"' he remarked admiringly.

CONFUSION
Women want to carry their own bags, men are afraid to open the doors for women, and people prefer to split the bill on dates. Although the ideals epitomised by the law of Jante have encouraged gender equality, they have also given rise to some confusion. Men, especially, are confused as to their roles. 32-year-old Annika is a pretty, petite nurse. She said, 'Some girls don't like it when guys pay. They want to be equal. A woman would be as likely to carry a heavy bag as the man.' Emelie, the cautious accountant is a case in point. 'There are still very traditional male roles. Guys still want to buy me dinner, but why should they? I have my own money. I want to pay half so I don't feel obligated.' Hugo, the chubby accounts manager, would agree. 'Why should I pay for dinner?' On the other hand, Eric, the café owner, had had a revelation, 'I am starting to realise that even though women want to be treated equally, they still appreciate the romantic gestures like holding the door open and compliments.'

These fluid gender dynamics do not mean that Stockholm is a feminist utopia. A few women mentioned that, 'It's not as equal as everyone thinks.' For example, it was pointed out that although Swedish women's salaries are high in comparison to other women, they're still not the same as men's. 33-year-old opera singer Johanna is thoughtful and measured. She summed it up, 'The male/female differences in Sweden aren't as obvious. Flirting is more boring; it's more difficult to understand what it takes.'

CONCLUSION
Flirting in Stockholm is governed by a unique confluence of cultural characteristics: an egalitarian society that places emphasis on the collective rather than the individual; a society in which women have financial independence and religious influence is neither pervasive nor persuasive. Thus, in contrast to the gender and religious bias of a city like Paris, where women play the passive roles and men the active ones, in Stockholm women call the shots. Nonetheless, despite being the flag bearers for women's liberation, Stockholm women prefer the men to make the moves, not because it is not socially accepted, but mostly because they just don't want to! This is not to say that women don't make advances, they do if they feel like it. The women of Stockholm know what they want and how to get it. Unlike their New York counterparts, that's not necessarily a husband, father or provider. The men know that their best chance with these independent women is to put up or shut up!

FLIRT FILE

To help make your way in Stockholm, follow these guidelines:

When in Stockholm … DO:
- Have a few drinks at home first. Or mortgage your flat to cover your night out.
- Flirt with someone at your own risk and choose wisely, my friend. You only get one chance in a night, apparently.
- Make eye contact from afar first, if you want to follow procedure.
- Feel free to approach guys, buy drinks for guys and have sex with guys. No judgment involved.
- Step out of your comfort circle. C'mon, someone has got to make the first move!

When in Stockholm … DON'T:
- Flirt with more than one person in a night. This ain't New York, you know.
- Insinuate that a woman can't do everything a man can do. Do you like to feel pain?
- Drool. Yes, they're tall. Yes, they're gorgeous. But, they're human too.
- Blink in your target's general vicinity more than a couple times. You don't want to be too obvious, you hussy.

MONEY, SEX AND THE SINGLE WOMAN

If the essence of flirting is playing on gender difference, can there be flirting in a society which stresses gender equality? Does female economic independence have an impact on the mating game? Stockholm has been leading the gender equality index, according to the United Nations Human Development Report, for over ten years now. The report measures factors such as reproductive health, the labour market, education and governmental representation. The index rates Swedish women as having the highest standard of living among all the women in the world. Globally, they enjoy the closest pay parity with men. The consequences of this economic equality are played out in the flirting culture. In Stockholm, constructed gender roles are understood but mostly disregarded.

GENDER ROLES
Like the Parisians, the Stockholmers are very aware of the roles traditionally expected of men and women. The difference is that they don't feel obliged to adhere to them. Stockholm women make their own living, pay their own way and are not subject to stringent religious or cultural expectations. They often choose to be single rather than part of a 'conventional' pair bond. Like their Stockholm sisters, New York women are confident, high-earners, they take the initiative, they like to have sex, and freely admit it! Yet New York women's earning power has ironically made it harder for her to fit into the traditional roles. If she still wants to be looked after, she must find a man who's earnings are even higher than hers. In Stockholm, financial freedom has had the opposite effect. She doesn't want to fit into those roles. 'I can buy my own drink!' the independent Stockholm women say.

BEING SINGLE
In Sweden, the institution of marriage isn't popular. This may be due to a less religious society, a different idea of what 'success' and the perfect life means, or pay parity between men and women. Unlike their New York counterparts, Stockholm women don't seem to be after a wealthy man with whom to play house. While the women of New York still face social pressure to pair bond and reproduce, the women of Stockholm are free to be single and have sex without stigma. And because Swedish society pays for costly health insurance and child care, a single woman can choose to have children, because she does not have to be financially dependent on a man. As Eric, the café owner, pointed out, 'Women want to choose these days and they don't need a good provider.' This, combined with a society that is not particularly religious, means women in Stockholm have the freedom to make their own choices, without needing to find a partner.

Besides just flirting for the fun of it, it is often the hope of having a relationship that encourages women to be receptive to men's advances, or to make an effort themselves. In many cases, this is also why men flirt. However, in Stockholm, many women did not seem very interested in being in a relationship. This woman employs avoidance tactics. 'I try and not see if someone is flirting with me; I am afraid maybe they want more than I have to give,' said Emelie, the accountant.

I met one Swedish woman, Anneli, at a party. She had a partner and two kids and was nonplussed by the question. 'Why don't you get married?' She shrugged, 'Why should I? We get the same benefits whether we are married or not.' In fact, many women interviewed preferred the single life. It was the men who seemed more interested in settling down. Bjorn, the PhD student observed, 'It seems women these days aren't looking for a boyfriend, they are just looking for fun.' Eva, the press officer, explained, 'Men are more likely to approach because they are looking for relationships. They need a woman to fulfil their lives, but women don't, they have already achieved fulfilment.' Annika, 32, a pretty, petite nurse agreed, 'There are so many singles in Stockholm that a woman has a lot of choices. They are content with their lives.' Annika was one of the many Swedish women interviewed who expressed a fear that being in a relationship might force them into traditional gender roles. 'When you start to go out with men, all of a sudden you are forced to "be the woman". It's only okay if I choose to be the woman. Being single is a lot easier. We show more of our masculine sides.'

Kristina, the HR manager, thought it is best to stay away from relationships all together. She doesn't see herself participating in any of the traditional roles. And, with financial freedom and less stigma attached to her choices, she doesn't have to compromise. She said, 'I have been single a long time. This relationship thing isn't for me. I don't see myself as a mother or wife. I want to choose my own life. I have different boys for different occasions. If I want my back scratched in front of a movie, I know who to call. If I want sex, I know who to call.'

Women are rejecting the institution of marriage and taking on 'male' roles. Thus, Swedish women are able to have 'free sex' without the stigma. The people of Stockholm don't take much stock in those time-worn categories of mistress or mother-of-my-children.

WHO MAKES THE MOVES?
In the dating game, whether or not it is acceptable for a woman to approach a man reveals much about gender relations in a society. You would expect that because of the egalitarian nature of Swedish society and the freedom from censure, women would be flirting with blithe abandon. And some do. Jenny, the PhD student in biology, and her friends, know what they want and go after it. 'My friends and I don't play games anymore. If we want to call, we call.' Kristina, the global HR manager, pointed out that men were expendable, 'If I was with friends we might have a bet and I would go up and ask him. If they don't get the joke then they're out.' However, as we have seen in flirting cultures as disparate as Paris, New York and London, here too, it is usually the men who must make the moves, not because it is their role or duty, but, because the women often don't want to do it. They are too busy having fun with their girlfriends!

Henrik, the blue-eyed banker, explained, 'Women aren't that desperate. They don't need to make the first move. They can sit back and take it easy.' Hugo, the accounts manager, agreed, 'It's not common for women to make the first move. Men do the work and the women choose, they are always in control.' It's certainly not unusual for Stockholm women to make their intentions known. Johanna, the opera singer, had no qualms about it, 'When I am attracted to him, and notice he is shy, then I will do it. I can take no for an answer.'

Clare, the air traffic controller, was one of those women who prefer not to make the first move. Yet, she's certainly no shrinking violet. 'I'm not the approacher so it depends on the guy's pace. Or, you just tell them what you want.' There is no place for Parisian coyness or London delicacy in Stockholm, although things do take longer to heat up. Geographically, almost 15% of Sweden lies north off the Arctic Circle, after all!

How do the men feel about the women usurping their traditional hunting grounds? Henrik, the banker, was a fan. 'You respect women more. They are equals in the flirting arena.' Other men, however, like Per, the virile Viking, who works for an internet start-up company, agreed, 'Women want careers, maybe a kid in their mid-30's. What's left for us men? Men are having plastic surgery to keep up. There is a big confusion of identity amongst men. The media is having a big influence.' Bjorn, the doctoral student, elaborated on the same theme, 'The last decade has changed, with women becoming more independent. It puts more pressure on men. We have to be interesting in other areas besides just providing food and money. We have to be good conversationalists and work harder on beauty. This is more obvious from the adverts, probably because women demand it. In an economic way, a woman's beauty was traded for economic security. Swedish women are more independent and don't have to find a man. They have other values besides trying to have a family. Because it's not as urgent as before, it means they can be pickier about it. This puts more pressure on the man. In my father's generation, being a 'good man' was enough. Now we have to know about wine and art, be good dressers, etc. It's recognised how much it's changed for women in the last decade, but often not how much it's changed for men. There's no previous experience which dictates how men should be concerning these new issues.'

CONCLUSION

In the case of Stockholm men and women, they both know that either one of them, at any time, can do anything. Because there are no set gender roles, a woman, would be just as likely as a man to initiate an encounter, be that a chat, a date, or a one-night stand. Both genders seem to be happy with this, if not a little confused, as they forge on into that brave new world of real gender equality.

FRIEND OR FLIRT?

There is a fine line between flirtatiousness and friendliness. Many people were unsure of how they could tell the difference. This uneasiness was even more pronounced in cities like London. The average Londoner is like a pre-booked restaurant table – clearly marked 'Reserved'. As a general rule, the more obvious the flirting is, the easier it is to tell the difference. Let's face it; it's kind of hard to get a mixed message if someone says to you, 'You're hot. Let's go back to my place.' The presence of sexual undertones also had a significant influence when trying to determine which side of the line one was on. Unsurprisingly, cultures that flirted with little or no sexual undercurrents, were the most likely to have problems negotiating the flirting/friendly border.

NEW YORK

New Yorkers are a friendly bunch. Random strangers smile and say 'Hello' on the streets. However, New Yorkers don't make a habit of relating to each other as human beings. Men see women firstly as women, and secondly as naked women. Women see men firstly as men, and secondly, as men who want to get in their pants. Since most flirting seems to be done with sexual intent, there isn't much chance it will be mistaken for friendship. When asked how he could tell the difference between someone being friendly and someone flirting, David, the 28-year-old architect, said, 'If my friend walks over to a woman, I know he's flirting.' Marie, the former sales assistant, said with a roll of her Rimmel-etched eyes, 'If they come over and start talking to you, they are flirting. Why else would they come up to you?'

Both men and women were aware of your average New Yorkers' dishonourable intentions. 'Rarely does an interaction between men and women start on just a friendly level,' said Corey, the actor/fire-fighter with smokin' good looks. Lisa, who works for a large credit card company, supported this view, 'I've never had a guy come up to me on a friendly level, so I can always assume he is flirting.' Indeed, New York men seemed to think they were as skilled as mentalist Derren Brown when it comes to figuring out the ladies. More often than not, when asked how they could tell when someone was flirting with them, they responded, 'I can feel it.'

Okay, let's assume there might be an occasion where a New Yorker was a bit fuzzy as to intent, then how could one tell? New York males are proponents of the 'Act first, ask questions later' school of cognitive behaviour. Thus, they often make a move first, judge her reaction next, and thereafter gauge which side of the line he is on. For example, Bryan, a tall and lanky musician, said, 'I'll put out feelers. I'll steer the conversation towards the sexual and see if she reciprocates or backs off.' Rebecca, who is in recruitment, was on to this modus operandi. She said she can tell when men are interested because, 'In flirting they will eye you up and down, the conversation will steer towards a sexual remark.' Some men said they could tell the difference depending on how 'persistent' the woman was. New York females are not afraid to go after what they want. Chris, the environmental engineer, said, 'She'll put her hand on yours and leave it there. It depends on how hard she is trying.' Some men gauge the situation based on how hard a woman laughs at his jokes.

Unsurprisingly, New York women don't have much difficulty telling when a man is interested in them. After all, if someone is licking his lips as though you are the main course, you can assume he's not looking for a life-long friendship. How do the women discern male intent? Most women said they can tell by looking at the guy's body language and by assessing how much attention he pays her.

Andrea, who works for a charity, said, 'It's the wandering eye which is checking out my body, the level of their interest, and the amount of interest they are paying to the conversation.' The men don't try to hide that they're giving you the once-over. 'Sometimes, I can feel myself blushing,' she admitted.

PARIS

Because men and women are mostly regarded as different species on Planet Paris, the idea of being friendly towards one another without sexual interest is as likely as eating a pain au chocolat without un cafe. This was exemplified by Jean-Luc, who worked for a large French bank, when he said, 'I don't believe there is a real friendship with men and women. It's always flirting, with a sexual undertone.'

The Parisian males had very similar attitudes to their New York brothers-in-charms. However, in a more restrained European fashion, they weren't as blatant about wanting sex. That would be gauche. The Parisians test the waters of the Seine with a cautious toe. New Yorkers jump head first into the Hudson and make a big splash. Frederique, the 28-year-old sales manager, looked too young to be so wise in the school of flirting. He insisted that 'The only time a Parisian male is being friendly instead of flirting is when he is not attracted to the woman.' One Parisian guy chalked it up to intent. 'Friendliness is with absolutely no underlying purpose. Flirting has a slightly opportunistic feeling in the mind.' Guilluame, the bookseller, spelled out the difference, 'When you're flirting, you are approaching each other in a way that you want to love together. Friendship is meeting and occasionally enjoying moments'.

Unlike in New York, where both men and women could be the initiator, in Paris the women had to be much more subtle in their intent. Could the men of Paris identify any clear indicators of female intent? Most men were aware of the nuances. ' Mathieu, the artistic director, said the difference was conveyed through body language. 'It's the way a woman walks. If she is attracted to you, she will give it a bit more effort and walk sexy. If the wind blows and she puts her hair behind her ear; if she is flirting, she will hold her hand there, touching her hair a bit longer.'

For both the New York and Parisian men, a no-fail way to ascertain the difference between friendliness and flirtatiousness was to act first and adjust the behaviour according to the woman's response. Take Nicolas, the project manager for a software company, for example. 'To find out if it's flirting,' he said, 'you move in and see her reaction. If she doesn't pull away then you can get an idea.' In order to do this, one must have the confidence not to feel hurt, if she does pull away.

The Parisian women didn't have to be sassy French detective Aimee Leduc, to figure out if the men were flirting or just being friendly – mostly because it always seemed to be the former. They could tell from the sexual undertones. Isabelle the librarian said, 'It's a physical attraction, you can just feel it.'

Monique with the small gap between her front teeth, was in sales herself, so knew when the men tried to sell her a line. 'In flirting they will talk about a hint of what their intention is, it's not just talk about the weather.' Most women concluded that it was the way a man looked at her that revealed his interest. They also could tell because of touch. Martine is a logistics coordinator and explained, 'With flirting there is more touching, and in different places, more south of the body, and the touches last longer and happen more often'. Just how far 'south' are we talking?

LONDON
There is a fine line between flirting and being friendly in the Big Smoke. Londoners find it difficult to distinguish between friendship and flirting. The reasons for this obtuseness include: a socially subtle culture, the impartial charm of London's ladies and the fact that so often the sexes related to each other as people first and potential sexual partners second. Platonic friendships between men and women are common.

In London, you hold your cards very close to your chest and never overtly show interest. Therefore, it's no surprise that a quarter of the women and a third of the men interviewed said they couldn't tell the difference between friendliness and flirting. Adrian, a real estate agent, admitted, 'I have so many female friends, I just assume this will be another one.' He went on to say, 'I always think it's friendliness until I am hit over the head that it's flirting.' In London, if you have a behavioural thermometer, and are able to accurately measure these almost indiscernible changes in degrees all will be fine. If not, read on for life-saving insights into the murky waters of London's flirting scene.

Alistair, the broadcast journalist, who looks as good as he sounds, explained, 'There is courtesy and courtesan, and this is the difference between friendliness and flirting.' The way he sees it, on offer is either politeness or prostitution. Londoners seem to regard flirting as contrived, and being friendly as sincere. They regularly pointed out that they didn't mean to flirt, but they were 'accused' of it, as though they had been indicted for flirting and were currently awaiting their sentence. People also seemed to want to distance themselves from not only the word flirting, but also from the behaviour. Both men and women would say things like:

- 'I have a natural flirtatious personality. I get told off for flirting, I don't realise I'm doing it.'
- 'More often than not, I think I am being friendly and people accuse me of flirting.'
- 'I relate to everyone on a friend level, so I think they are being friendly with me'.
- The friend defence seems to be a protective mechanism.

So unless there's a town crier ringing a bell and yelling, 'Hear ye, hear ye, ye are being flirted with in Olde London Towne and she fancies the breeches off you,' this man simply won't get it. He wasn't the only one.

The men said they could tell if someone was being friendly if:

- There was a lack of sexual innuendo in the conversation

- The other person and the exchange felt sincere
- There was a level of reserve
- Friendly questions were asked.

OK, so these guys hardly need Sherlock Holmes' powers of deduction to work out when someone's just being friendly. It's pretty obvious – a conversation that's limited to genial enquiries about the weather isn't going to lead to anything much hotter than a lukewarm cup of tea. Unlike the New Yorkers and Parisians, who were most likely to be flirting, especially if the woman was attractive, Londoners were more likely to assume people were just being friendly.

Individual viewpoints contribute to the confusion. Christopher, the 32-year-old ex-military man, said 'One reacts to the world the way one looks at the world.' If you are not flirting with sexual undertones, than you don't assume others are. Anthony is an IT guy who makes geek look chick. He agreed, 'I think everyone is just being friendly. Because that's how I approach everyone and that's how I think they are approaching me.'

Possibly due to the 'unwritten rules' which dictate their behaviour, London guys think it best to tread carefully. 'I err on the side of caution,' said one, 'I'd hate to make a mistake. It's not fair on her. A certain degree of caution is good.' Yes, that's right. He has just said that it wouldn't 'be fair' on a lady to flirt with her, if she wasn't interested. If there was ever a case of being too gallant – or too gutless? Another said, 'I can only tell with difficulty. There's always an unwritten code which one can very often misinterpret.' It seems like the men are missing out on many opportunities by being so guarded. One of the guys explained, 'Sometimes I can't tell if someone's flirting and it's gotten me in trouble. I have been friends with someone for a long time and people have said "She likes you".' How different this is from the New York attitude of 'Try first and worry if it's working – or not – later!' Or, the Parisians who only need a hint of eye contact from a woman before they close in for the kill.

So, we've established that London men know when someone isn't flirting with them. But can they tell when someone is, and if so, how? Some said they could tell if a woman was flirting with them if she 'flipped' her hair. This was the number one indicator for the London men. When I asked the women about this, they said they flip their hair all the time regardless of whether they are flirting or not. It's not surprising then that the London men rated themselves the worst at telling when someone was flirting with them.

London women, in contrast, appeared to be more adept at telling the difference between flirtation and friendliness. This had less to do with the nature of the conversation or any physical gestures. For them, it was all about proximity; the closer he stood, the more interested he was. Claire, the red-headed accountant from Devon seemed equally adept at maths and men said, 'When flirting, people are moving close and into your space. He is interested and flattering. Guys are crap at being interested unless they are interested in you.' Alice, a brunette beauty who works as an investment banker, said, 'When they're flirting they invade your space, you either mind or you don't'. Mary, an astute personal assistant, said she can tell by a shift in the manner of communication. 'If he goes from being cheesy to reaching out to you on a human level, that is flirtatious because he is bothering to understand you.'

While many opportunities may be lost, it's understandable that Mr London treads so carefully in his Oxford Brogues. It seems to be quite common for London females to claim they are only being friendly and for others to think they are flirting. Time and time again I heard that the women weren't intending to flirt, but it just appeared like that.

- 'I don't think I do, but I get told I do.'
- 'I don't know though because I don't know when I am doing it.'
- 'I think I do (flirt), even if I don't mean to.'
- 'I tend to be quite friendly and not know that I am flirting.'

Anoushka, the solicitor with unruly curls, was aware her friendliness could be misconstrued by the men. 'I'm told I flirt and I don't even realise it,' she said. 'Guys will take it the wrong way.' And the males were aware of this too. 'Sometimes girls are just being friendly but boys think they are flirting. They get the wrong idea,' said one. It seems like everyone in London is busy being friendly and not flirting. Then who exactly is flirting? Just hop on the Eurostar to find out. You will be in Paris in about two hours.

STOCKHOLM

For the men and women of Stockholm, it's all or nothing. It's either a 2am, drunken invitation to 'Let's go home together' or it's a humdrum 'Let's be friends'. The Stockholmers' regulation frosty demeanour is usually only thawed by alcohol. While there are 24 hours in a day, the Stockholmers only find their bottle for a fraction of that time. It's understandable, then, that distinguishing between friendliness and flirtatiousness is confusing for these chilly Scandinavians. On the flip side, presumably, they have a lot of friends!

Rather than moving into flirting straight away, the Stockholm males saw friendliness as the first step in flirting. Affable Mattias, the 28-year-old MD of a soft drink company, pithily explained, 'Friendly is the ladder to flirting.' Bjorn, the Physics PhD student said, 'I start as friends and then see what happens. If you agree to meet again then you know it's flirting. Women are good at setting limits'. In the opinion of Andreas, the personal trainer, 'In flirting one makes a somewhat 'unnatural' effort when we interact – jokes with sexual content. In a friendly interaction someone talks to you as a person, rather than as a man.' His point is clear – flirting is about emphasising gender differences. Some men favoured the comparative method in determining a woman's intent. Mattias said, 'One could also compare her behaviour with me to her behaviour to others. Does she act differently towards me?' Frederik, the law student, also mentioned this, 'You can feel it', he said, 'But it's different from person to person. Sometimes someone thinks they're flirting and I don't think they are. It's very hard to tell.'

The women of Stockholm, unlike their Parisian sisters, did not have an easy time tellingg the difference between friendliness and flirtatiousness. The Stockholm females were the most likely, out of all the cultures researched, to have a hard time deciphering intent. This is probably due to the fact that Stockholmers are adept at concealing sexual undertones. Also, the modus operandi of many Stockholm males is to be amiable before getting amorous, if, in fact, they ever do. Emelie, the cautious 32-year-old accountant is not one to make rash decisions. She said, 'That's difficult to tell because people have different ways of behaving.' Katarina, who is so gorgeous she makes the flowers in her florist shop look like weeds, said, 'I'm flirting so I know when it's flirting, but it's harder to tell when others are.' This conundrum was often the case.

- 'It's really, really hard'.
- 'I don't think it's possible'.'
- 'Sometimes you don't know, but I guess with friends, you joke more'.

Some of the Stockholm females interviewed admitted to taking years to figure out that they were the object of some man's desire. Annika, the pretty, petite 32-year-old nurse, said regretfully, 'It's so difficult to tell. I was hanging out with boys and years later they told me that they had been in love with me.' Maria, the 33-year-old project manager, is hopefully only this clueless in her personal life. She admitted, 'I've had problems with this for years. All my guy friends tell me they have had crushes on me. It has to be obvious for me to see. Most contact is with alcohol. If I make a strong connection with a friend then I don't want to see it, as I want to keep him as a friend. Friends you can have forever; relationships end.'

CONCLUSION

There are several factors affecting the ease with which a culture can tell if someone is flirting or being friendly. Cultures in which there were more sexual undertones in flirting, like New York and Paris, were also most likely to be able to tell the difference. They were also more likely to view an encounter as a potential flirting opportunity, rather than just a friendly interaction. In cultures which are reserved, and less flamboyant with their gestures and intentions, it is harder to tell the difference. For example, Londoners were not ones to make obvious gestures, and often kept their true feelings well hidden, making it harder to decipher their intent.

Other cultural nuances also played a part. In Parisian culture, it seems very clear-cut. Man sees attractive woman, man approaches attractive woman, man flirts with attractive woman, with underlying sexual undertones. Both men and women understand what is happening – mostly, because they are well versed in their roles and know what to expect and what is expected of them in return.

The Londoners preferred to be seen as friendly rather than flirtatious, and seemed to think if someone was flirting, that their intentions could not be genuine. Not surprisingly, many Londoners, especially males, admitted to having a very hard time telling the difference, possibly, because they were just not aware of the female nuances, or perhaps the women were just too subtle!

In 'Let's be friends' Stockholm, it was also hard to identify dishonourable intentions, especially because the men purposely approached on a friendly level first, with the hopes of ramping it up later. Unfortunately for them, they were often relegated to the 'friend zone' forever! Consequently, the women had a difficult time telling when someone was actually flirting with them. Thank Thor for vodka, which gives people the courage to clear up any confusion.

FLIRT FILE

- The difference between friendly and flirtatious is the absence or presence of sexual undertones. If you feel like they want to move in for a smooch, it's probably flirting.
- An interaction has at least two people, so what you're feeling is probably not one-sided.
- One reacts to the world, the way one interprets the world. Just because you are not flirting, don't assume they aren't either!
- Understand that some people are pretty clueless. If you are flirting with them, make it easy for them to understand.
- If you know you have the 'clueless' affliction, get your friend's take on the situation.

Chapter 11: Sex in the City
ALWAYS READY FREDDIES

Is flirting a pleasant pastime or time to make a pass? Sexual intent reveals whether people view each other as fellow human beings or the means to an end. Flirting can be playful or provocative depending on whether sexual attraction plays a part. The difference between flirting with the happily married 60-year-old shopkeeper on the corner and flirting with someone whose bones you'd like to jump is sexual chemistry. Ok, so you don't have to be Dr Ruth to come up with that insight. The presence or absence of sexual undertones helps us understand how a society flirts. Do they have va va voom on their minds when they initiate a chat, or are they simply looking for a pleasant diversion?

Each city had its own special distinction. New Yorkers flirt to hook up or find a potential marriage partner. Parisians flirt to test their powers of seduction. Londoners flirt for fun and enjoy making someone else feel good, while in Stockholm, the progression goes from a quick blink in your target's direction to knocking back shots to knocking boots.

NEW YORK
New Yorkers are sexy. In answer to the question, 'Do you prefer women who are natural, or well turned out?' one New York Lothario replied, 'I like it all. A girl in sweats is one step closer to being naked.' Geesh, is it getting hot in here? Likewise, New York women are not afraid to use their sexuality to their advantage. However, if you are not a fan of fondling at first sight, you have two options: put up a barrier (and be prepared to hear the line 'You're such a New Yorker!) or distinguish flirting from 'just being friendly.'

Summer in New York. Bare flesh as far as the eye can see. You can't help but feel the city's sticky heat – and I'm not just talking the humidity. When it comes to flirting, New Yorkers put out a lot more than just 'hot air.' As Dana, the pretty business analyst put it, 'Flirting in New York could most likely lead to a sexual encounter.' Unlike their European counterparts, who flirt for the fun of the social interaction, New Yorkers want a tangible result to come out of their flirting.

Joel, the entrepreneur, said, 'In New York it's easier to find quantity than quality. Everyone flirts to hook up. There are 8 million people, you can flirt, hook up, bang em', and never see them again. Guys are like dogs, they will look at any girl who gives them attention back. The girl gives the okay back. Guys are always on for flirting, always looking for the next 'bang'.

And, indeed, sex , it seemed, was one of their main motivations for flirting. Mike, a strapping, handsome banker, with the confidence to match said, 'If you're single and my age it's assumed you're going to have sex if the opportunity arises.' The men of New York flirt openly, with their eyes, their words, and their bodies. One man summed it up, 'We're young, we're single, we're financially stable. Let's have fun!' And he wasn't talking about playing dominos! 'However, at least one lusty New York male defended himself against this stereotype, 'Once in a while when I go out I think "I need to get laid", but it's always secondary.'

When the men of New York flirt, there is almost always a sexual nuance. Diana, the events planner, had their number, 'Guys like the possibility of sex when flirting.' A hefty 80% of the New York men interviewed believed flirting had sexual undertones. While flirting in New York most often had a sexual nuance, only 33% of the women believed that it actually did. This was surprising due to the fact that the New Yorkers flirted like they did everything else: fast, furious, and in your face. Perhaps the women's denial of the sexual aspect in flirting was because many of them didn't want to liken the kind of flirting they did to the kind the men did.

PARIS

Oo la la, the French have got one saucy mother tongue. And they know it! Anne, a woman as elegant as her words, pointed out the use of the word 'wine'. 'To talk about a glass of red wine you can say, Il a de la cuisse, which means "Top of the leg". Or you could say, Une belle robe, (has a beautiful dress) to describe the wine's rich colour. See? It is a sexy language.' Clever conversation and innuendo plays a big role in Parisians' flirtatious encounters as Geraldine the jeweller explained, 'Conversation is very important in Parisian circles. Our language is sexy so we can talk about anything when we flirt.' Isabelle, the willowy librarian, claimed, 'We're Latin, we talk. Flirting is a shadier way to communicate. In Latin countries you can be talking about politics and still be flirting.' And talk they did…of love, passion, and destiny, and this was before we'd even ordered our Perrier. Word play is important in Parisian flirting. Isabelle explained how the most sombre of subject matter can be sexed-up. 'The conversation can be about anything, it's the undertones that overtake.'

There's a 'frisson' between the guys and girls of Gay Paree as discernible and distinctive as the Eiffel Tower – there can be no more fitting symbol for the Parisian males' permanent state of sexual readiness. In Paris, the men are predatory, and the women proper. Thus sexual tension is high. Sure, Parisian women are sexy, and part of their allure is because they play the role of being unattainable. However, they aren't 'allowed' to be sexual, unless they are prepared to be labelled promiscuous and give up on ever being married. Thus, many Parisian women just don't play the game. And if they do, they are cautious. The knowledge that flirting comes with sexual undercurrents often clouded women's feelings about flirting and even stopped them from wanting to flirt. This was especially true in the case of Parisian women, who are aware that flirting in the City of Love always comes with sexual intent. Maybe this was why there was a direct correlation between women who thought flirting contained sexual undertones answering 'No,' to the question, 'Do you flirt?' They did not want to be classified with the group who flirted with sexual undertones.

Like their New York counterparts, Parisian men seem to have a permanent 'on' switch. And like their New York counterparts, almost every Parisian male interviewed said flirting had sexual undertones. Similarly, Parisian women were the most likely of all the females in the study to say that flirting had sexual undertones. Two-thirds of them were convinced that it did. There seemed to be a direct correlation between a woman's tendency to admit to flirting and her views on the sexual implications at its core. The more she thought flirting had sexual undertones, the less likely she was to say that she flirted. Veronique , the PhD student in French literature, was one of the many people who provided a reality check during the interview process. She said, 'My female friends don't flirt because they don't like the stigma that comes with it. In France when you are a 'flirty' girl, you also have to be a 'sexy' girl,' and we don't always want that.'

For Parisian women the end goal of flirting is a relationship. For Parisian men, the end goal of flirting is sex. Alexandre, who works in business tourism explained, 'I will approach any woman for flirting but only one kind for my wife.' If you're a woman in Paris you are likely to be put into one of two groups: 'Virgin' or 'Whore'. Nicolas, a 32-year-old project manager for a software company, freely admitted this when he said, 'The women are separated into two different categories. We respect the wife almost to a religious iconic level.' A woman who is open about her sexuality is swiftly labelled a 'whore'. A woman who politely gives off don't-touch-me vibes is promptly classified a 'virgin' and that's kind of woman men marry. The Parisian men unabashedly said things like, 'I make love to my wife and fuck my lover.' The stereotyping is so extreme that Monique, the sales rep, said, 'Some French people think that if women like sex then they have psychological problems.' A man is free to follow his sexual urges, while a woman's sexuality is decided by the role a man allows her to play. Such perceptions do not encourage men to be accountable or responsible for their sexual behaviours.

The terms 'bitch', 'fashion girl' and 'mistress' were used in reference to the more openly sexual or flirtatious women. Charlotte, the 32-year-old editor who actually makes smoking look sexy, explained, 'My male friends think the top models are very pretty and want to have sex with them, but they call them bitches.' Clearly, women who are categorised in this way are disapproved of, but the men aren't averse to associating with these women on some levels. 'It's OK to have sex on the first night with the mistress types,' said Nicolas, the project manager. When it comes to marriage, it's very easy to be considered for a full time position; there is only one requirement, as Guilliame said, without hesitation, 'For a longer term relationship, a man wants someone who is perfect.'
The women were well aware of the two roles available to them. Time after time, I heard them recite a litany of men's preferences:

- 'Men don't like too much makeup, stupid girls, laughing loudly, or women who are too girly. But to have sex with these girls is okay.'
- 'The French men love to look at these women and have sex with them, but they view them as mistress material rather than potential wives.'
- 'Fashion girls are admired, but guys aren't interested in that kind of girl long-term. They like girls who are comfortable in themselves and try to do the best with their bodies, but not too much.'
- 'If a girl's miniskirt is too short, they will think this girl wants sex. She is a girl for the night, but not for life.'

So the shorter the skirt, the shorter the relationship! In short, the Parisian woman has to be either sexual or chaste and she strives religiously to play this saintly role.

Sexuality might run rampant in the Parisian flirting culture, but it is at the women's expense. It is not surprising then that Parisian women struggle to carve out a place for themselves somewhere between the two extremes of sex goddess and vestal virgin. In Paris, it's angels and demons, with nothing in between. Nonetheless, one cannot deny that the atmosphere is electric. When the flirting is good, it is really good. Do high levels of sexual frisson mean low levels of gender equality? It seems in the case of Paris – yes.

LONDON

While the Parisians use their 'sexy language' to make double entendres about red wine and the top of a woman's leg, the Londoners knock back pints with the hope of some Dutch courage. In London, there was less obvious sexuality than in New York or Paris. Yet England is only a short ferry ride away from France. Could the Calais-to-Dover wine run carry more nuances than half-price bottles of champers?

Of all the cities studied, the London males were the least likely to say flirting had sexual undertones. In fact, 34% said they thought that it didn't. The reasons for this range from ideals of respect and not wanting to 'cross the line', to being too shy to show sexual interest. Recall how the Parisian women all said that flirting had sexual undertones and were the least likely to say they flirted. London females, on the other hand, all said they flirted, and were the least likely to say it had sexual undertones. Londoners inhabit a flirting culture where no one wants to be caught out. Londoners prefer to flirt alone. They don't like being watched. To use sexual undertones in flirting, therefore, is not only too obvious, but could also be considered impolite. In contrast to the Parisians who referred to their language as sexy, this Londoner viewed her mother tongue as being as constraining as Guinevere's corset. 'The language was very restricted as well and so is the way we pronounce things.' The trick is to disguise sexual interest with witty banter.

What motivates Londoners to flirt? On the surface Londoners seemed to be happy to flirt just for the sake of it and many stressed that nothing had to happen other than the flirt. Could this be because if there were no expectations, they couldn't be disappointed? Anoushka, the petite solicitor, said as much. 'I love the idea of flirting when there are no expectations that it has to turn into something more,' she confessed. 'I suppose it might be a safe way of doing it.' There were many fans, both male and female, of flirting for fun. 'Flirting is about enjoyment, the chase, the fun of the flirt itself,' said Georgina, the bubbly secretary. Charlie, the floppy-haired entrepreneur agreed. Flirting is '…just an encounter for the fun of it. See what happens after.' This wasn't 'flirting for the sake of it' in the self-motivated way of the Parisians, by playing the 'game' or testing to see if they've still got that je ne sais quois. Instead, this was flirting with no hidden agendas, no expectations, and no chance of getting hurt. Anthony, the IT guy summed up the prevailing view, 'It's not just a desire to sleep with someone. It's the company. It's nice to make people feel good.' Yasmin in PR admitted that she does flirt, '…but not with intent. It makes you feel good if you don't have a goal in mind. Two people communication is a positive thing."

London women did not seem especially concerned with finding marriage partners, unlike their sisters across the pond. However, both men and women did express the wish to find a relationship. Duncan the journalist explained the London approach to flirting. 'No, the intention isn't to go out and have a one-night stand, it's to have a relationship.' Anoushka the solicitor agreed, ' I don't necessarily look at a guy and think "He's fit!" it's more about if I think he could be a good companion, someone I could have fun with.'

The women interviewed were divided in their desire for a physical outcome to a flirtatious encounter. Some London women responded in a style more typical to New Yorkers. Rachel, the children's book illustrator said, 'The end goal is to get them to chase me. I expect them to ask me for my number, them to pay for my drinks.' Some had no goal in mind at all: Annette, the sultry-voiced jazz singer said, 'I don't do it with intent. It makes me feel good that I don't have a goal in mind.' 'Sometimes it's just nice to have a chat,' said Emma, a presenter on late-night television. A chat? Isn't that what you do with your Grandma, over a cup of tea and a plate of biscuits?

Others showed they were hot-blooded women: Kissing and having sex were common goals. Jane, who works in the financial district, said her aim was, 'To get off with them and if you really like them a date'. 'To try and not sleep with them but definitely kiss them,' said Liz, who works for a big advertising agency. Stunning Yasmin, who works in PR, simply wanted to 'create some kind of an obsession'. Anna, a voice-over artist was willing to wait. 'If not a kiss than the expectation of a kiss in the future, that will lead on to a longer-term relationship.'

A few women mentioned the importance of taking things slowly, 'Not too full on straight away. Exchange a number, start a friendship, not a full-on snog straight away'.

But, more often than not the women echoed the men's sentiments that flirting didn't have to have an end purpose. 'No, there's not always an end goal,' said Gemma, a television producer for a morning breakfast show, 'Sometimes I just flirt for attention. And I love people, giving them an extra spark.' 'Only flirt for fun,' said Catherine, the IT whiz, listed her rules of thumb. 'Never have an agenda. If you do then it becomes something other than flirting. It's thinking about what you are trying to achieve rather than enjoying the flirting.'

Like the women, London males seemed to be split as to whether the end goal of flirting was physical interaction or an extended engagement. Some didn't necessarily have goals. Ex-military man Christopher was easygoing. 'The fun part is the flirting. If you get a snog out of it, that's fine.' 'Just to make people feel good is my goal,' said altruistic optician James. Other men simply wanted to bask in the glow of female appreciation. Alex works in import/export for a large beer company. He strives to 'Curry favour. It's like in a restaurant. You want to get a good seat. You want them to think nicely of you.' Others made their decision according to the conversation: Simon, the PR executive, said 'If I am deeply interested then either a kiss and a phone number if they are being shy. Or sex if they are being slutty.' Max, the music publisher, was of like mind. 'If it's sexual, then sex.' But then there were men like Samuel, the furniture maker, who summed up his flirting goals, 'Rocking chair, the old folks home'. While David, the recruitment consultant, is not one to turn down a sexual encounter, he is also looking for something more. 'If the conversation is sexually related, then sex. If she is intelligent, then a date. I wouldn't want sex the first night with someone I really liked'.

Perhaps because there are fewer sexual undertones in London's flirting culture, and sex is not the end game, many Londoners view each other as people first, and potential lovers second. As Jennifer, the down-to-earth business analyst said, 'No, I don't approach men thinking "You're cute". It's not on my radar. I just see them as people.'

STOCKHOLM
Take a liberal culture where men and women consider themselves equal. The women are financially independent. There is not a strong religious influence provoking guilt and shame. The people are reserved and it's too cold to wear skimpy clothing. What you get is immoderate alcohol consumption and freely available sex, but not a lot of sexuality. Overt or

undercover, sexuality didn't seem to play much of a role in the Stockholm flirting scene. This could be due to a number of factors: gender equality, a reserved culture, and the perennial cold! Yet, once you have a Stockholmer warmed up, the next step is a waltz towards the waterbed. Maria explained, 'At a club, once you break through the barriers, people say "Let's go home."' Henrik, the banker, admitted, "It's not a big deal to have sex, but it's not easy to pick up.' Girls are always thinking I am just talking to them because I want to have sex, but that's not always my intention.' While sex doesn't have a stigma in Stockholm, it still seems to get in the way.

When answering the sexual undertones question, at first interviewees seemed to feel it politically correct to say that there weren't any. The answer was always a prompt 'No'. However, as the interview progressed and it became apparent from their responses that the sexual aspect could not be denied, they would begrudgingly change their answer to 'Yes'. In every city researched, more men than women said there were sexual undertones in flirting. In Stockholm, it was almost completely even – 53% of men and 47% of women said sexual interest was present in any flirting encounter. This was just the first indicator of many that seemed to show that the men and women of Stockholm were on the same wavelength. These Scandinavians do not think that they behave differently from, or desire something different to, the opposite sex. They interact with each other as people rather than potential sexual conquests. Annika, the nurse, pointed out, 'I am a human first and a woman second.' 'I know a woman is flirting with me when she is talking to and about me as a man rather than as a person,' said Anders, the 33-year-old sales rep.

Gender equality means there isn't much hip swaying and lip pouting and coming on strong is a no-no. Why? The women don't want it! Maria the project manager, when asked about how people in other cultures flirt, said, 'In Spain they grab your arm, come up to you more, shout, "You look good!" I like this, but I wouldn't like it if a Swedish guy did it.' The men realise the women's aversion to the home-grown, hard sell. Mattias, the MD of a soft drinks company, explained, 'On vacation the Swedish women love flirting with the foreign guys but if a Swedish guy did that they would just think, "He wants to sleep with me".'

However, this didn't mean people weren't having sex. It was repeatedly stressed by both genders that part of being an 'equal' society meant that women could have sex just as easily as men and without any stigma attached. Johanna the opera singer said, 'Sex is very accepted. As a woman, you are supposed to do whatever you want, to love your body. There is no religion in the culture so we can protect ourselves with the pill, condoms...' While it might take than more than a few drinks to get there, Stockholmers, both men and women, are not averse to having sex, and lots of it. 34-year-old Eric owns a café. He said, 'Going out on the weekends is about going out, getting drunk and getting laid.' If you think he is just being a 'typical' male by saying this, think again. Ava, a 29-year-old dentist said, 'If my friends have been drinking, they will walk straight up to any guy they want and say, 'Let's go home'.'

So, while it might take the reserved Swedes until well into the morning to get warmed up, they certainly are pretty hot once they get there. Yes, the sex is free and easy, coming without much stigma or judgement. However, there is little room for the back arch, chest swell and cleavage show of courtship display. In Stockholm, it's pretty much 0 to 60 mph in 60 seconds.

CONCLUSION

When it came to flirting, New York and Paris were the most overtly sexual cities. Unsurprisingly, the possibility of sex was also a main motivator for them when flirting. The New York and Parisian males seem always to be 'up for it'. New York females would often meet the men halfway, matching their overt body language and sexual talk. Parisian women, on the other hand, could only display their sexuality if they were content to play the role of mistress rather than wife. Parisian women know the score. They were the largest group of women who believed flirting had sexual undertones, yet were the least likely to say they flirted.

In contrast, London men were the least likely of all the men interviewed to believe flirting had sexual undertones while only 25% of the London females interviewed believed there was a sexual undercurrent to flirting. London men were also less inclined to use flirting to gain sex. London's more flexible approach to gender roles may explain the difference. In gender-neutral Stockholm, on the question of whether flirting in their city had sexual undertones, the Stockholm males and females were about even.

Cultures such as New York and Paris, which thought of sex as an end goal in flirting, were more likely to believe flirting held sexual undertones. Cultures that were least likely to say flirting had sexual undertones were more likely to relate to each other as people first, and prospective lovers second, as observed in London and Stockholm. The more sexual undertones there are in flirting overtures, the more the culture is probably aware of, and acting on, the differences between men and women. The more a society separates men and women into distinct groups, the more likely it is to think of them as sexual beings first, and as people, second.

Sexual tension runs high in New York and Paris. The forthright New Yorkers flirt to hook up and make no bones about it. Parisian men are looking for either a wife or a mistress, and the women know it. The chorus of Parisian women is, 'If you like it you better put a ring on it.' Londoners flirt for fun and with the hope of a longer-term relationship, while the Stockholmers don't flirt, they just have sex if they feel like it.

FLIRT FILE

- You can flirt with sexual intent, without using sexual undertones, but you probably won't get very far. This is usually true for men more than women.
- The best way for a man to seduce a woman is for him to make sure that she knows that he is sexually attracted to her. Be cool or funny about it. If you go over the line into crass or rude, it will backfire.
- If you do nothing about it, you will probably be cast in the role of friend where you will languish forever, or until she one day wakes up and and realises she fancies you.

Chapter 12: Obvious Vs Subtle
STRAIGHT TALKER OR SMOOTH OPERATOR?

Different cultures have different ideas of what constitutes 'being obvious'.

In New York the women will show ample cleavage; in London, a glimpse of cleavage; in Paris, a glimpse of her neck above the polo neck sweater and in Stockholm, it's too cold to reveal much at all. The confusion lies in identifying the boundary between being more obvious and being too overt.

Whether people flirted openly or obliquely was often directly related to whether their social culture valued what is said more than what is not said. The New Yorkers believe straight-forward is best because it's the easiest to read. In a culture where time is money, who has time to hang around trying to decipher intent? The Stockholmers' initial shyness may appear as coy, but give them a few drinks and the mild-mannered Scandinavians turn into the most direct of them all! London and Paris, however, operate by not being obvious, although, with different motives: Parisians so they can look good in front of others and Londoners because there's no excuse for bad manners.

NEW YORK

In New York, responses to the question, 'How do you get to your end goals?' ranged from 'Just ask', to 'By any means necessary'. There's no place for subtlety in this city. As Lisa, who works for a large credit card company, said, 'You always have to be on the offence and direct, otherwise you will get lost in the shuffle.'

Among the men of New York, it seems there are two camps: those with the moves, and those without. Chris, the environmental engineer of the curly brown hair explains that he has two groups of friends. 'One group will go up to women and hit on them. They are direct. They just walk straight up to women. They're not subtle. If they walked over to her, I knew they would be flirting. The other group flirts by trying desperately to make eye contact, and if by some chance they get it reciprocated, they have another drink and decide what to do.' These two men are clearly in the former camp. Corey, the hunky actor/ fire-fighter disclosed, 'I'd just go up and introduce myself or sometimes if she is at the bar, I'd just say to the bartender, "Two shots of Jack", or "Want a drink?" If I'm on the street I would catch someone's eye and say, "Hey, where are we going?"

Joel, the 33-year-old entrepreneur declared, 'I would indirectly say (at a volume level that she could hear), "There are some good-looking women around here!"' And that was a New Yorker trying to be subtle!

The women of New York don't mince their words or mask their intentions, either. One of the ladies' favourite ways of getting the flirting started is to walk up to a guy and introduce themselves. 'I just say 'Hi, I'm Rebecca, who are you?' Another variation: 'Hi, my name is … wow, it's so hard to get a drink around here'. If smart and sassy Sarah wants to see a guy again, she would say, 'It's been fun. We should really hang out sometime.' Susan, the budding journalist, shared some tips, 'You don't have to be dazzling in your opening line.

Then he has no pressure to respond in a witty way. Natural and situational are best, like "Damn, it's hot" and "This sure is a long line". And if that doesn't get the ball rolling, then simply say, "You're cute."

The New Yorkers had an uncanny ability to turn any answer into something sexual. When asked 'What non-verbal techniques do you find most effective in getting a woman's attention?' one guy answered, 'Making out.' These sexy citizens take body language to a whole new level. Both men and women openly admitted to eyeing – looking or staring someone up and down in a sexual or suggestive way to express interest. Eyeing was also a useful gauge as to whether someone was flirting with them. 'Sometimes men just stare directly at your chest,' said Alexis, the research assistant who should have been a J Crew model. 'They don't even look you in the face.' Some men knew that the women were onto them. Corey, the fire-fighter and part-time actor said, 'Women don't like it when you're looking at the body and not the face.' Yet the New York women admitted to similar tactics. Alesha, the striking, broadcast journalist, shared her favourite flirting technique, 'You just look them up and down like you are checking them out.'

Because New Yorkers are so 'in your face' they know exactly how to use and read body language. Well over half of the interviewees claimed that they were good at reading people and picking up on signals. Men said that they not only recognised when a woman was flirting with them, but that they enjoyed it if she was 'behaving in a sexual way', or 'drawing attention to her best assets' – as the New York women were well aware. Diane, the events planner, clearly knew her stuff. 'Men love my librarian or school marm look. Sometimes I lean over so they can see the small of my back.' Both men and women claimed that when they were interested in someone, they ensured that they had 'open body language,' that they were 'directly facing someone' and that they would 'move closer' or 'lean into' someone they were flirting with. One guy was so body conscious, that he even noticed the difference between when a woman was 'crossing her legs towards me rather than away'. Unsurprising then that when asked, New Yorkers said the worst flirting faux pas was, 'Not being able to read the signals.'

Like the raunchy body language, sexually charged conversation is also common flirting practice in New York. Men use this technique as a tool to gauge a woman's sexual interest – the theory being that if she is willing to talk about sex, then she will be more willing to have it. They said:

- 'I'll steer the conversation towards the sexual and see if she reciprocates.'
- 'I'll talk about sex and see if she is welcoming the conversation rather than changing the topic.'
- 'I gently go into the topic of sex and test her reaction.'
- 'I can tell a woman is flirting by her suggestive jokes,'

The women used similar tactics. Alesha, the striking, broadcast journalist said, 'I might up the ante by being willing to turn it into a more sexual stage of banter.'

The direct approach has its drawbacks. It is generally accepted that when a man is flirting with a woman, he is most likely trying to ascertain the possibility of sex. 30-year-old Andrea works for a charity. She said 'In New York, when girls notice a guy is flirting, they become standoffish because they know what they want…sex.' Stacey, the make-up artist, agreed, 'Women have to be convinced you are worth their time because there are so many dogs out there. They will say no more often than yes'. The men realise the odds are stacked against them. Jason, the high-school science teacher, said, 'My default setting is women aren't interested and think all men are scumbags and have one thing on their minds'.

The sexual tension is tangible in New York, and women are the targets of unrelenting male attention. Affable Andrea, who works for a charity, said, 'In New York, you don't want to be bothered and have to keep your guard up because there are so many crazies.' The attitude is if you have made an effort to dress up and go out, then you are open to meeting people. This is very different to English culture, where privacy and space are so deeply respected that it's not very easy or common to meet new people, especially if they haven't been introduced to you by a mutual friend. Thus, while it might be easy to mix with new people in New York, what if you don't want to talk to every Tom, Dick, and Mehmet who wants to talk to you?

Oversized sunglasses and iPods tucked firmly into ears are one way New York women avoid attracting attention. The look is so distinctive that one man referred to such women as 'aliens'. Parisian women, who are also under siege by persistent males, employ similar tactics, by wearing conservative clothes in dark colours and avoiding eye contact. Don't give the men anything to look at and they won't look at you. While this may be intimidating for some men, take heart from this handy tip from a New York gal who recognises the challenge: Stacey, a 28-year-old make-up artist of Puerto Rican descent, said 'The women in New York are guarded. The more normal he talks to me the more willing I am to respond.'

Yet, the women use the male preoccupation with sex to their advantage. New York women are not afraid to use their sexuality in flirting. In fact, they seemed to enjoy being sexual, and not just because it's what the men want or expect. Women admitted to 'touching hair, flipping hair, dancing provocatively, showing off cleavage'. Dana, the pretty brunette analyst, explained 'You always have to make the guy think there is the possibility of sex, you have to look, talk and act in a sexual way… engage, lean in, sit with your legs straddled…' Toto, we're not in London anymore. We're in Now York — no need to wait to get home to straddle, just do it at the bar. Do it now!

PARIS
How do you tell if a Parisian man is flirting with you? That's like asking, 'How do you tell when someone has thrown a brick through your window?' Charlotte, a 32-year-old editor explained, 'It doesn't take long for a woman to figure out if he is one of those flirty guys or not.' Clearly, Mathieu, the dishy artistic director, is one of the former: 'She'll give me an opening or a look. If she sends me one sign, I will take it.' One man's assertiveness is another woman's headache. Many women complained about how strongly the men came on to them. 32-year-old Claire, the assistant to a CFO, said 'Of course, I can say yes, it is easy to tell, because they are very obnoxious and make it obvious.' The women bemoaned the fact that the men don't give up easily. Willowy Isabelle the librarian lamented, 'French guys will start at the beginning and try until the end.' Swedish Kristina, a global HR manager also recognises this kind of flirting, not from Swedish men, but from her experiences in Africa. 'Flirting is more on the male side. It's a game they play with women. They get rejected and they just keep trying. Sometimes they win, which is positive reinforcement to

keep playing.'

The good news is that the Parisian men aren't oblivious to their reputation. 'Women quickly get fed up with basic questions because they are so used to being chatted up,' said insightful Laurent, a 30-year-old architect. Alexandre, who works in business tourism was also empathetic and intimated that he'd like women to take a more active role in the flirting process without other people judging them for it. 'Girls are fed up with men approaching because they think they just want to have sex. I would like a woman to be able to come up to me without people thinking she is x, y or z.'

While the men are forceful and persistent, the women dare not express their interest overtly. Unlike New York men who, on the whole, seemed happy for women to be as assertive as they are, not many Parisian men shared this view. Most echoed this man's sentiment about being approached by a woman. 'If it was just for sex maybe, but not a serious relationship,' said Antoine the banker who is clearly not a Simone de Beauvoir fan.

LONDON

Londoners don't do 'obvious'. Both the men and women have a reserved sexuality about them, courtesy of the English preoccupation with good manners. As Sophia, a lithe, 28-year-old dance instructor said, flirting shouldn't be , '… too forward. We like 'polite' flirting.'

Thus, while you'll have no problem knowing if a man is coming onto you in Paris, in London it can be hard to tell.

Characteristics which are universally prized in males in flirting cultures include: assertiveness, confidence, and the ability to approach women. English men, however, lack most of these traits. Not to mention, to be upfront would be an affront for Londoners, who pride themselves on their mastery of undertone and innuendo. However, this lack of straightforwardness can be a handicap in the dating game.

Unlike their upfront brothers in New York, the men of London are fans of nuance. Most stressed the importance of subtlety and described their flirting techniques as:

- 'dipping in and out of areas that might seem playful.'
- 'not saying exactly what you want to say, but alluding to things.'
- 'breaking down barriers without being direct'.

Anoushka, the sexy solicitor, is well aware of this, 'Men like subtlety', she stated simply. Annette, the soulful jazz singer agreed, 'A man doesn't like you to be too full on, but they would like to know they are in with a chance and that they won't be rejected.'

The sort of subtlety the Londoners employ takes immense skill, sensitivity and practice. While the New Yorkers will be the first to tell you about their finest attributes, the Londoners have their own special way of doing it, as Christopher, the former British soldier, said, 'It's about being self deprecating, taking the piss out of yourself, bigging yourself up and then talking yourself down.'

Alistair, a 32-year-old broadcaster offered this advice: 'The trick of English flirting is to make yourself look desirable without actually pointing out that you are.'

Also, it's important that both people understand the understated cues. While she might think she is wildly batting her eyelashes and giving her best 'come hither' look, he thinks she has something in her eye. While she thinks she is tossing her designer tresses with abandon, he thinks she has problems with her neck. The results of these actions might be nothing more exciting than recommendations for effective eye-drops or a reputable chiropractor on Harley Street.

One beguiling Queen of Hearts shared her passive flirting technique. 'I look at them; I don't need to do anything physical. The fact I'm listening makes them feel important.'

And, if you want to be really subtle, do nothing! Samuel, the charming cabinetmaker, said, 'The classic English thing is to not do anything at all as the signal that you're obviously interested.' There is truth in this. Sometimes people, especially women, mistakenly give off signals of interest when they are not interested. In an ode to politeness London women will smile, nod in agreement, ask questions, and stay talking to a man she is not interested in. In contrast, it is equally possible for someone who is interested not to give any sort of clue as to their real feelings. The Londoners hold their cards very close to their chests, and it wasn't just because that's where the men's eyes were resting already. Both men and women seemed to prefer not to let on that they were interested, when they really were. Confused? You aren't the only one. Sam, the website designer, acknowledged that a woman could still be interested in him, even if she didn't show any signs of flirting. 'If that person doesn't openly flirt, it can be hard to tell,' he admitted. Another way to decipher someone's interest? Bring a thermometer! Max the music publisher explained, 'In England you get a subtle change of temperature – the cold shoulder. No woman would ever say, "I'm not interested." If you know the London rules, you understand how the game is played. If you don't, you've lost before you've even started playing.

STOCKHOLM
The Stockholmers are as reluctant as the Londoners to make their true intentions known, but add 20 degrees colder weather, and the effects are even icier! To the cautious Stockholmers, you shouldn't ever look like you're flirting. Why? Because the women don't like that! However, there is an exception, you can if you are not a Stockholm male. I suppose, it's because they should know better. Kristina the HR manager spoke of her time in Africa and said, 'In Africa it's easier to flirt. I loosen up more and get more attention.'

As Clare, the air traffic controller, said about what she responds to when a man is flirting with her. She likes them to 'Not to be too open about it, don't look too obvious. You don't want to know he is interested'. The men are aware of this. So how's this for subtle? One man's strategy is to let her smell him first. 'I stand so close that she can smell my aftershave. I stay on the outside border, like 30cm, for her to smell my aftershave or feel the energy. Let her know I am not afraid of her.' He is a brave one, as Stockholm females have been known to bite. Like the Londoners, alcohol loosens the inhibitions and then there can be no doubt about lascivious intentions. It's hard to miss someone groping your chest.

CONCLUSION
The New Yorkers are obvious. Why wouldn't they be? Time is money and it certainly saves time if you make your intentions clear. The Parisian males don't seem to hold back

either – they have the women to do that for them. Not only are New Yorkers not afraid to be direct, but, they are not afraid to talk to each other either. However, addressing an innocent 'Hello, how's it goin'?' to a stranger on the street in London, could be considered a deplorable intrusion on someone's space, although, a brief 'Morning' and a smile could make someone's day. You're forgiven if you're finding it hard to see the difference. The Londoners have a complex system of social intricacies, all of which favour not letting your intentions be known, while the Stockholmers' signals are subtle to the point of non-existent before the addition of alcohol – and impossible to miss after.

FLIRT FILE

- Being obvious helps both parties recognise interest.
- The preference for obvious or subtle is most likely due to what is most common in the culture, rather than what gender you are.
- The scale is relative, what we might think of as being too obvious, someone else might think of as being too subtle.

RULES OF ENGAGEMENT

Some cities were keen on candour; others appreciated the understated while others understood what was left unsaid.

In New York, if you don't tell people how great you are, how will they know? Here, both men and women are forthright in their flirting approach. In London, it's polite to keep flirting; even when you get the feeling the person isn't interested but whatever you do don't tell people about your accomplishments. This would be seen as bragging. Stockholm is similar. They shouldn't 'take up too much space'. In Paris, the men are direct and the women decorous and in Stockholm it's best to grab a drink before you even think about flirting – or just wait until spring.

In the flirting game, New Yorkers play by set rules that everyone understands. 38-year-old Dana, the pretty brunette business analyst, said 'In New York, it's not about getting to know each other, it's about gamesmanship. Trying to one-up the other. It's like chess and you shouldn't show your real feelings. The pros are that everyone plays by the same rules and knows what to expect. The cons are that no one is really themselves. It's an act. People aren't concerned about who you really are, but more about how sparkling and wonderful you are.' The PC Parisians are also concerned with appearances, if only for appearance's sake. Appropriate behaviour is valued in this structured, formal society. Martine, the logistics coordinator, compared Parisian flirting culture with that of London. 'In London it's more friendliness and flirting mixed together. Londoners are much more relaxed than the Parisians, more open.' Yet unwritten laws of polite consideration govern Londoners' social interactions, and make it almost impossible to know whether someone finds you attractive or is just being friendly.

Alesha, a New York broadcast journalist whose work often took her to London, said, 'In London, people embrace the 'oddities' more. But because there are no rules, you can't tell if someone fancies you.' At least, there's no mistaking the sexy signals in New York. 'In New York, you talk to a guy …and if he likes you, he will ask you for your number. You have a way of knowing. In London, you don't.' She spoke from personal experience. While in London she was flummoxed by three English men, whom, after speaking to her at the bar for five minutes and not asking for her number, she assumed simply weren't interested, despite their obvious admiration. In Stockholm the rules for flirting behaviour vary according to whether you are at home or abroad. Jenny, the biology student admits, 'When I am travelling, especially in countries which are hot, like Brazil or something, I feel much more open and am definitely more likely to flirt! I guess it's the cold weather that makes us so closed.' The road to true love is beset with obstacles and obfuscation. Best we acquaint ourselves with the diverse rules of engagement in the universal game of love.

NEW YORK
You can belong to New York 'as much in five minutes as in five years' because it is a city of rules so straightforward that they are easily learnt. Don't turn on red. Don't honk. Don't show up to an art opening late because the champagne will have run dry, and the

Who's Who will be long gone – one way or another. Do not, ever, make eye contact on the subway, but do huff at tourists who get in your way, and there you have it, you're a New Yorker. The result of the visionary Commissioner's Plan of 1811, New York is built to one of the most famous grid plans in history. Provided you know Broadway is the only street that cuts across diagonally, it is impossible to get lost. But how you make your way up the subway stairs, or down the wide, right-angled streets, is only one small chapter in the giant rulebook of New York. The chapter we're concerned with is the flirting one, of course, and these rules mostly revolve around sex and relationships.

Americans are passionate about baseball. Don't ever put a Mets fan and a Yankees fan next to each other at dinner and mention the words 'World Series'. Baseball is a useful metaphor for life, for work, and for flirting in New York City. From their very first kiss, New Yorkers fit the dating game neatly into bases:

- 1st base: Kiss
- 2nd base: Make out, i.e. kissing/snogging and 'over the clothes' action
- 3rd base: Make out heavily, i.e. heavy kissing/snogging, under the clothes action.
- Home base: Get laid

The rules of baseball dating more or less continue to apply well beyond elementary or high school. However, the adult version is slightly more complicated and intricate, as Susan of the systemic smile explained.

- '1st base: Meet and talk for 30-60 minutes. (Although, with a New Yorker, this meeting could take up no more than 10 minutes.) If he's interested, then he asks for your number; if he doesn't, you know he's not interested. If you are a 'modern' woman, you take his number.

- 2nd base: First date. If he's really interested, he will suggest dinner. If not, he will suggest drinks or coffee. (This is insulting, as it means he won't even spring for dinner). You spend time trying to be interesting and charming, but not too much. You want him to think that you meet people like this all the time. It will end with a good night kiss. If you do really like someone, it's a good idea to date a few other people who completely adore you as well, just to take the edge off. You don't want him to know that you are too interested. It might scare him off.

- 3rd base: Second date. At a restaurant – hopefully in the same week. He'll pay again. The plan of action is to be everything he wants in a woman. You will kiss and make out a bit, but not much. You don't want to be slutty.

- 4th base or home base: Third date. One of you cooks dinner and you watch a movie, thereby presenting the opportunity for sex. If this is still a little too soon for you, this could be the meet-the-friends session, instead.

In New York, if you are woman, 'Giving it up' on the first date is considered too easy. Time and time again in interviews, the women cited the 'three to six dates' rule. It's all well and good that they all want sex, can all ask for it, and do often get it, but if they want anything more than sex, the rule is as follows: Don't indulge in the pleasures of the flesh until you've gone on at least three dates. If you do, you can pretty much assume that the sex is all you're going to get. Wait three dates, ('screw the hot bartender in the meantime), then have sex, then get married. Dana, the 38-year-old business analyst, explained the 'Ten Guy Theory', 'You can only sleep with ten guys before you meet your dream man. One friend was at slot 7 and was hesitant about giving it to this guy with the knowledge that she would only have two more until she had hit her 10.' Apparently, if you exceed 10, you get struck down by a taxi.

While New Yorkers are synonymous with straight talking, they are also creatures that thrive on challenge. Life in gutsy and competitive New York is tough, and the inhabitants are used to having to work for things, wait for things, dream of things, whether it be on Wall Street or Broadway, or out on Saturday night. There is a fine line between being extroverted/expansive and being easy, and New Yorkers, both male and female, constantly perform a behavioural trapeze act in order to negotiate the precipice. No woman wants to be perceived as easy, and no man wants to sleep with easy – unless it's just for the night.

'If this happens, then do this.' New Yorkers have a contingency for everything. When asked if he'd ever been rejected Mike, a tall, handsome banker, with the confidence to match, explained 'All the time. But before I start, there has to be a sequence; first eye contact, then a smile, accepting of my initiating of conversation, open body language. If there is a blip in the sequence, you quickly abort.' Joel, the 33-year-old entrepreneur from the Mid-West, explains his system for meeting women, 'Eye contact first, then approach. If that goes smoothly, then buy them a drink to break the ice.' David, the 28-year-old architect, has an eye for lines…and curves…and shapes. He also has his own methods. ' I like it when she has hot friends so there are more to choose from. I always hit on the second hottest girl as she isn't used to having as much attention and will be easier to hook up with.'

New York women also have systems when it comes to putting on the moves. While budding journalist Susan is from Ohio, she seems to have adapted to New York admirably. She doesn't just smile, she smiles with intent. 'First I smile. I don't show teeth at first. Then, if I really like them, I will show them my teeth and smile.' Marie, the out-of-work sales assistant, explained her flirting procedure 'You just keep upping the ante. You look, and they look. They move closer and then you move closer. They touch your hand, you touch their shoulder. They say something cute, you laugh and flip your hair. They move closer again, so you end up with feet or legs touching' Serve it up hot, this recipe for flirting flambé.

PARIS
The Parisians are PC. They are sticklers for Parisian Correctness, resolutely conscientious when it comes to living up to their idea of the proper standards of behaviour. Ask a Parisian if he or she flirts at work and the answer is always a resounding 'non!'. In fact, some of the women were quite emphatic on this point. 30-year-old Sandrine, with the sleek brown bob, is a director's assistant. She said, 'It's not a good idea to date someone at work, unless it's serious, or you will get a reputation.' She goes on to explain, 'But we do give compliments. There are ways to be nice, and not to flirt. I flirted with a colleague for months, but we were only playing. It was just a game.' So, you can flirt at work, as long as it's only a game? Drinking too much also goes against the laws of Parisian Correctness, especially for a woman, who will likely be branded a lush if she so much as sniffs the cork from a bottle of Chateauneuf de Pape. Frederique, the 28-year-old sales manager said, 'French women

aren't hard work, just Parisian women. This is due to the pressure of the rules. They are trying to be PC all the time.' And yet, you'll hear one thing from a Parisian and witness them do another. They say they are single when they're not. The men say they like to prolong the chase, but they will always give it their best shot. When women were asked if men really wanted to wait for sex, they scoffed at the idea. 32-year-old Claire, the assistant to a CFO of a large bank, said 'This is only the image of what they want, but the reality is altogether different.'

The Parisians' special charm lies in their contradictory behaviour. Veronique, the PhD student in French literature summed it up, 'The Parisian culture is complicated and it takes time to understand.' Willowy librarian Isabelle explained why things were so confusing, 'France is a country of paradoxes and that's why it's so charming. We never know the rules. We like to be mysterious.' Parisians view the aloof subtleties adopted by the women as stimulating. To non-Parisians the signals are confusing. Shy Laurent, the 30-year-old architect, explained why Parisians act disinterested, 'It's a way to hide ourselves. To show what you want is like exposing yourself and then we can feel vulnerable.'

LONDON
Given the Parisians' preoccupation with mystery and morality, at least at face value, it's not surprising that they should find London's flirting culture more outgoing. Antoine, a 35-year-old banker, with impeccable dress sense enthused, 'London is easy. I wouldn't talk to as many people in Paris. I wouldn't know what to say, but here in London there is always something to say. Light-hearted, not too serious, being friendly, "How's it going?".'

However, unwritten rules of etiquette feature strongly in English culture and if you aren't aware of them, any amorous advances are doomed. Concepts of personal space, politeness, not mixing with strangers, and over-familiarity impinge on the flirting arena. If a conversation with a stranger is an invasion of personal space, there isn't much scope for meeting new people. However, the biggest social rule working against the London flirting scene is the notion of politeness. And, the London females are the biggest culprits. Even rejection is softened by good manners. Being polite means it's hard to know someone's real intentions.

Baby-faced Sam, the website designer, said 'In England we have boundaries. It depends on how well you know someone and what their status is in order to negotiate these boundaries.' Unlike the New Yorkers who had their rules well-signposted, the rules of the English are only learnt over time. As Alistair, the 32-year-old broadcast journalist, said, 'Americans follow the written rules and the English only follow the unwritten ones'. Unlike PC Paris, these unwritten rules are not there to help you present the proper public persona, no matter what your really think or feel. Londoners grease the wheel of social interaction with politeness and consideration. Sophia, the flexible, dance instructor said, 'If someone says something you agree with it, even if you don't. You talk about the weather. It's about being overly polite.'

Being polite isn't enough. There was more advice along these lines: Don't blow your own trumpet. Don't say sorry before you need to. Saying 'Sorry' in New York is a deep, personal, acknowledgment of wrongdoing, and only used for special occasions, like when someone reneges on an agreement to allow you to sublet their rent-controlled apartment in

Manhattan. This is when a New Yorker might say 'Sorry'. In London, saying 'Sorry' is a built-in reflex and, therefore, it doesn't carry a lot of weight. This 'It'd be rude to/no to…' attitude permeates the culture and is what gets so many English people stuck in conversations they really don't want to be in. This same attitude also makes it awfully hard to tell the difference between someone who genuinely interested in you and someone who is just 'being polite'.

Simon, the dapper-looking PR exec, said 'In England, you get a slight change in temperature. No one would ever come out and say 'I don't like you.'' Self-assured Jane, who works in the financial district, confirmed this impression. 'If it's not working, I will keep trying for politeness, but will back off.' Rachel, the 29 year-old children's book illustrator, explained how to let them down easy. 'If someone is too interested in you, you have to use different techniques. In order to save face you have to continue to flirt but tone it down so they think you are just being charming and not really flirting. You must back down gradually.' In the name of good manners, London women relinquish their own desires, not realising that the man would much rather have them be honest than polite. Again, this leads us back to the question: Do London women really know what London men want?

Here's a classic example based on personal experience. I used to help a friend out at her singles events. I would introduce people to one another and make sure there weren't any lost souls lurking in corners. I introduced one woman and man. An hour later I checked back and they were still together. I pulled her aside and demonstrated a range of movement with my eyebrows that I never knew I had. 'So, it looks like it's going quite well.' 'Mmm,' she said, with a distinct lack of enthusiasm, 'I don't really fancy him'. 'Well, then why are still with him an hour later? This is a singles party and you are surrounded by available men!' 'Well, I don't want to be rude,' she said. 'Honey, the rudest thing you can do is waste his time by pretending you're interested, when he could be finding someone who really is interested!'

STOCKHOLM

On the surface, your interaction with a Stockholmer is going well, so why is it that you've just been knocked to the ground? One man, originally from Morocco, had this to say about the people of the country where he had lived for the last 20 years: 'There is an invisible barrier. You have to know the rules. It's like an invisible electric fence. You don't know it's there until you have crossed it. Language and culture make it slippery. There are no clear words for "Yes" and "No". The rules of the game are hard to learn.'

Here there are no long, smouldering looks like in Paris, or witty repartee like in London. The Stockholmers don't do innuendo. It's all or nothing. You would expect the reserved Stockholmers to keep their heads well below the passion parapet. However, wait until they're liquored up. From a shy glance during the day to the direct approach at night, the Stockholmers will walk straight up to someone and say, 'Let's go home'. But what's the protocol before the vodka kicks in? It seems the Stockholmers and Londoners share much in common in their attitudes to dealing with strangers: don't get too personal, don't offend anyone – best stick to neutral ground – and don't big yourself up.

Like the Londoners, there is an imaginary line with the Stockholmers that you don't cross. While always polite and helpful to people they don't know, it would take a couple of years before you were invited into their homes. Things take time here. Per, the virile Viking, explained, 'We need to plan our dinner dates for a long time in advance and tend to have a problem being spontaneous!' Once again, like the Londoners, the Stockholmers take care not to offend people they don't know. Eva, the press officer said, 'We would shy away from talking about things such as politics or money with people we don't know. You wouldn't want to offend anyone.' Then she added, with a hint of sarcasm, 'However, a nice conversation about the weather sounds great, doesn't it?'

Bjorn, the brainy PhD student, explained the finer points. 'There are some unwritten rules here regarding when you are supposed to say "Hi" to people you don't know, that may be very confusing for foreigners. For example, if you take a stroll in the nearby woods, it is totally normal to say "Hi" to a person you meet a few trees away. If you are walking in one of the city parks and say "Hi" to a stranger, you are creepy and considered mental. And, god forbid if you would start a conversation to person next to you on the subway. Which prison did you just escape from?' As if that wasn't confusing enough, he then added, 'Starting a conversation in the line at the supermarket is much more accepted by some reason.' But when in doubt, an unchallenging conversation about the weather is a safe bet, just as long as you don't make it too personal, by asking 'What colour is your umbrella?'.

Let's not forget the one-size-fits-all law of Jante, which underpins Swedish thinking and dictates so much of a Swede's behaviour! Hugo, the chubby accounts manager, offered this pearl of wisdom. 'It's fine if you are successful or have achieved something really big in life, but whatever you do, don't mention in it to a person you just met at a party. Chances are that the person will just see you as an asshole.'

CONCLUSION

The New Yorkers' rules are straightforward, just like them. Just be sure to ask for a playbook though, so you can follow along. The Londoners follow codes drilled into them since birth. They could write them down, but then everyone would know. This isn't New York, you know. The Parisians understand the rules but don't always play by them. While the Stockholmers, like the Londoners', have unwritten rules, but they will only reveal them over a double vodka or two.

FLIRT FILE

- If you're not interested in someone, being polite is not efficient; it's wasting people's time.
- You could be insulting someone's mother, cousin, and favourite butcher, and not even realise it. Pay attention to others' reactions and you could be walking through a field of daisies, instead of a minefield.

THE RADAR OF ROMANCE

There was a direct relation between the frequency of flirting and the ability to recognise when someone was flirting. Those cultures, like New York and Paris, which operated in high flirt mode, had a more finely tuned romantic radar. Unsurprising, really, since they get more practice. In Stockholm, however, such interactions were rare – and probably more meaningful – but hard to come by. The men especially were no good at deciphering flirting behaviour. Why? Because they knew the women were not, most likely, interested!

How easy it is for people to tell if someone is flirting depends on whether the culture is outgoing or reserved and, to a point, how confident and expressive they are as individuals. The majority of New Yorkers interviewed, both male and female, were convinced they had a sixth sense when it came to discerning amorous intentions. New Yorkers' brazen approach to the mating ritual may have something to do with such perceptiveness. The Parisians were even more adept at picking up on sexual signals even though their flirting culture is less overt than in New York. However, Parisian men were not as assured as the women when it came to recognising when someone was flirting with them. Londoners, in contrast, were at sea when it came to rising to the bait. What began as a confident, theoretical list of recognisable flirting behaviour, suddenly came to a screeching halt when asked if they were personally good at telling if they were the tender target. This was also true for the Stockholmers who admitted they didn't have a clue.

NEW YORK
When asked if they were good at telling if someone was flirting with them, 60% of the New Yorkers interviewed said 'Yes'. Both men and women said they were in touch with their feelings and could 'just feel it'. One man said he was perceptive to '…being in the energy of the situation'. Other men's responses included:

- 'I am good at reading people. I pay attention to detail.'
- 'I have a good sense if I click with someone or not.'
- 'I am perceptive to people's voice and body language.'

Some people are easier to read than others. Some people don't put themselves on the line and thus there isn't much with which to work. Unlike Paris, where a woman may be considered 'easy' if she so much as looks directly at a man, the New York women gave as good as they got. Thus, the men sometimes did not necessarily know how to react when the women were flirting with them.

Bryan, the lanky aspiring, musician said, 'I'm oblivious, friends have to tell me. I think she might be, but it's not directed towards me. Sometimes I ignore it because I don't know what to do.' C'mon, Bryan. Is that any way to treat a fan?

Jason, the high-school science teacher, said, 'If I have decided to flirt back, I usually have more successes than failures.'

Mike, the tall, handsome banker, doesn't have this problem. 'I'm too busy flirting to recognise they are flirting. You don't think a lot about that part. As a male you pursue without thinking.'

Emblematic of the common female response, Stacey, the 28-year-old make-up artist of Puerto Rican descent, said, 'It's intuitive. I'm good at sizing people up'. Andrea, the 30-year-old who works for a charity, added her voice to the chorus of 'I can feel it.'

Such pervasive perceptiveness may have something to do with the fact that New York is the most populous city in the United States. If you're sitting in a half-empty café, expect a New Yorker to sit as close to you as he can get. Londoners, on the other hand, would consciously sit on the other side of the room and maximise their personal space. Stacey explained why New Yorkers don't seem to value personal space, 'In New York everyone shares the same space. I share my front steps with a hundred other people. It helps to develop people skills. In New York, sharing space doubles as an opportunity for self improvement.

Not only did New Yorkers congratulate themselves on their perceptiveness, but in this competitive city, they couldn't help but compare themselves to each other.

Alesha, the broadcast journalist, was upbeat. 'I understand. I am more aware than others.' Corey, the actor/fire-fighter, asserted, 'I am more perceptive towards the subtle signs that women give. I have experience with women'. No doubt!

Curly-haired Chris, the 30-year-old environmental engineer, pronounced, 'If you are not a moron, you can tell.'

This could also be because New Yorkers are extroverts. They always want to be where the action is. Alexis, the research assistant, described her friends, 'The crowd I hang out with is very outgoing. Not a reserved atmosphere'. Because of the high levels of social fluidity in New York, interacting with strangers is commonplace. Thus, when asked 'What makes a good flirt', outgoing people were the yardstick. Such attributes as: 'the life of the party', 'good at making connections with people they've never met before', 'being able to walk up to anyone and start talking', were mentioned. Characteristics like 'charisma', 'assertive and outgoing' were common responses, particularly for men because they were the ones expected to make the first move.

Despite the fact that New Yorkers pride themselves on their intuition, they have a major advantage when it comes to picking up on those sexy signals. New Yorkers are not the most subtle of seducers. Charity worker Andrea relied on New York men's understated body language, 'I look at their body language. Or they try and hug you, put arms around you, try to touch hand and kiss you'. This is a far cry from the Scandinavian squint that signals interest! As Mike, the all-American banker, remarked, 'It's in no one's best interest not to be obvious. A girl is going to throw out an obvious thing at me, so it's not hard to see.' London men, on the other hand, would love more evident signals of interest.

New Yorkers of both sexes rated themselves as equally good at telling if someone was flirting with them. They relied on their intuition, although New Yorkers' straightforward style, and unequivocal body language probably had more to do with this aptitude. Once again, this points to the fact that New York men and women behave in similar ways, although both also often embrace typical gender roles.

PARIS
The Parisians were the most confident in their ability to identify a come-on, with the women more attuned than the men. Although the men flirt compulsively, they find it harder to discern when they are the object of attention. Of the Parisian women interviewed, 95% said they could tell if someone was flirting with them compared to 63% of the men.

Parisian women are fine-tuned to detect flirting, but this may be because the Parisian males were always coming on to them. Lorraine, the author said, 'We learn early how to handle the men. As a child walking down the street I learned how to deal with the men's comments in a nice way. We learn how to volley back.'

Bar one, every Parisian woman said she could tell when a man was flirting with her. 'Of course, I can say yes, it is easy to tell. French guys are very heavy,' said Charlotte, a 32-year-old editor. Sophisticated Stefanie, the business analyst, agreed, 'It doesn't take long for a woman to figure out if he is one of those flirty guys or not.' However, at least one woman admitted to a crises of confidence when flirting with someone she really likes, 'I can always tell, except when I am really interested in him; then I am not as confident.' Welcome to the club, lady.

The one woman who claimed she couldn't tell was 32-year-old Claire, the CFO's assistant. She said, 'It's because I do everything I can to make it not happen', although she could tell when someone was flirting with her on the metro. 'Because they are very obnoxious and make it obvious.'

While the men make their interest obvious, they prefer the women to be mysterious and aloof. 'If a woman is too open and shows herself then there's no mystery,' said Alexandre who works in business tourism. 'I like a woman to be shy, subtle, and mysterious', echoed Mathieu, the artistic director. Yet, ironically, this makes it harder to tell when she is genuinely interested.

Despite their reputation as ladies' men, Parisian men are not as cocksure as they seem. On the question of whether he could tell whether someone was flirting with him, Laurent, the 30-year-old architect, said, 'Sometimes I can feel it but I don't believe it is really happening'. Greg, the communication student, expressed self-doubt uncharacteristic of Parisian men. 'I don't believe I am that attractive.'

Some men expressed uneasiness because the women might just be 'playing with their hearts', as Antoine, the dapper banker admitted, 'I can see strong clues but still can't be sure they are flirting with me particularly because there are girls who flirt with everyone'.

LONDON
Londoners have a hard time decoding the lexicon of lust. 43% of women and 65% of men threw up their arms in despair and said, 'You can't tell!' Both men and women agree that it's much more difficult to detect when a woman is flirting than a man. Anthony, the IT guy, claimed he can never tell if a woman's interested, '…either because it doesn't happen, or

because women are not shouting it from the rooftops.' He was talking about women like Anoushka, the curly-haired soclitior, who insisted, 'I'm not one of those obvious flirts.'

'Girls are more discreet,' agreed Charlie, the 30-year-old entrepreneur.

Another common indicator for men and women, that showed when someone was flirting, was when the expected social niceties were not followed. For Alistair, the broadcast journalist, the giveaway was the fact that '…she's giving you 100% attention. You know how much time you should be spending, and aren't. At a dinner party, for example, you should be speaking with everyone equally and you are only speaking with one person.' Liz, the accounts manager for a big advertising agency, uses the interaction in a group as a test for a man's interest in her as an individual. 'In group conversations the conversation is directed at you. You are the person in the group who gets told the interesting story.'

Men
Only 35% of London males said they were good at telling if a woman was flirting with them. They attributed their success to a number of factors, saying:

- 'I have people skills.'
- 'I know through experience.'
- 'I am socially aware.'
- 'I have confidence.'

Some of the men answered this question with insightful lists. However, despite seeming to be well-versed in theory, it was a different matter when it came to practice. When asked, 'Are you personally good at telling when a woman is flirting with you?' the same men who had just rattled off considered and accurate lists of indictors would scratch their heads. Max, the music publisher, said, 'It's easier to see two halves rather than just one. I am better at telling when people are flirting with others than with me.' The London males knew what the flirting signals were, but when it came to using this knowledge, they were the first to admit that they were clueless! They found it almost impossible to tell when someone was flirting. Take Sam, the website designer, for example. He was frank about his shortcomings. 'I don't think you can tell. I'm quite bad. It has to be something very obvious, like how I met my last girlfriend. We met a dinner party. I asked her to pass the salt. She did and I said, "How can I ever repay you?" She said, "I can think of a few ways".' And the rest is history.

Many of the men mentioned proximity and physical contact as aids in discerning interest. For these London lads, physical proof was the best indicator that someone was flirting with them. Daniel, the astute bar manager, said, 'I am never entirely certain. I think at a certain point you can tell with a lot of physical contact'. Obvious clues are welcome. 'Sometimes they will deliberately do something like put their hand on my knee or they will tell me', declared Duncan the journalist. Proximity too helped get the message across. Christopher, the former soldier, summed it up. 'It's when we start at opposite ends of the sofa and end up hip to hip.' Or, if not proximity, the fact that she's still around is seen as a good sign. Alex, who works in import/export, said for him the indicator was that '…she's still talking to you after an hour. It's 11:30, the pub is closing and she is still there.'

When women showed interest, many of the men simply assumed that 'they just want to be friends.' The men tread carefully and take nothing for granted, not even one of the top five sexy signals favoured by women around the world – the hair flip. As Alistair, the broadcast journalist explained, 'They could flip their hair but it doesn't mean they are interested in you, they are interested in their hair.'

Some men said they just weren't thinking of flirting and others pointed out that women weren't obvious enough. This was a common observation among the men. If the woman is being too subtle, it makes it difficult to read her intentions. As Anthony, the IT guy, complained, 'I can't tell unless it's completely obvious. I need walls with signs along the road…The only point I can tell is the moment before the snog'. He wasn't alone. 'It would have to be something quite obvious, a taxi ride to their house or an invitation to bed', said Samuel, the charming cabinetmaker. James, the optician, wanted women to '…express more interest; make it more obvious to the men that they like them.' Alistair, too, had no time for beating around the bush. 'I would like a woman to say, 'Yes, we can go home now.'

But, are the women any better at picking up the signals? The answer is yes, although they're still less skilful than the women of New York and Paris.

For bubbly Georgina the secretary, 'It has to be an obvious cheesy chat up line. For example, after coming back from sailing one morning a guy said, "Are you going to have a shower? Do you mind if I come and shampoo your hair"?'

However, in London, such quips are humorous rather than sexually-charged as in Paris or New York. Had she replied, 'Yes, I hope you're good at getting the knots out,' the poor man would probably have been rendered speechless.

A relatively modest 57% of London females could tell when someone was flirting with them. The reasons they gave were:

- 'Men are crap at being interested unless they really are interested.'
- 'I know through experience.'
- 'I'm good at reading body language.'
- 'I'm in the mood.'
- 'I can tell because guys are obvious.'

But were the men really so obvious? When asked for a definition, some of the men said flirting was:

- '…breaking down barriers without being direct.'
- '…dipping in and out of areas that might seem playful.'
- '…not saying exactly what you want to say, but alluding to things.'

Whew! With all the alluding, dipping and barrier jumping, it's no wonder there's a problem deciphering intent.

43% of the women interviewed said they weren't good at telling. Their reasons were:

- 'I assume men are just reciprocating friendliness.'
- 'I am thinking of them as people, not men.'
- 'I have low self-esteem.'
- 'I'm not open to it.'

In London she who asserts wins. However, this isn't New York. Walking up to a timid Timothy in London and saying, 'Seven minutes in heaven, baby' will probably frighten the brogues off him. Some men love it when a woman approaches, others say they might 'feel affronted' or caught off guard when it's done in an obvious way. However, the men do agree that when they are actually in a flirting situation with a woman they like, they like her to 'come on strong' and be obvious about her interest, because they find it so hard to recognise the signs.

It's not an easy task finding a balance between being obvious and seeming predatory in a culture which prides itself on discretion. So, how do the women manage? Mary, the personal assistant, admitted that 'I would find it hard to be openly flirty but they would know if I was interested or not.'

Rachel the illustrator said she wouldn't have to do anything special because he would know she was flirting because she was listening to him.

This approach may be too indirect for the kind of man who only knows a woman wants him when she's bundled him into a taxi and is taking him back to her place.

What a woman might think is obvious, might not be to a guy.

'I'll use obvious body language, like pointing my knee towards the guy,' said Catherine in IT. For most London males, lips puckered in their direction might be more effective. So is it that the men are obtuse, or are the women too obscure? Daniel, who manages a bar, thinks it's a bit of both. 'Women shouldn't be so subtle and men shouldn't be so insensitive.'

In a city filled with women who tend to charm any Charlie with a stiff… upper lip, how can your average London male be sure if a woman is particularly interested in him? This breeds uncertainty in London men who have turned 'look before you leap' into 'wait until the rigamortis sets in'. Thus, the women need to be bold in their overtures. Mixed messages are another challenge for the bashful London male. Picture the scene: A man and woman … she is nodding, smiling, asking questions and, most importantly, still there. He assumes that she is interested. No necessarily so! These charming London ladies act towards men they don't like, as they would towards men they do. Even if the intent is 'I'd rather be at home in a bubble bath with a nice glass of wine' the women are reluctant to end conversations with men in whom they are not interested. Thus, the London woman plays out the scenario, and agrees to exchange phone numbers with no intention of ever returning the guy's calls. Confusing? Imagine how the London males feel.

STOCKHOLM
The singletons of Stockholm need to get on the flirting train to fun town. 77% of men and 65% of women said they can't tell when someone is flirting with them. A common

reason, for both genders, is because they think everyone is being friendly. This excuse is used as a safety net, forestalling failure. It is also used to categorise someone when you are not interested. As 33-year-old Johanna, the opera singer, said, 'It's a safety mechanism to pretend he is just being friendly. I might actually realise they are flirting but then reject it if I am not interested.' It seems the men lack confidence because the women aren't really interested in flirting!

When asked whether they could tell if someone was flirting with them, the men had a common refrain.

- 'I'm terrible.'
- 'I often have no idea.'
- 'I have low self-esteem.'
- 'I'm too naïve.'
- 'I am slow in this area.'

Andreas, the personal trainer, summed up the problem. 'I'm naïve. I have the Stockholm syndrome where I think everyone is just being friendly. Maybe it's lack of confidence.' Mattias, the 28-year-old managing director of a soft drinks company was in the same boat as Andreas. 'I'm bad at that. I usually don't assume the person is flirting. Other people have told me. If I wasn't focused on that interaction then I wasn't open to signals or maybe didn't expect it. I have many female friends so interacting with females is normal for me'. Café owner Eric echoed this sentiment. 'I think everyone is just being friendly. I think, "Why would they be flirting with me?"' Free muffins, perhaps? Per, the hunky accounts manager, lamented, 'Sometimes I can objectively see she is flirting, but I still can't think she is flirting with me. Maybe it comes from low self-esteem. I don't see myself as someone who approaches but rather as someone who someone else flirts with.' And this guy is drop-your-knickers gorgeous!

It seems the self-effacing Stockholmers get by with a lot of help from their friends.

Frederik, the 28-year-old student, said, 'Friends have to tell me. I am critical about my own ability to attract'. Frederik must have friends like Hugo, the slightly chubby, bearded, accounts manager, 'I often help friends. I like meeting people. I'm very social and like to be in control. Self-confident Stefan was also one of the rare exceptions to this drove of unsure Stockholm males. 'We know we can flirt. We know how to get into the game. If you can't win the game you must resign at once.' Most, however, seemed to think that it's easier to give up before you've started. Banker Henrik said, 'I tell myself I will be very disappointed if it's not true. Save myself from disappointment.' What was the source of all this self-doubt? Could it be…the opposite sex?

It seems the women of Stockholm are just not interested:

- 'I am just not open to that. I'm not looking for it.'
- 'I don't give them a chance.'
- 'This relationship thing isn't for me. I don't see myself as a mother or wife. I want to choose my own life.'

Fortunately for the future of the Swedish population, there are a few women in Stockholm who can pick up the signs. Eva, the press officer, said, 'I can feel it. I do interviews. I'm good at reading people but I'm curious about people and sometimes they think I am flirting'. Johanna the opera singer attributes her aptitude to experience, 'I am more aware of it, older, more experienced'.

Like the men, some of the women lacked the confidence to read the clues.
Maria, the 33-year-old project manager, said, 'I am sure it's low self-esteem. Even when I know they are flirting, I rationalise it can't be happening'. 'I've missed it so many times that I don't trust myself anymore.' said Annika, the pretty, petite nurse, 'I just always think they are just interested in the subject we are talking about.' Kristina, the global HR manager said, 'I don't go to places where they flirt. There is no flirting at conferences.'

Any flirting that does happen in Stockholm relies heavily on eye contact. Thus, it appears that it is those people with 20/20 vision who have the greatest success in the flirting stakes. Emilie, the cautious, 32-year-old accountant, explained that she has a hard time telling if someone is flirting because she is near-sighted. Katarina, the florist, also has this problem. She said part of the reason she has trouble telling is because she has bad vision. In Stockholm, you are definitely at a disadvantage if you've forgotten your glasses!

CONCLUSION
The New Yorkers flirted with pride, as flirting is a way of life in the Big Apple. The Parisians flirt as instinctively as they breathe, so it is easy, especially for the women, to tell whether someone is flirting with them. In places like London, where overt flirting is considered to be impolite, the inhabitants go so far the other way that it is all but impossible to distinguish flirting from friendliness. This was also true of Stockholm, where the men especially had a hard time telling. Did they think flirting interfered with gender equality? Perhaps this was a reason most Stockholmers stuck to being friendly.

The more a culture admits to and engages in flirting, the more obvious it is to see, because it's deemed 'socially acceptable'. In those cities where people wore their hearts on their sleeve and did not value subtlety, it was easier for individuals to tell if someone was flirting. Additionally, it appeared the more outgoing people were, the easier it was for them to read others. As the definition of an extrovert is one who gets their energy from others, it is understandable why extroverts have the advantage.

FLIRT FILE

- If you think they are flirting with you, they probably are.
- Many people err on the side of caution, but that only leaves you wondering, 'What if?'
- If you happen to be one of the people who consider themselves 'clueless' in this area, ask your friends what they think.
- If all else fails, just ask them in a flirty voice, 'Are you flirting with me?'
- 'Why can I flirt with someone that I'm not interested in, but I can't flirt with someone who I am interested in?' The obvious answer is because you have nothing to lose with the person you are not interested in. However, it's also not nearly as fun and exciting either!
- One reason we are often nervous in flirting interactions is because we are not sure what to expect, or even say, and we certainly don't want to make fools of ourselves in front of someone we fancy. But, if we practise enough, and become more familiar with the tools in our 'flirting arsenal' we will be better equipped and feel less nervous when flirting with the person we really like.

Chapter 15: How Can You Tell?
DECODING DESIRE

'Time, touch, attention' was the way that Maria, the 33-year-old Scandinavian project manager, summed up the telltale signals of romantic interest. Universally, the main indicators for most of the interviewees in all of the cities studied were: eye contact, smiles, physical contact, attentiveness and women laughing at men's 'bad' jokes. However, eye contact in Stockholm means a quick blink. In Paris, not looking at someone may indicate interest, while in New York you may find yourself being undressed with a steamy stare.

Each city also had its unique indicators, from the women being funny in New York, to the Parisians provoking each other to show interest. In some cities, where bigger is better, like New York, it was a matter of exaggeration; doing what you usually do, but with greater effect. For example, you wouldn't just laugh at a joke, you would laugh hysterically. You wouldn't just stand near someone, you would stand on top of them. However, in other cities, such as Paris, it was more a matter of 'almost', but not quite; she almost touched you, but didn't. The trick is knowing when these seemingly innocuous signs are not as innocent as they look.

NEW YORK
The men and women interviewed in New York identified three main flirting signals:

1. Physical contact
2. Body language
3. Eye contact

When it comes to showing – and recognising – interest, New Yorkers both the men and women emulate Olivia Newton John and get physical. Touch was one of the many ways that New Yorkers received and interpreted interest. Physical contact is usually reserved for women to initiate, because it may be construed as too aggressive coming from a man. As some of the males pointed out, it was the woman's prerogative to break the 'touch barrier'. Yet, New York was the only culture studied where the men were as touchy as the women and sometimes even initiated physical contact. Mike, the highly confident banker, said he sees his friends, 'Touching women on the arm, hand, finding a reason to touch them.' Gina, the occupational therapist of Chinese descent, said, 'Guys will be bold and touch the knee.' In equal opportunity New York, the women, too, aren't afraid to be overt. Doug the dentist said of women, 'They will touch you when flirting. They will position their body towards you'.

Body language 101 seems to be a required course for all inhabitants of the Big Apple. Both the men and women were equally astute students of expressing attraction without words. Stacey, the 28-year-old make-up artist of Puerto Rican descent, can tell by '… their body language. Or they try and hug you, put arms around you, try to touch your hand and kiss you'. Well, that's a bit of a give-away! Corey the handsome actor/fire-fighter is obviously a student of the unsaid. He can tell if women are interested if they are '…crossing their legs towards me rather than away'. Other very good indicators of interest are, 'Touching, moving closer, intense eye contact, facing straight on, legs straddled,' explained Marie, who doesn't miss a trick.

Eye contact was another important signal of sexual interest. Stacey, the make-up artist, knows when she's in someone's sights because 'His eyes are roaming up and down my body.' Bryan, the aspiring musician, said of women with flirtatious intent, 'They are less guarded and closed off in the way they are holding themselves. They face me and lean towards me more. They hold eye contact for longer'. This strategy was more pronounced in Paris, where they have at least 453 different ways of making contact. Acting chivalrous was another way that New York women could tell if someone was flirting with them. They said that the man would 'take care of you'. This included, but was not limited to, the following: 'Buys you drinks', 'Rescues you from creeps', and 'Puts his arm protectively around your shoulder.'

Smiling and laughing were also semaphores for sexual interest. Both male and female interviewees noted the importance of both in any flirting encounter, with 'over-laughing' and 'over-giggling' at jokes often listed as ways to tell someone was flirting. New York was the only city where the business of being funny wasn't strictly the man's domain. The character Big in Sex and the City admits that Carrie's ability to make him laugh is one of his favourite things about her. Many of the men expressed a desire to be with women who made them laugh, and even praised them for having the wit to do so. Corey said, 'If we're on the same page, she makes jokes and I make jokes.' One woman echoed that sentiment by saying she can tell a man's flirting '…if he laughs at my jokes'. Beyond the jokes, New York women were also praised for being articulate and eloquent. So, not only do New York women know what they want, they know how to ask for it.

PARIS

In contrast to the forthright Americans, Parisians adopt the less-is-more approach. While New Yorkers blatantly confess the secrets of their hearts, the Parisians deplore such lack of finesse. They adopt the 'almost, but not quite' approach and place a high value on holding back. Many men mentioned they could tell if a woman was flirting because she was 'almost' touching you. A Parisian will put his/her hand near you, but not actually touch you. He or she might stand close to you, but not next to you. Shy Laurent, a 30-year-old architect, explained, 'The ideal is to come close to the line but not to cross it. Create a borderline.'

In the context of a culture where women show interest by not looking at the person in whom they are interested, the Parisians have to interpret subtle clues. Antoine, the well-dressed, 35-year-old banker, knows just what to look out for. 'It's in the eyes, but they don't look at you. Maybe they are blushing and sneak a coy glance.' The Parisians have elevated eye contact to an art form. Sandrine is a 30-year-old director's assistant, 'It's in the way you look at him, that can translate to words without saying anything'. Juliette of the big brown eyes is a social worker. 'The way he looks at you, you can read it in his eyes; it's in the eyes. His gaze rests on you for a long time. In a group the eye contact is on you, there's more staring. He makes you understand with his eyes that he wants to talk to you, everything happens in the eyes, playing with the eyes'. People were described as having 'dancing eyes' or 'smiling eyes'. Carefree Geraldine is a jewellery maker, 'Especially when you are dancing and watching him; it's an invitation.' Eccentric Olivier delivered this unforgettable image, 'She looks at me as if she will eat me like a biscuit'.

While such subtlety adds mystery, it can also create misunderstandings. The men of Paris err on the side of daring and pursue even those women who seem unmoved by their charms. After all, a woman in Paris shows she is interested the same way she shows she is not interested – by not looking at a man.

LONDON

Chivalry is not dead, you'll be happy to know. New York women could tell a man was flirting when he amped up the 'manly, protective vibe'. The London ladies also found this a telling sign.

Yasmin, the brunette beauty who works in PR, explained, 'I can tell when they are getting protective, like putting their arm around your shoulder or back, like it's a statement, "I own this person. I'm protecting them"'. One woman could tell if he was acting 'frightfully respectful' and, another signal was if he bought the drinks.

Most men agreed – at least in theory – that sure signs of flirtation were as follows:

- 'She laughs at my crap jokes.'
- 'She's happy to be with me.'
- 'She's mirroring my body language.'

Unlike in Paris, where both genders remarked that flirting was often a 'male monologue', London men mentioned things like 'mirroring' or that fact that women will say things like, 'Me too.' One perceptive man said he even noticed if a woman was drinking at the same pace as him. And, being a fast drinker himself, he took this as a good sign. Unlike Paris, a well-sozzled lady in London is far from a turn-off. A woman who can match a man pint for pint is more welcome than a London cab after closing time.

In London, as in Paris, eye contact was key, as both sexes agreed. However, the English are not aficionados like the French or Americans. Absence of eye contact is more telling than long, smouldering looks, as Georgina the secretary, explained, 'The shy ones will nervously look away'. 'Guys aren't generally good at eye contact so they are either a salesman or flirting,' agreed Jane, who works in the financial industry. You'd think, at least Daniel, who manages a bar, would have an advantage. 'I see flirting and people giving each other the eye in here night after night. I should be better at this, but maybe I'm immune to it now.'

The next biggest indicator for both sexes was proximity. The Londoners' have a wide-ranging sense of personal space. Someone entering your space is very noticeable and usually not appreciated. Adrian, the real estate agent, shared an early lesson he'd learned on the subject. 'My first lesson was slow dancing. You hold them tight and move in as close as you can. If you move your hands lower and then they move their hands lower, you're in!' Sofia, the lithe, dance instructor, knew all about men like Adrian. 'He will invade your personal space. You either mind or you don't.'

There were other, more obvious, signs besides eye contact and proximity. One of the most frequently mentioned ways that a woman knew a man liked her was because he was paying attention to both her, and her chest. Annette, a sultry voiced, jazz singer said, 'I can usually tell because he sneaks a look at my chest'. Other women said they could tell that men were flirting with them when they were 'looking at my chest' and 'commenting on my body'. Sam, the website designer, acknowledged that, 'Women want men to look at them rather than their breasts. You want to make it clear you are looking at their body, but not in a sleazy way. People want to feel attractive but not an object of your lust.' However, the women admit to using this mammary fixation to their advantage. Anna, the voice-over artist said, 'I'll let him get a glimpse of cleavage. I see nothing wrong with showing my god-given assets.' Alice, the glossy-haired investment banker said she uses her ample charms to good effect, 'I give them a glimpse of my cleavage, you know, show my best assets.' Yasmin's friends are more forthcoming. 'I know my friends are flirting when they use their bodies to their advantage.' And how do they do this? 'Boobs out, move hips, show necks, arch bodies.' That should be obvious enough. Claire the accountant said she could tell her friend is flirting because 'She has her boobs out and faces the guy she likes' Apparently, this only works for her friend for short-term encounters. 'But she only gets one night stands'.

STOCKHOLM

Of all the cities studied, the Stockholmers were the worst at deciphering the lingo of libido. Only 24% of men and a measly 34% of women said they were able to tell whether someone was flirting with them. Mia is the buyer for an art gallery. When asked the question 'How can you tell when someone is flirting with you?' she had to first clarify, 'When you say 'flirting' do you actually mean talking to a guy?'

Stage 1 in the mating game in Stockholm entails eye contact, and a lengthy spell at that. As Eva the press officer said, 'It starts with strong eye contact. The first thing you do is make eye contact, then look away. After a while, you just keep looking.' Jennifer is a PhD student in biology. She elaborated, 'It's a procedure; we start by making eye contact. He looks, then I look'. When asked why eye contact is the first point of contact, Eva explained that unlike Latin cultures, where it's easy to make physical contact because of the dancing, they didn't have chances like that in Sweden. She added that Swedish boys don't give you the same attention. However, if they did, the women wouldn't like it. Eva agreed, 'No, Swedish boys couldn't do that'. Flirting from afar allows the reticent Stockholmers to gauge potential interest, reducing the chance of rejection. As Clare, a 30-year-old air traffic controller said by way of explanation, 'The reason we are subtle is that if the other person isn't interested in you, then no one will notice. You don't want to make a fool of yourself.'

Mostly, the Stockholm men, like their London brothers, were at a loss when it came to deciphering female intent. Bjorn, a 31-year-old doctoral student drew comfort from facts and figures, 'I notice the behaviour, but unless it's totally obvious, I don't make the connection that she is doing it with me.' It is his faith in physics that keeps him going. 'The statistics show that we will eventually get together.' Henrik the banker would also appreciate a formula or two to help him with this problem. 'It's hard to tell if she is flirting or just good at socialising and meeting new people.' Personal trainer Andreas looked at it as a puzzle that must be solved, 'I don't know for sure, which is a big problem in life. You have to try and figure it out. It's like a game. It's a mystery and you don't know for sure. But focusing of attention, or if you feel a hand on your leg, then you know.'

Many of the males seemed keen on the direct approach, as were their London brothers, who were equally stumped by subtlety. For Mattias, the soft drinks MD, it's about having self-belief. 'I have no idea. It's about confidence. People want to flirt to build confidence. They might see the signs but think, "No, that's not true". She would have to be very explicit. I only could tell with my last girlfriend because she touched my arm and we kissed.' He wasn't the only one, Eric who owns a café, admitted, 'I need it direct and obvious'. Failing the direct approach, a sure sign that a woman was interested was if she was nervous, or blushing.

So, did the females fare any better? Did their 'female intuition' save the day? Not exactly. The women said: 'I just don't know'. 'Sometimes my friends say "He's flirting with you". I don't see it.'

This woman also gets by with a little help from her friends

'You don't know until after when someone else has told you. It's so ambiguous. Maybe I am just too cautious.'

If they did notice, it was mostly because of the attention from the man. As Emilie, the 32-year old accountant, said, 'If he talks to you for more than 15 minutes, then he really likes you.' If they could tell, it was mostly because he was paying attention to her and was asking personal questions. Clare, the air traffic controller, said, 'I'm not interested in flirting, so I don't pay that much attention, but if a guy is flirting with you, he's probably going to be extra nice.'

But take heart. After spending a good deal of the night eyeing each other from afar, eventually – usually with the aid of alcohol – one person will approach the other and then you don't need to be pyschic to read the signs.

CONCLUSION
All cultures seemed to have the same standard indicators of sexual interest. One of the most common signals was eye contact and its many uses. Other people could tell by physical contact and proximity was another important sign. In fact, physical contact was a very important clue for men to show that women were interested, as it was the only indicator that could not be misinterpreted! Most cultures said they could tell by the body language of a person, but the levels varied. The New Yorkers certainly weren't shy about using their bodies to display interest while the Londoners' were much more subtle. To the English, 'obvious' is pointing your knees in a guy's direction.

FLIRT FILE

- There are six universal signs for flirting: eye contact, smiles, touch, body language, proximity and attention. Use these to notice if someone is flirting.

1. Eye contact: It is longer, more intense, and happens more frequently. If you are starting with eye contact from afar, the rule is if they look three or more times, it means he/she is interested.
2. Smiles: Open and easy smiles, especially ones that show teeth
3. Touch: In most cities, it is the women who do more touching and are first to break the 'touch barrier'. New York males were the exception. Touching on the hand, or close to the hand, are considered to be more intimate places to touch than the shoulder or arm.
4. Body language: It is open, the arms are uncrossed and shoulders are facing your way. Look at the direction of the feet. Where they are pointed, so is the interest.
5. Proximity: They have moved closer to your proximity or, if you are already engaged in conversation, they are standing very close to you. This also enables them to smell you, which is a very powerful tool in attraction.
6. Attention: If you are getting a lot, especially in comparison to others' who might be in your group, means they like you!

- Be flexible and open-minded as to the level or intensity of how these signals are displayed. Don't expect a toothy smile at the beginning of an interaction, if a cities' inhabitants save that one for people they know well.

NEW YORK

How men can tell:
- Body language
- Eye contact
- Touch
- Over giggly at stupid jokes

How women can tell
- Intense eye contact
- Body language
- Attention
- Protectiveness
- Laughs at my jokes

PARIS

How men can tell:
- Eye contact, or lack thereof
- Attention

- Almost touching
- Acting shy or coy

How women can tell:
- Eye contact
- The way he speaks/provokes
- Attention
- Makes me laugh

LONDON

How men can tell:
- Eye contact
- Proximity
- Playing with their hair
- Laughs at my 'crap jokes'
- Mirroring

How women can tell:
- Eye contact
- Proximity
- Undivided attention
- Looks at my chest
- Buys drinks
- Acts chivalrous

STOCKHOLM

How men can tell:
- Eye contact
- Proximity
- Blushing/acts nervous
- I need it to be direct
- Most of them couldn't

How women can tell:
- Eye contact
- Attention
- Asks me personal questions
- The way he looks at me
- Length of time he spends with me
- Most of them couldn't

Chapter 16: Do You flirt?
NAME IT TO CLAIM IT

'Do you flirt?' – three little words that stopped people in their tracks. Hot on the heels of that humdinger, came this one ... 'Why?' We'd defined flirting, distinguished it from friendliness, identified underlying sexual undertones and assessed whether you knew it when you saw it – all safe speculation. Now, there was no denying personal culpability. The quickness and content of the response depended on the flirting culture of the city in question, and whether flirting was regarded in a positive or negative light.

NEW YORK
In New York, 'Do you flirt?' could have been substituted with 'Do you draw breath' so often was the answer 'Yes'. An astonishing 93% of men and 94% of women answered in the affirmative. No other city so proudly and willingly claimed itself flirtatious. And why? 'Fun' was the reason most often mentioned by both the men and women:

- 'It's fun. A mini exploration of someone. Delving into an unknown person or situation.'
- 'It's my source of entertainment.'
- 'It's pleasant to interact with someone you are attracted to, it's pleasing.'

Both the men and women used flirting as a tool to look for relationships as well as sex. The Big Apple is jam-packed with people wanting to make, build and develop relations in the city in order to get ahead.

New York men are a results-driven bunch. Many of the men had an end goal in mind. After fun, the next most cited reason for flirting was as 'a means to an end.' Mike, the self-confident banker who is, no doubt, having lots of it, said, 'You get to have sex if you're good at it,' – good at flirting, that is. The question of 'good at sex' didn't come up, although I'm sure had they been asked, New Yorkers would have given a resounding 'Yes' to this too. New York males flirt for sex, as the women are very much aware. Lisa, who works for a credit card company, said, 'You want flirting to be fun and light, not that the guy has to 'achieve' something by the end of the night. Guys feel if they don't get something, there is no point to it. No prize at the end.' The men were more open about looking for sex than the women, perhaps because it seemed almost expected of them.

The women, however, didn't admit to flirting so blatantly for a 'prize at the end' – except for the woman who flat out said she flirted to get drinks. But that's just common sense, right?

New York women flirt to secure a date or a phone number, with a view to consummation no sooner than the third date. Most said their end goal was 'To have him ask me for my number' or 'manipulate the situation to get him to ask for my number'. Although the women don't like to ask outright, they will, if he's proving slow on the uptake. As Sarah, the smart and sassy fashion buyer, admitted, 'If they don't have the smarts to ask, then I hint at an activity.'

In New York, much as in Paris, flirting is wielded as a weapon in the power struggle between the sexes. 'It's knowing that you can get them. It's a power thing,' revealed Stacey, the 28 year-old makeup artist.

While the men flirt because they enjoy sex, they are also looking for a willing partner, often to confirm their own attractiveness. I'm also looking for sex, to see if I am desirable,' admitted high-school science teacher Jason. 'I'm interested in having relations with somebody, physical and otherwise: there is a psychological need to feel attractive,' confessed Doug, with a smile that helped advertise his profession as dentist. This is not surprising in this competitive city, where everyone is striving to be 'the best'. Notches on bed posts are a tangible way to measure success. The men also wanted to start relationships: 'I am looking to find my significant other and looking to see if we are compatible,' said Bryan, the musician.

Only 7% of the men interviewed said they didn't flirt, saying they weren't sure of what they were doing, or were worried if their attempts would be well received.

Women whose families were second or third generation New Yorkers were noticeably reluctant to admit that they flirted. Some substituted 'being friendly' for flirting with the sort of ease they'd display when switching from sugar to low-calorie sweetener in their double, no-whip, skinny macchiatos. It seems they wanted to distance themselves from the sexual nature of flirting in the city. When asked if she flirted, Gina, a 33-year-old occupational therapist of Chinese heritage said, 'I don't flirt a lot but maybe it's because I am Asian'. Stacey, the make-up artist of Columbian descent said, 'I wouldn't say that I necessarily flirt, I am just very friendly.' Faced with a choice between sexual flirting or no flirting at all, substituting words like friendly allowed the women to flirt on their own terms. The 6% of women who said they didn't flirt claimed they were too shy.

PARIS
'Do you flirt?' I asked one Parisian man. He replied, 'Right now?' The Parisian men interviewed, with the exception of one, all said they flirted. In fact, as a group, the Parisian males rated themselves the flirtiest of them all. Like their New York home boys, they had some very broad criteria when it came to flirting, confessing they did it, 'Extensively', 'Everywhere,' 'With anyone, of any age, in any situation'. In all the cities surveyed, most males perceived flirting as a means to an end. Parisian males, however, were the only ones to stress that nothing had to come out of flirting. It could just be done for the fun of 'the game'.

The phrase, 'Flirting is a game' was a constant refrain. And the object of the game? To best the opponent; to be the supreme seducer. The person who shows real interest in the other is the undisputed loser. This isn't always easy, Sandrine, the director's assistant with the sleek brown bob said, 'The danger is that you'll forget it's just a game and get too involved.'

The Parisians are in it to win it. For both the men and women, there were two main reasons for flirting: fun and to test one's powers of seduction. 32-year-old Claire, who works in finance, explained, 'The main reason is to give yourself confidence about your capabilities.

It's the question of can you attract people? Are you still good-looking? But, it's also a game because you are bored and want to have fun.'

Both men and women said that their greatest reasons for flirting were:

- to see if people liked them
- to test their ability to attract/seduce
- to make themselves feel good
- to build confidence.

The genders differed on two counts. The game aspect was more important to the males – every man interviewed mentioned it. The women had two additional motives for flirting:

- as a tool to get what they want
- as a way to feel feminine.

Flirting for the Parisians is almost entirely self-serving. They don't do it to make others feel good, help smooth social relations or meet new people. It's not about kissing, dating, or even bedding their sparring partner. Parisians view flirting as seduction and people don't usually use seduction as a way to meet new people – they join a book club, buy a dog to walk, or take an evening class in extreme knitting. A very Parisian sentiment was 'You feel powerful that you can seduce someone.' Sophie, the primary school teacher said, 'It's a fun game. I use it to get something when someone is resisting me.' PhD student Veronique, said, 'It's fun, it boosts your ego. I like to see men desire me. Men often like my mystère.'

The Parisians flirt to establish how others see them; where they rank in relation to everyone else. Do they have what it takes to score? Isabelle, who gives new meaning to the stereotype of the sexy librarian, said, 'Sometimes you just want to know more about your ability to attract.' There seemed to be a lot of prestige in one's ability to attract the opponent. Without this ability, one resembled a bottle of champagne without the fizz; tempting on the outside, but no sparkle on the inside. Isabelle summed it up nicely, 'On the one hand, it's a selfish game to see if one still has it, but flirting is also light, fun and pleasant. It's like champagne or a dip in the pool on a hot summer's day.'

However, if the other person knows you are genuinely interested, then you have lost the game. Antoine, the banker with fashionable flair, described the key to success as, 'To try, but not to want.' 28-year-old sales manager Frederique said 'Parisian flirting is rather like a series of techniques used to make another person understand you are interested, but it must be subtle, otherwise the person will understand and just run away.' According to the confusing Parisian rules of flirting, you're better off using flirtation with someone who isn't tagged as a favourite. That way you don't risk letting any real feelings get in the way of things. After all, if the situation gets serious and you show your vulnerability, you not only lose the game, but you drive away the object of your desire. Greg, a student of communication, who had difficulty understanding women, explained, 'We wait because we want to be sure. It's difficult to know because girls like to play.' This wariness is inevitable in a society that insists on traditional gender roles and encourages game playing in their personal interactions. Not surprisingly miscommunication and manipulation is common. One interviewee described certain flirtatious interactions this way, 'When you say "No", they say they were just being friendly and when you say "Yes", they say they were just being friendly!'

All the participants agreed that an easy win is as bad as losing. Don't ever give in too easily. The surest way to ensure 'game over' is by prematurely thinking the game is over. As Mathieu, the artistic director, said, 'Keep in mind this is a game and it's not interesting if you win too easily. I don't want them to immediately say, "Do you want to go back to my place?"' In contrast, a lot of New York males would want someone to be this direct, and they'd certainly appreciate this fast-paced, cut-to-the chase approach.

The game has some unwritten rules. The men did not want to be seen as 'Le Dragueur' – a womaniser. Romantic Guillaume has eyelashes that would make Joan Collins jealous. 'I am not the kind of guy who looks at the girls without knowing her and just intrudes into her life. Often the seduction begins with a friendship and the seduction comes over a period of time. I might be seduced by her looks the first time, but I don't flirt with someone I don't know.'

In most cultures, if women said they didn't flirt, it was usually because they were too shy or insecure. This was not the case in Paris. Here the reasons for not flirting were vastly different:

- 'It's misleading.'
- 'I am not good at it.'
- 'It's a boring game. '
- 'I'm with friends and not thinking about it.'

Of the Parisian females interviewed, 78% of them said they flirted. This might seem like a high number, but Parisian women were the most likely to say they did not flirt, out of all the people studied. This might have something to do with the fact that flirting is so prevalent in the culture that the women don't have a choice but to flirt. The ability to attract and beguile is an integral part of being Parisian, but even more so for the women. There is great pressure put on Parisian women to arouse and seduce men. However, the women have to navigate the fine line between flirtatiousness and salaciousness. Monique, a 28 year-old sales rep, pointed out that, 'Men are not happy when they want to take it further and you stop it. The game is to play with their masculine expectations, but not to take it too far.'
The women are the ones charged with making sure an encounter doesn't get out of hand and that men didn't get the wrong idea. 'In France you have to put a limit on the French boys,' said Sophie, the 34-year-old primary school teacher. Some women admitted to backing off if they realised that the man was actually getting into it more than they were. The women were aware of the risks of gaining a questionable reputation and most took full responsibility for not leading the man on. Juliette, the social worker, said, 'A woman must take care not to flirt with a man who likes her. It's very easy for women to get a bad name in French culture.'

This explains why some women were not proponents of flirting; they were wary of it! Some even seemed to have a major dislike of the practice. Isabelle, the French librarian working in London, said she did not flirt. 'Flirting is bad. She did not flirt. 'Flirting is bad,' she said. 'Flirting is misleading. When you flirt, you show the best side of yourself, it's light, cheerful, and happy but it's not the reality of things in the long-term. Many people start a relationship based on flirting and sexual attraction and spend a lifetime trying to live up to the promises made in that moment.' 35-year-old Francine, who works in publishing, simply doesn't want the effort and hassle of beginning a game of seduction. 'Sometimes I just can't be bothered!' she said, 'It's boring; I would only flirt with someone that I am already in a relationship with, whom I already know. I don't want to flirt and give them false hope.

While it seemed the Parisians were as likely to flirt as they were to buy a baguette, both sexes were aware of the implications and for the women, it came with an extra burden – being mindful of the man's ego. So what's the score when someone really likes someone else? And what happens if, fortuitously, two people like each other in equal measure? No satisfactory response was ever forthcoming. Everyone seems to abide by the rules of the game, but does anyone really win?

LONDON

It seems that no one, native or not, believes English flirting actually exists, and, more specifically, that English men actually flirt. That is probably because of guys like James the optician. Explaining why he doesn't dabble, he said, 'It's like being scared of spiders. I just am. I don't know why.' When he does manage to overcome his phobia, he soon scuttles back to safety. 'I might test the water, stepping over the mark from formality to flirting and see how it's received. If she's frosty, then I won't try anymore.'

When asked if they flirted, Londoners often feigned innocence. Georgina, a 28-year-old secretary who punctuates all her answers with a laugh, said 'I don't think I do, but I get told I do.' The chorus continued. 'I don't think I do, but people say I do,' said David, a recruitment consultant with expensive tastes in wrist watches. 'Sometimes women think I am flirting because I give them compliments like nice shoes. I am just telling the truth and don't have any intentions.' Claire, a flame-haired accountant admitted, 'I think I do, even if I don't mean to.' Simon, who is in Public Relations, said 'Sometimes I have been told off for flirting inadvertently. People misconstrue being nice.' Poor bloke – he's probably just doing his job! Emma is a presenter for one of those TV stations you come across at 2 am while you're flipping through the channels. She has a similar problem. 'More often then not I think I am being friendly and people accuse me of flirting.'

The men couldn't offer a definitive answer to the question 'Do you flirt?' While 85% of them said 'Yes', they also pointed out that flirting wasn't something that had an on/off switch. They didn't consciously think about it. James the optician might have an advantage when it came to recognising eye contact, but he also said, 'I don't flirt deliberately. I don't think "Right, I am going to start flirting now." It's a subconscious response to someone who is flirting with me.' The Parisians also said they don't consciously set out to flirt – it was just something they were born to do. The Londoners, on the other hand, make flirting sound like something that happens by accident. 'Whoops, I'm terribly sorry, but I've accidentally flirted with you!'

The 15% of London males who didn't answer 'Yes' didn't necessarily say 'No'. They also said, 'I don't think so'. David, the recruitment consultant said, 'I suspect I do flirt, but I don't know if I do it consciously. I don't intend to. It doesn't occur to me.' 'It has to naturally escalate. I don't think, "I'm going to flirt now",' said Adrian, the real estate agent.

The men also said that they would feel uncomfortable if the flirting became a conscious effort. Sam, the website designer, said 'The flirting takes over by itself. If I start thinking "Where is this going?", then I become nervous. It becomes unnatural.' Chic geek Anthony is another proponent of the natural method: 'I feel like I'm having a normal conversation. I don't think much about the flirting or the how or the why.' This is very different from the New Yorkers who flirt with force and fury. In fact, the Londoners often mentioned that the American flirting style was too full-on for them. Joey's 'How you doin'?' routine from Friends just isn't going to work in London.

As in the other cities, the number one reason for flirting for both genders was because it was fun. Rachel, the illustrator of children's books, said 'When it's reciprocated, you get a buzz and feel high and excited. It's fun and it's quite risky'. Alex, who works in import/ export agreed, 'It's fun to have an interaction with someone you are sexually attracted to. Something different in the mundane path through life'. But the Londoners had other reasons for flirting. Unlike their Gaelic cousins, Londoners were more likely to use flirting as a social lubricant or to boost someone else's ego, rather than their own. Daniel, the bar owner, serves up compliments with his cocktails. 'The end game of flirting is to get someone to think of you favourably, the other extent is to give people a boost. English women often have low self-esteem.'

Londoners mix business with pleasure. While the Parisians would swear they don't flirt at work, both London men and women admitted to this. It seemed like the polite thing to do. Alistair the broadcast journalist said, 'It makes for a productive work environment. It just makes things easier.' Duncan, the journalist, can always get behind enemy lines. 'I flirt in my job. There can be an end result getting people to do what I want them to do.' Alex, the import/export man, thinking of more customers, said, 'Sometimes it leads to business.'

The women agreed that flirting helps grease the wheels at work:
Yasmin, the PR stunner said, 'I flirt if I want something from the guy, like if I want job contacts.' Jane works in the financial industry: 'I use it if I want something or need something like work done quickly. I notice other women in my office also do it.' Duncan the journalist was also aware of this ulterior motive, 'Some women use flirting to be more social in society. When used in the media and in a professional way it can be fake. It's hard to tell the difference'.

Englishmen do flirt, but without the assertiveness of the New Yorkers or the suaveness of the Parisians. The techniques range from distant to downright crazy. Guys seem either to be gazing wistfully in the other direction or slipping on banana skins and shouting 'whoops' in order to attract women. The clowning and affected ineptitude are used, to good effect, to inspire sympathy. The men seem to favour mirth as a fast train to Flirtland.

Simon, who works in PR, said, 'You'd use slight innuendos, slight rude remarks which are intended as a joke but with a hint of truth.' Christopher, the 32-year-old ex-military man said, 'I like the playfulness and the banter. I have a technique of disagreeing and women love it!'

Just as not all New York males are egomaniacs named Joey, and not all Parisian females want to channel Coco Chanel – although they might all want her wardrobe – not all London males are shy, bumbling Hugh Grant characters in the flirting game. There are many charming, captivating, and very adept male flirts in London. So, it might be more subtle than you're accustomed to; it might not be as obvious as you'd like, but if you pay attention to the signs and embrace the charm you'll find that the English do flirt, in good form and good humour.

STOCKHOLM

The majority of Stockholmers said they flirted. Like the other cities studied, the Stockholmers' main reasons for flirting were excitement and ego. Maria, a 33 year-old project manager said, 'I do it on the train. I look and smile and know it's not going further. If he responds, it's good for my self esteem.' They claimed to flirt in the shops and on the street, and as Maria said, on the train. However, evidence of such amorous behaviour was lacking. Flirting by night was easy to detect. When a man paws at your chest, it's pretty apparent that he wants to make contact – in fact, he has made contact. For Stockholmers flirting means a quick blink in your target's direction. The Swedes were used to such minute gestures of interest, although that didn't mean anything would be done about it.

In line with the majority male view of all the other cities, except London, the men of Stockholm were more likely to say they flirted than the women. However, at 88% compared to 80% of women, the gap wasn't significantly large – not like it was in cities such as Paris. The Stockholm males were most likely to flirt as a way of meeting people, because it was exciting, and as a confirmation of their attractiveness. Per, the virile Viking said, 'It's exciting, even if you don't have a plan for more. It's a confirmation that you are okay and attractive.' Mattias, the MD of the soft drinks company said, 'It makes an ordinary day more exciting.'

While the men might be more likely to say they flirted, they also pointed out that it wasn't necessarily in a 'pro-active' way. Bjorn, the PhD student, said 'I guess I do flirt, but it's not "I'm going to start flirting now". I don't do it in an active way.' Stefan, the bicycle store owner, was cut from the same cloth. 'Normally, I don't take the initiative but I respond if I can'. Displaying astonishing powers of deduction, café owner Eric said, 'I'm not particularly active right now, but I am dating so I must be flirting.' Like the London males, the Stockholm men were happy to be the subject of feminine interest. However, if the woman waits for the man to take the initiative, she could be waiting a long, long time.

80% of the Stockholm women interviewed said they were willing flirtatious participants. They gave reasons such as 'It's fun', 'It's exciting,' 'It's good to get feedback from people'. Annika, the pretty, petite nurse echoed these reasons when she said, 'If people flirt back, it's a good feeling.' And then, as if she were reminding herself, said 'I should flirt more. It feels good.' And, because we are in self-aware Sweden, one woman said, 'I flirt to show I'm not the stereotypical feminist.' In Stockholm, a sizeable proportion of men and women admitted to flirting for fun but many of the women, also admitted to not having an interest.

The women who said they didn't flirt gave reasons such as:

- 'I don't care anymore.'

- 'I am picky. It has to mean something.'
- 'I have passed the flirting stage. I would think about it for two weeks and come back and say "Here's the situation. I find you really attractive...".'
-

CONCLUSION

The Stockholmers claim to flirt, but, don't be surprised if they flirt with you and you miss it. A blink of the eye and it's over! Parisians males flirt all the time. Hence, Parisian women showed the most caution towards flirting. Parisian women were less likely to flirt than their male counterparts, or New Yorkers or Londoners. New Yorkers, too, are always flirting, but no one flirts as much as the London women, who use flirting to brighten a rainy day, get what they want, but in a charming way, and usually at work. Parisians use flirting to see if they are attractive. New York males flirt in order to have sex to see if they are attractive. Flirting, like many other things in New York, is a means to an end, a step towards the pursuit of a goal. In contrast, Parisian men claimed not to have any end goals in mind, but the Parisian women think differently. Londoners are just happy to be asked.

FLIRT FILE

- Almost everyone flirts. Whether they admit it or not, is another issue.
- People might not outwardly claim that they are 'flirting', some due to cultural connotations and others because they don't see it as something to switch on.
- You don't have to label it. Just enjoy the moment.

WHAT LIGHTS YOUR FIRE?

Some may like it hot, others not. If you are a hot-blooded New York male, you'd like to see a little sample of the goods before buying her a drink. The strong, independent New York women like a man to be assertive, but if he's slow off the mark, they'll let him know what they want, in no uncertain terms. What comes easy is considered 'easy' in Paris. The Parisian men like working for it and even expect to be rejected initially. Parisian women were looking for someone to approach them in a creative, unique way. If it's happening fifty times a day, a little ingenuity can't hurt. The women want someone to 'act like the man' and intelligent discussion is a no-brainer for both men and women. In contrast to the Parisian penchant for being carefully contrived, for Londoners, flirting has to be genuine. Both genders need to know that they aren't just a number in the flirting stakes. The ladies love sincere compliments while London men like women to make their interest obvious. Of all the men interviewed in the different cities, it was only the London males who displayed an understanding that a flirting encounter is a shared experience. For these men flirting was about what was happening between two people, with the emphasis on whether the woman seemed happy. Stockholm men and women seem to share similar turn-ons and want someone to make them feel special. The women want things done their way, or the highway!

Every culture mentioned 'humour' as a key component in flirting, although who was allowed to 'be funny' varied. The New Yorkers gave funny men and women a high-five. In Paris, humour was firmly kept in the male domain. There was no place for a funny mademoiselle (although she was free to tantalisingly titter at the mens' jokes). For the Londoners anyone one who was clever enough could play. In the case of Stockholm, it is important to note that Stockholm women didn't necessarily not like humour in flirting. But, when presented with many options, it was telling which qualities were repeatedly selected.

NEW YORK
It is all about presentation in this competitive city and what is flirting but a sales pitch? So don't expect sincerity in Sin City. The New York Times bestseller The Rules, written by Ellen Fein and Sherrie Schneider, encourages women not to follow their instincts. According to the authors, in order to attract his interest, ignore him, don't call him and resist all your urges. There's a reason the book was a bestseller. It seems New York women follow The Rules religiously, if the men's responses are anything to go by. Their biggest turn-off was women who put on an act.

As Chris, the curly-haired environmental engineer, said, 'Be sincere; be a real human; be honest. If you are really interested then ask questions. People in New York have an issue of just being themselves.' Doug the dentist agreed, 'Just be a real human being and not fake.' Jason, the high-school science teacher, provided a checklist, 'Be clear, be direct, don't play games, be natural and be consistent with who they are and how they act with their friends.' Interestingly, it was only the men who stressed the importance of just being true to who you are.

Besides urging women to be their real selves, what else tickles the men's fancy? The men of Gotham City like women to use their sex appeal. Corey, the fire-fighter and part-time actor, admitted, 'I like it when women show off their body, and use sexuality with postures and movements.' The effective female flirt, according to Joel the entrepreneur, '…knows how to use her body and fulfil the guy's fantasy,' while her male counterpart should be smart and confident. However, some men also appreciated cleverness as well as comeliness in a woman. In addition to good looks, the 'ideal' women described were 'intelligent, witty, quick on their feet'. They had 'humour, confidence, intelligence', 'a goal and a purpose,' and 'something to say'. David, the 28-year-old architect, likes women who '…try to up the ante with every witty thing I say. And, add to the excitement or fantasy that it might lead somewhere'.

The men were divided at just how explicit they liked the woman to be. Some New York men liked the women to make their dishonourable intentions plain. Jason, the teacher, likes his women to be assertive. 'If you like something you should go after it.' Other men liked women to give out clear signals so that they wouldn't miss an opportunity. Doug the dentist admitted, 'Clear signs are helpful. I don't mind if someone is direct because there have been times when I have been interested and they have been so hard to read that I have opted on the side of politeness.' Russell, the 28-year-old graphic designer was of the same persuasion. 'I don't pick up signals so well, but if it was too obvious then I wouldn't like it.'

A little sexiness is good according to Joel the 33-year-old entrepreneur. He likes his women to '…be sexy without being explicit,' as does Andrew, a 34 year-old attorney. He prefers his women to 'Play hard to get a point. If it's too easy then you lose interest. I like them to initiate… However, after that, you should make me work for it or I won't be interested any more.' Justin, a 38-year-old literary agent, was also middle-of-the-road. He liked his women '…not to be too forward but to let me know in our own dynamic that she is interested. Don't be overly aggressive or passive.' What does overly aggressive mean? Remember, inhabitants of this city have been known to straddle their victims while sitting on the bar! So, there you have it, from the men themselves. A New York man's ideal woman is genuine, not too sexy nor too shy, and loves to laugh, especially at his jokes.

On the one hand, New York women refuse to conform to gender roles. On the other they demand them! Like the men, some women expected tangible results in the flirting stakes. 38 year-old Dana, the pretty brunette analyst, didn't mince her words, 'Close the deal. If you are going to flirt with me all night, something better happen. I don't want to waste my time.' Like the men, the ladies were also fans of humour. 'Being funny' and 'making me laugh' were top of the list. But, whatever you do, don't bring up business! Laura is a high-powered New York female who works for a large credit card company, 'Don't go into what I do or how much I make. Don't talk about work,' she insisted. And keep your eyes where they belong – on her! Here's Gina's advice, a 33-year-old occupational therapist of Chinese descent. 'Be interested in what I have to say, without a wandering eye checking out who else is around'. However, as independent and sexually liberated as the New York woman is, she also expects the man to buy her drinks. Smart and sassy Sarah, a fashion buyer said, 'I expect the guy to buy drinks, if he doesn't then I don't want to talk to him.' The women want their men to be strong and decisive and protective. Peonies may thrive in Central Park, but wallflowers get trampled. The women were looking for assertiveness. Alesha, a striking broadcast journalist 'He has got to be assertive. No one likes a wimp!' If a New York woman smells fear, you're a goner. The New York woman wants her man to 'take care of her', 'to put his arm around the back of her chair as a protective thing', 'to tuck her hair behind her ear and rescue her from creeps.'

PARIS
In New York, PFO stands for Potential Flirting Opportunity. New Yorkers believe that any opportunity not acted on is a missed opportunity. In Paris, every person of the opposite sex is a PFO – a Potential Flirting Opponent. Alexandre, who works in business tourism, explained, 'In flirting 90% of the cases don't evolve. There is a difference in power when one is more attracted than the other. But then the power could shift when the one who is more interested thinks "She's not interested. I will go away." Then the other becomes more interested and the power changes.' This is an essential component of the Parisian flirting game. Who likes least, wins. Or do they?

In Paris, if you're interested in someone, act like you aren't. Unlike New York, where being upfront pays off, here the name of the game is 'Play Hard to Get.' The general consensus amongst the Parisians seems to be that if it's easy, then it's not valued. Consider this old proverb, 'Follow me and I will escape from you. Escape from me and I will follow you'. Antoine, a 35-year-old banker, explained, 'People are attracted to what they don't have and not satisfied with what they do have. You need to be rejected to be attracted to someone. It can't be too easy. It's best to show you are interested and then stop. Provoke interest and then desist.'

While the New York women are reading The Rules, the Parisian women have written it, and the Parisian men love this kind of behaviour. Perhaps this kind of game playing works best in cultures which regard men and women as different? However, in more reserved cultures where the men want women to have a greater role in the whole courtship, such as London and Stockholm, this behaviour would confuse and put off the men even more! Playing this game might very well help a woman 'catch a man' but, unfortunately, not a man one who best fits with the real her. Besides, once he is caught, she has to either continue putting on an act for the rest of the marriage or, have nothing in common with him.

Despite the fact that theirs is a culture that prizes the differences between men and women, both sexes identified similar desirable characteristics in a flirting encounter. 'Natural', 'nice' and 'intelligent' were some of the words that were repeatedly used. Both men and women also appreciated humour, in their different ways. One woman said, 'With humour, he is halfway through the door.' The men had a similar outlook. 'Women who laugh are halfway to bed.' Raucous laughter and cheesy pick-up lines is not the Parisian style. However, innuendo is. Many women mentioned that men would 'tease' them. 32 year-old Claire, who works in finance, said, 'I like it when he teases me, but I don't like flattery.' In this land of smooth talkers, it's not surprising that some women prefer it more real.

Carefree Geraldine, the jewellery maker, didn't mind '…a few compliments, but not be put on a pedestal.' Some down-to-earth women were aware of the dangers of this deification of women. They knew it was impossible to stay there once their partners inevitably learned that they were merely human after all. Claire agreed with Geraldine. 'For me the more a guy says compliments, the less interested he is. Or he could be putting you on a pedestal, which is also bad because it means you are not equals.'

In the same way that the men of New York like their women to be themselves, the French also favour looking and acting naturally. A common response to the question, 'What do you like someone to do when they are flirting with you?' was, 'Just be natural'. French men also appreciate 'natural' beauty. 'Do you have a preference regarding physical types of women?' 'She should look natural,' they said. Natural? Ah, natural. It may take two hours for a Parisian woman to achieve the casual, just-got-out-of bed look, but the fact that artifice is involved is irrelevant. This emphasis on the 'natural' has many different layers of meaning in Parisian culture, from wanting women to be 'natural' in their behaviour and their appearance – no matter how many hours it took for her to get that way – to their 'natural' or innate flirting instincts. Thus, natural means inherent, which leaves little room for individualism or choice. Destiny is inescapably linked to the genitals. This emphasis on 'natural' is used to defend traditional gender roles and maintain the balance of power. Whether someone was born male or female doesn't dictate their preference for the colours blue or pink, nor a pre-destined ability to excel at either mathematics or languages, or even an entire gender's desire to want to 'play the field' or 'settle down'. Try explaining this to the Parisians!

Niceness was another criteria shared by both men and women, while the men added 'mysterious' and 'distant' to their checklist. Laurent, the shy 30-year-old architect, admitted that, 'I am looking for a woman who is distant and nice.' 35-year-old Francine, who works in publishing said, 'I don't like it when they're arrogant. I like someone who is nice.' And yet, French women like their men to be masculine and assertive. Monique, the 28 year-old sales rep said, 'I don't want him to be too nice and at your feet.' Women expressed a desire for the man to take the 'manly role'. Juliette, the social worker, likes it when a guy, 'makes decisions and acts like the man'. Charlotte, the 32 year-old editor agreed, saying she wants him to, 'Take the initiative at the beginning. You want to know that he is able to lead'. So Parisian women are looking for manly men who are nice, but not too nice, while, as Antoine the banker pointed out, '…men like the woman to be quite feminine, mysterious, withdrawn. The image of femininity in France is still old fashioned.'

Do the men really want a woman who is 'mysterious and withdrawn', or is this just another example of a Parisian paradox? Martine, the logistics coordinator, said, 'The men want the image of the woman they can't have'. Veronique, the sexy PhD student elaborated that Parisian men, '…miss l'amour courtois of the Middle Ages, where a man would court a woman over a period of years. The girl never initiated, she just nodded yes or no'. Yes, you heard that right, l'amour courtois – courtly love! This literature derived from an era when the man was in control of the pace; he was the active pursuer and the female a passive receiver. Anthropologist Dani Cavallaro says, 'One of the main axioms of courtly love consists of the idea that the idealised lady is precious because she is unattainable and that the male lover should be inspired precisely by her unavailability'. Surely courtly love is outmoded in contemporary Paris? Not so. Then, as now, French men use the women as mirrors to help express their masculinity. They hunt and the woman wait passively to be caught.

Many Parisian men expressed immense distaste for women who were too pushy. That's his job, after all. Bespectacled and smouldering Jean-Luc likes his woman to '…be refined, not like she's driving a lorry'. Mathieu, the dishy artistic director, dislikes women who are '… too pushy and aggressive. I can tell in several minutes if she is a good person or not.' Aggressive women are immoral, it would appear. The men didn't like women to be too open about their feelings. They preferred it when women make them wait. Guilliame the Gallant said 'I don't like her to rush into things and make it too obvious that she is into me.' Mathieu the artistic director said, 'I don't like easy women. I would want to wait several times before kissing.' 'I generally don't appreciate a situation that's too easy,' said Nicolas, the matter-of-fact project manager. ' I don't appreciate it too much if I haven't made an effort.'

A woman should be sitting in the corner of the room acting sultry and aloof. Joan Rivers would certainly have been home alone on a Saturday night if she'd been born a Parisian. Despite the male preference for distant and mysterious, à la Catherine Deneuve, they weren't averse to women showing a little je ne sais quoi. The Parisian women knew how to accent their best features, however, there are no gauche displays of cleavage here! Alexandre who works in business tourism said, 'I like sexy women, and I don't mean the way they are dressed. It's like when she talks in my ear and slightly touches my cheek with her face.' Antoine likes it when a woman 'shows her neck'. How risqué!

Intelligence is as highly prized in Paris as beauty. Frederique, the 28-year-old sales manager, said, 'I couldn't date a beautiful but stupid woman.' Before engaging in a tête-à-tête with a Parisian, therefore, it's prudent to polish up on your Proust. Time spent reading le Temps Retrouvé will be time well spent. Want to really be a hit, then digest your Dostoevsky too – read The Idiot in at least two languages to avoid looking like one yourself. However, if you're not quite up to such heady intellectual pursuits, then you could just play it safe and keep quiet. The Parisians would prefer the sound of silence to the mind-numbing drone of someone talking about the X-Factor.

Paris is known as the City of Light, not only because it was the first city in Europe to have gas lamps, in 1828, but also because of its 18th-century reputation as a centre of education and art during the Age of Enlightenment. According to the 15th century French poet Francois Villon, 'Good talkers are only found in Paris.' Citing their 'sexy' language as playing a significant role, the Parisians were clear about the importance of verbal communication. Lucy, an English artist living in Paris, explained, 'Conversations have to be intelligent. There is no such thing as idle chitchat like we have in the UK. I was once sitting in a group of six Parisian friends and we sat for a whole minute in silence because no one could think of anything intelligent to say.' 'We like having big discussions and strong disagreements,' confirmed Charlotte, the 32-year-old editor.

Ironically, having an argument is what turns on these citizens of the Capital of Love. The more heated a debate, the greater the indication that some proper Parisian-style flirting is taking place. In his Paris Diary, Ned Rorem wrote, 'Quarrels in France strengthen a love affair; in America they end it.' Antoine the banker explained his modus operandi, 'I will start a debate with a woman in order to show I have a strong personality and am intelligent. We Parisians like to debate and can flirt while talking about serious issues.' However, revealing your serious side can sometimes be taken for show. 32-year-old Claire, who works in finance, said, 'I try to not flirt with someone who flirts. I can't take them seriously. I like them to be genuine and not try and show me their 'serious' side.'

Both men and women mentioned the importance of bestowing new ideas. Sophie, the primary school teacher said, 'A good flirt can bring something new to the discussion that you never knew before.' Lorraine the author, a Parisian native, said 'Debates show that the men have a strong personality and that people are intelligent'. Parisians like someone 'surprising them' with something they hadn't known, or catching them off guard. The ability to 'provoke' the other was continually mentioned by both genders. Sophisticated Stefanie is a business analyst. 'I like a man to surprise me, not boring, and as provocative as me.' Lorraine, the Parisian author, who makes her living from her command of the French language, said 'A good reaction to stimulation is quite stimulating. I like him to be as provocative as me in his words.'

The men agreed. Greg, the communication student, said, 'I like a woman to be provocative and surprising – someone who can turn around with a funny and striking line and be quite imaginative.' Handsome artistic director Mathieu said, 'I like her to surprise me by playing a game, pretending not to be interested, then doing something outrageous. She would say something that you wouldn't expect from a French girl. It wouldn't be so bold as a compliment, but it would be a little something unexpected.'

In Paris it's important to express strong opinions, but in truth you don't have to really believe in your declarations. This seemed to be an essential part of the 'provoking' process. Monique, the sales rep admitted, 'I like to provoke him. If he says white, I will say black.' Frederique, the 28-year-old sales manager openly admitted, 'I use rude or crude words to describe a situation in order to provoke.' Veronique, the PhD student knew the game. 'Men tend to say things to test how you will react. They can be a little provocative.' Sophisticated Stefanie, the business analyst, summed it up: 'Flirting is the perfect mix between attention and provocation.'

Given that most flirtations begin as a game that no one takes seriously, it is understandable that the Parisians exercise caution. If a Parisian man is simply attracted to a woman then he will want to seduce her as quickly as possible in order for something physical to happen. But, if he really cares about her, he won't want to kiss her until after an 'acceptable' period of time has passed. Frederique, the sales manager said, 'Often the seduction begins with a friendship and the seduction comes over a period of time. I might be seduced by her looks the first time. It takes time to know someone.' Slowly does it. The issue of time, and how much of it should pass before a flirting couple can respectably engage in physical relations, was part of Parisian charm. These Parisian men were eager to point out the importance of separating initial physical desire from other feelings about a woman. They want to make sure the connection is one that will endure. 'There is a separation between lust and love,' explained Greg the communications student, 'Either I want to have sex or if I really like her ,I couldn't even think about sex during the first few dates.'

The men often wait until several dates have passed before even kissing a woman. Antoine the banker said, 'The 'frontier' is not always clear. The first time you never know. It depends on the length of the experience with this person.' Alexandre, who works in business tourism, follows a similar approach. 'I stay distant the first few times. I might eventually take her hand. I have to see if I am interested in her more than just physically. I wait until she shows me signals so I can be sure.' Nicolas, the project manager for a software company, said, 'I would like a real relationship to start slowly, with not even a kiss, maybe a phone number.' How then could he be sure he'd see her again? He replied, 'If she's a friend of a friend, you know you will see her again. We don't need anything to happen right away because when it's easy it's not fun. The excitement you can gain if you wait is great.' He then added another favourite Parisian ideology, 'We always want what we can't have. Similarly, 'If I do like her,' said Laurent the architect, 'it will not be to have sex. Not even a kiss on the first night. The longer you wait, the better it is. After you have sex, it's easy and you're not attracted anymore.' Laurent told of meeting his new girlfriend while they were on a group holiday. 'I didn't ask for her number or email after the holiday was over, but I knew my friend had her details. I proposed a group dinner and she came along.'

So, the Parisians pace themselves. There's a slower burn, and this allows people to make sure they are not fooled by initial impressions.

It all seems very much left to chance, doesn't it? Can you imagine a New Yorker meeting someone on holiday and failing to get so much as a cell-phone number, e-mail address, Facebook friend guarantee, or a Twitter@name? The Parisians don't display the sort of 'want it now' attitude of the New Yorkers. Laid back? It's beyond even that; this patient, what-will-be-will-be attitude would seem to befit someone confident of living to be 200 years old. How and when does anything ever happen when Parisians flirt for so long and so slowly?

LONDON
While New Yorkers understand that any flirtatious encounter is as long as any good sales pitch, and something better may come along, Londoners don't think along the same lines. Both genders are looking for something more than a one-night stand. London women had several consistent preferences. They like attentive, complimentary, genuinely interested, funny guys who can hold their own in an intelligent conversation. London men love tactile ladies with a sense of fun and humour, who make their interest evident. For both men and women, being genuine in the flirting interaction was vital.

While it's impossible to be genuine in the Parisian flirting game, for a Londoner, 'keeping it real' is as important as finding a late-night drinking place after all the bars have closed. When Oscar Wilde said, 'To be natural is such a very difficult pose to keep up,' he could have been speaking of Parisians. Their version of natural is largely based on artifice and they work hard to keep up this illusion. Londoners, on the other hand, distrust fakery, and any sort of artifice is viewed with disapproval. The preference is for real, even if real is a bit on the bumbling side. Move over James Bond, your smooth talk leaves no one shaken or stirred; London ladies are more likely to warm to Boris Johnson, London's notoriously buffoonish mayor. Emma, a bubbly gadget presenter on late night television, delivered a somewhat backhanded compliment when she said, 'Englishmen are not very good at flirting, but when they do it, it does feel genuine. As in, 'it's so blundering, there is no way it could be an act!' Claire, the red-haired accountant, who was equally good at maths and men confirmed, 'Be interested in what I'm saying but not just because you think you should, but genuinely.' Annette is a sultry-voiced jazz singer with curves to rival J Lo: 'Show a genuine interest in me, what I do, what I enjoy, but not in a scarily, intrusive way.' Yasmin, the brunette beauty who works in PR, said, 'I like it when they pay you lots of attention, not just looking for a snog, but investing time.' Interesting conversation was just as important as a sense of humour to the women of London. 'I like someone who will flirt with my brain,' said Jennifer, the down-to-earth finance analyst.

Along with being themselves, being genuinely interested, and capable of intelligent conversation, the women said they liked men to pay them compliments. But not any old compliment will do. Catherine is in IT, but is far from what you'd call geeky. 'Compliment me, but in an intelligent way. I don't want standard compliments.' 29-year-old Rachel is an illustrator who shares this view, 'I love compliments, but ones which show thought.' Jane works in the financial industry and had very specific requirements. She said, 'Compliments are good. They can be blatant about the way I look, but not about the way I think. For example, if they say, "You look great", that's good. But I would prefer them to match me by mimicking my thoughts, rather than saying "You have a fast mind."' Did you get that, men?

Both sexes wanted to feel that they were singled out and spoke ill of anyone who was 'playing a numbers game'. The women said that they didn't want a guy who was 'hedging his bets'. Liz, an account manager for a big advertising agency, insisted that flirting must be about '…focusing on one person rather than 'hedging your bets'. Alice, the investment banker, said, 'I like it when a guy makes me feel like I am the only person in the room.' Anoushka the solicitor agreed, 'If he is flirting with you, it can only be you. You have to choose.' But it seems like the women weren't the only ones who liked to be specifically chosen. Women pointed out that paying attention to other men was a real turn-off for the London lads. 28-year-old secretary Georgina said, 'They definitely don't like you flirting with other men in front of them!'

Londoners share an appreciation of the self-deprecating and ironic wit for which the English are infamous. Both men and women felt humour had a big role to play in flirting. Alistair, the 32-year-old broadcast journalist, likes a girl, '… who can show she has a sense of humour. I like it when a woman makes me laugh.' Mary, the astute 28-year-old PA with mousy brown hair and sensible shoes said, 'I like banter, laughing, and them to be a little cheeky.' Emma, a bubbly presenter, likes, 'A bit of cheekiness just to catch me off guard, but not be too rude'. Samuel the cabinet maker said, 'I always have the best fun with people who can be my partner in crime, taking the mickey. If she says something witty and wise I will say "I'm sorry, you are wrong."'

The level of cheekiness, like everything else in London, is governed by good manners. Alistair, the broadcast journalist, explained, 'It's teasing, but no one really means it. You would do it with someone you don't know well. But you don't choose a real insecurity of someone's.' Subtlety and consideration are at the core of Londoners' behaviour and these characteristics are also evident in their humour. The basis of English humour, according to several respondents, is that everything can be funny if it's done in an ironic and self-mocking way. 'There is a massive current of irony which runs through our culture,' said Charlie, the floppy-haired entrepreneur, 'There is no situation in which humour is inappropriate. We love ridiculous understatements.' Sam, the website designer said, 'Irony is our amniotic fluid. There is a self-mocking irony about English flirting, looking at a situation in an amused way.' This irony is the perfect tonic for the Brits' worst nightmare… earnestness! Ex-military man Christopher said, 'Being earnest is unforgivable. You can't take yourself too seriously. We like bumbling amateurs. Being good at something is all right if you are reasonably humble about it.' The only Londoner allowed to blow his own trumpet is the royally appointed bugle boy. This attitude works as a protective mechanism for the men. If they're being ironic or self-mocking and things don't work out, well, they didn't really mean it anyway! Soft spoken Anthony in IT said, 'We're not good at being serious.

Instead of facing things head on, we go around it with humour. Part of this could be seen as guys being shy.'

Like the New York females, London ladies were also revered for their wit, although this wasn't so much to do with the woman laughing at the man's jokes, it was more about there being a feeling of togetherness. Samuel, the furniture maker said, 'I like a woman to smile, have fun, react. The banter needs to be back and forth.' Consistently the preference was for mutual understanding. 'She's laughing with you,' was Daniel the bar manager's criteria for a good flirt.

London women, however, didn't see the humour so much as 'back and forth' but, rather, as pretty one-sided. 'Men', they said:

- 'like people who laugh at their jokes.'
- 'like girls who find them amusing'
- 'like to think they are funny'
- 'like girls to laugh loudly at their jokes even if they're not funny'

While the Parisian men like their women to be mysterious and subtle, and wait for him to make the first move, the Londoners prefer their women to be move obvious about their interest. The men are hesitant when it comes to approaching women and thus they don't like to have to guess when someone is interested in them. Simon in PR is a man with an eye for detail. 'I like it if she uses little excuses to touch me or hold my hand…It's the little things, a quick glance and a smile, a light tap on the shoulder, coming over with a drink for you. Things that show you she is interested in you. I find it hard to notice clichéd flirting. I notice the little details.'

The men repeatedly stated they wanted women to initiate proceedings. Duncan the journalist: 'I like women to be forward, to approach, to touch. It's 'I like you', no guessing games.' In New York, full-on flirting is favoured for a reason; it makes things clear from the outset and therefore no one wastes time. The reason the London guys would like the girls to be more upfront has less to do with speeding up the process and more to do with making their lives easier. Although James is an optician, it seems he's no good at reading signs, 'I'd like a woman to give me more signs that she's interested.' Alex works in import/export. 'Some girls need to make it a little bit more obvious. Men are not as subtle and need a barn door open in their face!'

But how much is 'a little' more obvious? Samuel and Simon were on opposite ends of this spectrum: Simon in PR, said 'I like her to be attentive but not too forward – to me that says "Slapper".' Samuel, a charming, 38-year-old furniture maker, disagreed, 'I like a girl to say "Yes, we can go home now."' Admittedly, there were a few of men who still preferred to take the lead. Alex said, 'I like to know a woman is interested but not coming on too strong. I like to chase.' However, most of the men interviewed would agree wholeheartedly with James, the optician, who begged, 'Can you please tell the women that if they ask us to do anything: dance, date, snog, shag, we will say yes! Just have them ask us!'

Unlike their Parisian counterparts who like their women pliable, London men are drawn to outgoing, fun-loving, independent women. Adrian, the real estate agent, said, 'London women are hard work because there's a lot of competition amongst the men for the women. There a lot of good looking and successful women in this city, which makes them harder to please and with more barriers.'

Sam, a website designer, agreed. 'English women are very confident. They know what they want and usually get it.' Opticians, music publishers, journalists and recruitment consultants alike were unanimous in their admiration for women who '…have confidence, power, like a lead singer in a band. If someone is centre stage they catch your attention', said James the optician. Similarly, David the recruitment consultant, likes women who '…are the centre of attention, a bit loud, not in the corner. Max the music publisher chimed in, 'If she is having fun, centre of attention, sexiness, she would attract my attention' Duncan the journalist agreed, 'I don't like it when they are too quiet'. Daniel, who manages a bar, added his voice to the chorus, 'Ideally, she wouldn't let me get my way all the time. I have a tendency to date stubborn women, independent and strong'. Anthony, the chic IT geek, did not understand why the women weren't more forthcoming in their opinions, wants, and needs. 'Women have a strange view of the rules of engagement.' And so say all of us, said the London men.

London males seemed to have a genuine appreciation for women and who they are. When the men were asked if they had a certain type, most of the men said they didn't. Samuel the furniture maker was adamant that there are '…no such thing as types. You are attracted to an individual package…Brunettes, tall, slim tends to be my choice but that doesn't mean I don't like other types.' Others agreed that it had to be about more than looks. Alistair, the broadcast journalist, admitted to previous errors of judgment, 'A mistake I made in the past was going out with others only for their looks.' Simon is a reformed breastaholic. 'Big breasts used to be more important to me in my younger years.' Charlie, a 30-year-old, floppy-haired entrepreneur said, 'I wouldn't change much. Women as a species are doing alright!'

In another telling show of sensitivity, London men emphasised the importance of both people enjoying the interaction.

Anthony, the IT guy, said, 'It's about taking a step forward and a step back at the same time, so both are comfortable.' Some men also pointed out the importance of synchronicity in flirting, stating that the women would be:

- 'mirroring your movements.'
- 'doing what you are doing.'
- 'matching what you do, whether it's body language or saying 'me too.'

While the Parisian men and women were mostly flirting to improve their own positions at the expense of the other person, the London males often pointed out that they weren't the only ones in the picture. Sam, the website designer, said, 'There has to be an 'us' in flirting. 'You and me' is a shared experience.' The London lads were exceptionally good at pronouns, as Charlie the entrepreneur said, 'I would try to work out if there was a 'we' part of the conversation or just an 'I'.' Christopher the ex-military man poignantly declared, 'Flirting goes wrong when whoever the 'you' and 'me' are, don't know who the 'us' is.' This awareness of both people in the flirting encounter is a far cry from the self-proclaimed

Parisian 'male monologue'. And what's most interesting is that it's the men who are the most conscious of this.

STOCKHOLM
True to form, the most common response Stockholmers gave to the question, 'What do you like a man/women to do when she/he is flirting with you?' was 'The same as me'. Andreas, the personal trainer, even said, 'The stuff women like is what I like'. Anders, a sales rep, pointed out, 'Women should be as equal as the men'. So, it's clear that everyone likes the same thing, but what is it that they like? Mostly, it's to feel special.

The sensitive New Age guys of Stockholm like to be appreciated for who they are, and they like to take it slow. Bjorn, the doctoral student with the jet-black hair and aquamarine eyes, said, 'I am an easy person to get if someone recognises my self-concept and reinforces these things. I have values and am interested in someone seeing them.' Per is the epitome of a sexy Swede. He also happens to be an accounts manager. He likes women to, '…talk about me, focus on me'. Frederik, the older student, wants women '…to be interested in me and not arrogant.' Mattias, the MD of a soft drink company, said, 'I like compliments, letting me know I am special.' Eric owns a café. He likes, '..kisses, cuddling, being open'. Hang on a minute. Compliments? Kisses? Feeling special? We've heard all this before, but usually from women. Stockholm men certainly aren't afraid of showing their feminine side. Some of the men missed good ol' fashion courting. Andreas said, 'I like it when she doesn't move straight on to the sexual invite. It's like skipping the game'. Unlike Paris, where the men didn't like women to be too forward because it threatened their masculinity, Stockholm males don't like to cut to the chase too soon because it cuts short the pleasure of pursuit. Mattias insisted, 'She shouldn't be too pushy. If she is too eager it makes me feel like it's happening too fast. The women also wanted to feel special. Emelie, the cautious, 32-year-old accountant said, 'I like him to be interested in me as a person. What I think, what I like.' Maria, the project manager, agreed, 'Pay attention, make me feel special'. Yet, the women liked to be the ones calling the shots. Jenny, the PhD student in biology said she wanted to be the one to choose whether or not to follow up on a flirtatious encounter. Meeting again and letting me choose if I want to.' Likewise, Katarina the florist said, 'I don't like them to touch unless I have initiated it.'

The women also liked compliments, but it came with a Stockholm twist. Watch Johanna, the opera singer, try and rationalise her answer, as if she was trying to make peace with it. She initially said, 'I'd like more compliments' After a moment she added, 'But in my head I am thinking this is the negative side of equality. If you were equal, why would he give compliments?' In the end she concluded it would be acceptable if both men and women did it, 'I guess both sexes should give more compliments.' It's not easy trying to be an equal society, you know.

CONCLUSION
New Yorkers value looks over intelligence, but Parisians won't dally with a dunce. New Yorkers are all about carpe diem while Parisians believe in que sera, sera. In New York City, those who can negotiate the line between confidence and arrogance, and can be charismatic without being a show-off, were clear winners. Unlike the Swedes who favour discreet eye contact from afar, a New Yorker who has the social confidence to strike up a conversation with anyone is highly prized.

In New York, both men and women valued humour, the New York men wanted women to be themselves, and not be afraid to use their sexuality. The New York women wanted men to be assertive. The Parisians thought easy come should go. They did not value something that was caught too quickly, but they did value intellect and provocation. Both men and women claimed to like playing traditional gender roles in the flirting game. But, it's impossible to be truly genuine in the Parisian flirting game, no matter what the Parisians' claim they want. Londoners have a wary fascination with flirting. The women love it; at least the version they refer to as 'being charming'. The men seem to be less enamoured with flirting and some even consider it contrived, which was why all the Londoners' continually referred to the need for flirting to be genuine. London men seem to want their women to be both subtle and obvious and thus the women have to figure out how to behave in the space between subtle and slapper. It seems that the ideal modus operandi is if the woman subtly lets on that she is interested. Then, while the flirting is 'naturally' happening, and if they are getting along well, she makes it clear that she is into him so he doesn't have to worry about being rejected by her. Et voila, the ideal way to snare an Englishman. The egalitarian Stockholmers simply want to feel special. Perhaps they should buy a dog.

FLIRT FILE

- The best way to meet your perfect match is to behave as your true self. If you are loud and outgoing, don't try and be quiet and shy to impress someone.
- We are not trying to match with everyone, just one special person. Therefore, we will meet a lot of people along the way with whom we will not be compatible. Rather than viewing this as 'rejection, think of it as an efficient weeding out process enabling us to find someone who is really match worthy.
- No matter where you go in the world, one thing is consistent – people like to feel special and unique.
- Listening rather than talking, using empathy and being curious about people, all helps to create this feeling of being understood.
- Flirting, like ballroom dancing, tennis or even duelling is a two-person pursuit. Only an individual stuck on a desert island works in isolation from others. Human dynamics are dependent on those who are in that dynamic. Most often, we use others as mirrors for ourselves. And, we often choose our partners, flirting or otherwise, because we like how we look in those mirrors.
- The more you practise flirting with different people, at different places, the more you will start to understand what your personal preferences are.

TYPECASTING

In New York a man's street cred rises in direct proportion to the attractiveness of the woman on his arm. In Paris, women are also expected to uphold ideals of beauty; although an effortless natural look is the de facto standard to which the women are meant to aspire. In London, both men and women are judged on more than what they look like. In Stockholm, the men like their women in proportion, neither fat nor thin, but athletic, and with curves. And both men and women appreciate a well-kept appearance.

NEW YORK
Bryan, the aspiring New Yorker musician, quoted Ezra Pound :

> *'It rests me to be among beautiful women*
> *Why should one always lie about such matters?*
> *I repeat:*
> *It rests me to converse with beautiful women*
> *Even though we talk nothing but nonsense,*
> *The purring of the invisible antennae*
> *Is both stimulating and delightful.'*

The quest for beauty, or the quest to take the most beautiful woman home, is one of the biggest of the many battles raging in New York. To New Yorkers, you are not a red-blooded male until you are seen with a beautiful woman on your arm, and you only become the king of the jungle if you are observed taking her home. Conversely, if you are a rich, powerful woman, you have access to younger, good-looking men.

In New York, beauty is quantifiable, like an Olym$_1$pic sport. Because beauty is the benchmark of success, there is a constant pressure on women to look good. The women go on diets and spend countless hours at the gym and beauty salons. They don't leave their houses, even to go to the shops, unless they are immaculately turned out. In New York, these apogees of feminine beauty are sometimes called, 'Perfect Tens'. David, the 28-year-old architect admitted, 'Beautiful women get more attention. It's more exciting to flirt with a beautiful woman because you want to be seen with this girl. People assume that you must be doing something right if you make a beautiful girl giggle… No one wants to flirt with a fat girl unless she is a '12 beer' girl', he said, referring to the number of beers required to render her attractive. Temporarily under-employed Marie said, 'Beautiful women don't need to talk. There's an attitude that they don't have to do any work as the men are lucky enough just to be sitting with them.' Joel, the 33-year-old entrepreneur, was happy to settle for second-best. 'I like when she has hot friends, so there's more to choose from. I like to hit on the second hottest girl as she isn't used to having so much attention and will be easier to hook up with.' Poor girl number three is usually left wondering where all the men have gone.

The omnipresent impact of the media contributes to these unrealistic ideals of physical beauty. When asked what influenced their flirting style, half of the interviewees cited the

5 *Ezra Pound, 'It Rests Me To Be Among Beautiful Women', Tame Cat, Otttbir, New York, 1911*

media, movies or pop culture. This response was far greater than in any of the other cities studied. Studies reveal that when men are shown pictures of models, and then pictures of 'normal' women, the latter are rated as much less attractive then if the men were just asked to rate the attractiveness of the 'normal' women without the comparison of the models. With 99% of the population being bombarded with airbrushed images of 1% of the population, this sets an unrealistic expectation, which can never be attained by either men or women and, inevitably, leads to discontent.

Despite the fact that beauty, like most everything else in the corporate capital of America, is a commodity, the eye of the beholder is extremely selective and often roving. A New Yorker's definition of 'beautiful' differs according to the goal – copulation or cohabitation. Andrew, the 34-year-old attorney, listed his criteria, 'There are different standards for my wife because I want her to be tall as I want tall kids, but I would hook up with a short girl, C-cup or larger, athletic build, no smokers, slender body, no fat girls.'

New Yorkers had definite ideas about physical types. The men seemed to prefer petite, 'exotic', brown-skinned women. Most often, Asian and Latina were mentioned as far as physical ideals. The women, for their part, were looking for Mr 'Tall, Dark and Handsome' and stereotypically masculine. Stacey, the make-up artist said, 'I like a tall, dark, handsome, alpha male. Not a skinny white boy'. Andrea, who works for a charity, likes manly specimens, 'I like men who look like men and not boys. I don't like them androgynous or slim.' Many women also stressed that a man must be well dressed, citing nice trousers and a button-down shirt as something that would make then want to flirt with a man.

Almost all of the female interviewees specified that a man should be taller than them. Similarly, almost every man said that a woman should be 'shorter than me'. These physical preferences underline how New Yorkers still identify with traditional gender roles – the man, as protector, must be tall; a woman taller than him would somehow undermine those masculine ideals. New York women are looking for super humans. They allow themselves to move in and out of gender roles when it suits them, yet expect men to always be men. Is this what they call having their cake and eating it too?

PARIS
The clear separation of genders in Parisian culture was also evident in the Parisians' physical preferences. The men liked petite women, for fairly obvious reasons. The diminutive female form provides a stark contrast to a man's physicality, making him appear very obviously strong, powerful and…male, capable of taking care of his little woman. With the big-man, small-woman union it's easy to see who's in charge. The men also showed a marked preference for brunettes. Slim brunette Winona Ryder was held up as an example of the men's ideal. Interestingly, everyone vehemently denied the reports that she ever shoplifted. Jean-Luc echoed the sentiment of many when he said, 'I prefer feminine women.' Although, in true Parisian style, he also said, 'Physically, I could be attracted to most women.'

Women expressed similar stereotypical views. Sophie, the primary school teacher, said she didn't want a man who 'acts like a woman', also declared, 'I like them a bit hairy, a manly man.' The women stated their preferences for 'someone manly' citing the Die Hard hero, Bruce Willis, as someone who fitted their physical ideal. The character of Indiana Jones, played by Harrison Ford was also a firm favourite. The fact that both of these men could potentially be their grandfathers didn't seem to bother the women. Both of these 'ideal men', happened to be well-established seniors and would, consequently, be better suited to taking care of women – especially if those women needed advice about the effectiveness of prunes on a sluggish digestive system, or tips about Saga holidays for the over 50's.

Little Miss Pretty-But-Daft may struggle to get hooked up in Paris, whereas in New York she'd be hotly pursued. A beautiful New York woman is a trophy and the man will wear her on his arm for the same reasons he wears several thousand dollars worth of Rolex on his wrist – to show he's made it and that he can have anything he wants. Parisian men are different; they don't admire beauty for beauty's sake or because it represents achievement. Laurent, the architect, said, 'A woman can be good looking but if she is like a doll or a piece of paper it means nothing.'

One man admonished women who look high maintenance by declaring they couldn't possibly be intelligent. Olivier proclaimed, 'A woman too close to her physical side isn't too deep in her mind.' Does he believe that a beauty cannot be bestowed with brains? Or is he saying that a woman who expends a lot of time and energy on her appearance is shallow for doing so and therefore of lower intellect?

This is not to say that looks are unimportant in Parisian society. As in New York, in order for a Parisian woman to wield any power in society, she must have beauty. Looks are seen as a significant part of a woman's ability to attract and seduce, even if she's only doing so to boost her own confidence. As much as intelligence and substance are highly regarded, no one is fooled by claims that looks are not deemed important. So, what is a Parisian woman to do?

Well, it goes something like this: while she must be intelligent and pretty, she can't seem to be trying too hard with her appearance, and she must achieve and display the right kind of beauty. If she looks too highly styled she will be stigmatised as a 'fashion girl' or a 'bitch'. Alexandre, in business tourism, explained the preference this way, 'I would prefer a natural woman. It's nice to see a woman who's not wearing makeup because it says she's in her environment and natural.' The 'natural' beauty expected of Parisian women is even more of a challenge than the highly-styled look of their more glamorous New York sisters. Sandrine, the director's assistant, shared her secret: 'Women spend a long time trying to look like they got ready in five minutes.' In New York the men might expect a woman to look beautiful, but they wouldn't expect her to wake up looking the same as she did on a night out. He might have a preference for large breasts, but wouldn't condemn a woman whose large breasts he desired were fake. It wasn't just in terms of physical attributes that the subject of naturalness came up. Antoine, the banker, said, 'I want a woman to be natural when she is flirting with me, if not, she is playing a game like a mannequin.' The challenge is to contrive to look and behave naturally, while playing by the Byzantine rules of the Parisian mating game.

LONDON
Those of you not blessed with the gamine limbs of Giselle or chiselled jaw of George Clooney, have no fear. Unlike the New Yorkers who were constantly hedging their bets to see if they could secure someone better-looking, the Londoners were most interested in having a connection with someone. This was the case for both the men and women. The

Londoners said good looks weren't particularly important to them. Barkeep Daniel doesn't '...want the pin up girl because it's one dimensional.' He '...needs more than looks and a great figure; needs personality.' Alice, a brunette beauty herself, and an investment banker, echoed this sentiment, 'It's not about looks, it's about attractiveness.'

The general consensus of the men was that their preferences for women had to do with characteristics other than appearance. Contrary to what the biological scientists might say, it wasn't a certain hip-to-waist ratio, dilated pupils, or even a perfectly symmetrical face that lured the London males; rather it was how approachable a woman was. Being friendly and approachable were the most often mentioned characteristics that attracted a London male to a female. Anthony, the IT guy, summed it up. 'I need more than looks and a great figure. I need personality. She has to be approachable.' Duncan, the journalist, explained what attracts him to women. 'It's made up of several things: how they carry themselves, if they are relaxed; in general, someone who looks happy and open.' Alex, who works in import/export, also tried to put this ineffable allure into words, 'It's an air about them. Some girls just have something about them that makes you want to get to know them more; a whiff of vulnerability, awareness, confidence.' Sam, the website designer agreed, 'It's not just tits and ass. It's more about smiles, eyes and bodily confidence.' The men agreed that there had to be some sort of basic attraction, but as Alex, who works in import/export, said, 'I don't have a specific type. 'I'm not going to flirt with someone because she has a great body or is a great dresser.'

What women wear, however, was important to a number of the men interviewed. Men admitted to being attracted to women who dressed sexily – but not provocatively – many hastened to add. 'If she is dressing to impress, I will acknowledge it. I don't like a frump,' said 29-year-old Simon who works in PR. Anoushka, the sexy solicitor, was well aware of the London heterosexual male's preferences. 'Normal Englishmen, they like sexy but traditional.'

Not for the Londoners the natural look that takes three hours to achieve. Rallying fervently against the Parisian ideal of beauty, Anoushka acknowledged, 'Guys like that you've made an effort but not a dog show. The worst is a woman who tries to be casual but spends eight hours trying to look that way.'

Like the men, who stressed they weren't looking for Angelina Jolie, neither were the ladies looking for Brad Pitt. The London females interviewed emphasised that men don't have to be gorgeous to be appealing. 'There has to be a physical attraction, but that doesn't mean that they are really good-looking,' said Liz, an account manager for a big advertising agency. Jennifer, the finance analyst, tried to pin it down, 'It's a particular look they have... not necessarily handsome. There are certain people I feel naturally attracted to – maybe it's pheromones?' 'It's not pure good looks,' agreed Georgina, a 28-year-old secretary who answered all the questions with a laugh. 'I like people with 'a presence'. A certain je ne sais quoi.' The London sisterhood was united in this.

It's how they carry themselves, the whole package.' said Annette, the jazz singer. 'I don't tend to fancy people on sight. I have to get to know them before I find them attractive,' said Mary, the 28-year-old PA.

When explaining what would make them want to flirt with a woman, the majority of the London men and women interviewed were attracted by more than physical good looks. They spoke of character and honesty, sexiness, friendliness, and demeanour. One man had a particular penchant for eloquent women. David, a recruitment consultant, said, 'I like people who enunciate and pronounce things correctly.' Their cousins across the Atlantic place a stronger importance on good looks in both women and men – an unpleasant symptom of a media savvy culture. However, as supermodel Cindy Crawford famously said, 'Even I don't wake up looking like Cindy Crawford.'

STOCKHOLM

The Stockholmers generally agreed that it takes more than hot looks to melt the ice. However, even in this equal society, gender had a way of creeping in when asked about physical preferences.

I asked the Stockholm men if they had a physical type of woman to whom they were attracted. Like kids compiling their Christmas wish list, the men described the physical attributes they prefer in women: sporty girls, petite girls, girls with a 'latin look', red heads, blondes and brunettes…the list was diverse and seemingly endless. However, two preferences the men had in common was that a woman not be 'too much' of anything. And when in doubt, they preferred curves.

Henrik, the banker, summed up the dominant position, 'If it looks good, it looks good, as long as it's not too extreme. If someone is too fat, it makes me think they have a problem or if someone is too skinny, it makes me think the same thing. Everyone looks good when they are looking as they should. I discussed it with my friends and all but one said they don't like skinny girls.' However, 'I do like tits and ass,' he admitted. Similarly, Eric, the café owner, likes, 'Female forms, not too skinny, not too tall, and not too thin'. Affable Mattias, the soft drink company executive, shared this view. 'The body is important, not thin or too big. I also like big eyes with sparks and openness and a large curve in the lower back,' he added, either having given this a lot of thought or with a certain someone in mind.

So, the men were wary of extremes and liked things in proportion. All, except Stefan, the tall, slim, bicycle store owner, who simply liked 'Pretty girls. I don't care if they are fat, think, short, tall. I like a pretty face.'

In this sporty society, there was a preference for people who were physically fit. Per, the embodiment of the virile Viking, said, 'I like in shape, but looks get less important as you get older, and personality becomes more important.' Andreas, the personal trainer with the muscles to match conceded that, 'If I don't find her physically attractive than I don't want to flirt, unless my impression of her changes as we begin talking, which is common. I'm usually not that interested in looks and don't have a physical type.'

While 30-year-old Hugo, the slightly chubby, bearded accounts manager, was perhaps shooting for the moon, he likes '…the playboy model hair looks and body.' But, as this is Stockholm and not New York, he added, 'I am also interested in their psychology about life. She has to say something intelligent.' Other men reiterated this view that 'Looks aren't enough'. 'I like a beautiful voice and certain energy in the eyes. Looks aren't enough though.' said Bjorn, the PhD student. 'If a beautiful woman looks boring I would disregard them.' said Andreas, the personal trainer.

Like their men folk, the Stockholm women interviewed also emphasised that being attracted to someone was about more than just looks. They said things such as, 'It's more of a chemistry thing' and 'What is more important is a good presence'. Clare, the 30-year-old air traffic controller, likes '…interesting facial features. They don't have to be traditionally good looking, but have something about them that I would personally find interesting.' The women prized intelligence too. Mia, who works in a gallery, expressed her reservations about good-looking airheads, 'But if he looks good and is not intelligent, than no way!'

While the Stockholmers might not be hung up on good looks, that doesn't mean that they shouldn't look good. Both the men and women stressed that what someone was wearing and the way he or she presented themselves, was very important. As Bjorn, the doctoral student, explained, 'The way people dress is an expression of their attitudes and personalities'. For Eric, the café owner, 'It's the way she dresses, if she spends time dressing up.' Stefan also likes his women to look womanly, 'A bad attitude is never interesting. Skirt and high heels would catch my attention more than a unisex outfit.'

Henrik, the banker, agreed, 'She has to look classy. It's how she moves, how she acts, can't be too loud, and has a feminine way.'

Like the men, when it came to physical preferences, the women also let down their gender guards and said they preferred men who were 'tall', 'masculine', 'hairy' or 'had stubble'! While Scandinavian culture pays more than lip service to gender equity, and it takes more than good looks and a pretty face for both the men and women to fall for someone, androgyny was not high on the list of physical preferences.

CONCLUSION
New Yorkers place more emphasis on physical appearance than do Parisians or Londoners. While New York men like their women to strut their stuff and vice versa, Parisians go for the natural look that takes three hours to achieve. Londoners thought that 'good looks' weren't that important and weren't looking to flirt with the most attractive person in the room. Even in gender-equal Stockholm, they thought that men should look like men and women like women, but attraction depends on more than just good looks. Perhaps the last word belongs to 32-year-old Annika, a nurse in Stockholm. 'When you are in love with someone, the looks don't matter.'

FLIRT FILE

- If you're not blessed with the tall, blonde looks of a Swedish Viking, have no fear, people will stiall find you attractive.
- Approximately half the interviewees said they didn't have a physical type. They were equal opportunity flirters.
- Many people said looks had become less important as they got older

TURN-ONS –TICKLE MY FANCY

To flirt successfully with someone, you need to know what floats their boat. How well did the genders understand each other's flirting preferences? Comparing what men and women thought the opposite sex liked produced some interesting results. Some cultures had it spot on. The New Yorkers and Parisians share a penchant for traditional gender roles and thus seemed to understand perfectly what the other gender liked. In other cities, like London there was some confusion. While the Parisian men seek affirmation of their manliness in the femininity of their women, London men never mentioned the importance of making her 'feel like a woman' or wanting to 'lead' or 'be the man'. Yet, the women of London thought that the men wanted demure, ladylike woman. In fact, the men regarded excessive 'girliness' as a turn-off. In contrast, Stockholm men proved very perceptive about women's needs and the women were equally insightful about the men's preferences. Perhaps, because they always like the same things!

NEW YORK
In Stockholm, if he spends 15 minutes talking to you, it's the start of something serious. For a New Yorker, this is just a warm-up until something better comes along. Amiable Andrea, who works for a charity, summed up the female perspective: 'It's easy to think, "Am I just one in a long string of women"?' In New York, people change their flirting partners as often as they refresh their drinks. Joel, the 33-year-old entrepreneur, spoke for the men: 'Is she just passing her time with me getting drinks until a better prospect comes along?'

Because this is a culture of 'easy come, easy go' the majority of the men and women interviewed identified a need in the opposite sex to feel singled out. For the men, wanting extra attention had a lot to do with getting 'props', or respect from his friends; for women, male attention was a reassurance that she was not just one of many.

So, how do you flirt with a New York male? According to the women of New York flattery will get you everywhere. As Gina, the Chinese New Yorker, said, 'Men like looking good in front of their friends'. 'They like women who pay attention and are impressed by a myriad of things about them. Flirting is a refined form of flattery,' said Rebecca, who works in recruitment. 'When flirting, it's important to make them feel manly by boosting their ego', added Sarah, the sassy fashion buyer. She gave examples like, "Could you open this for me?" and "Wow, that sounds so dangerous".' The only way it can get better than being flattered is if you're flattering him in front of his friends – and you're hot! As Alesha, the broadcast journalist, said 'All men like to feel flattered, manly, and virile. It's an ego boost if a hot woman is paying attention to them.' 'They gauge their own ability by the quality of the woman who's flirting with them. It makes them feel and look good in front of their friends. It's a very New York thing', said Alexis, the research assistant. 'They want to be zeroed in over their buddies, made to feel as though they were selected,' agreed Lisa, who works for a large credit card company.

In many cases, the men interviewed were aware that women also like to be noticed and need attention too. Justin, the literary agent said, 'Women like to be noticed; to be seen as desirable. They want attention; want to earn your first kiss; want to attract the opposite sex, and don't want to feel like a slut.' Bryan the aspiring musician was obviously successful with the ladies due to his insightful observations. 'They like attention; to be listened to; to be made to feel special; to be treated differently than everyone else.'

Joel the entrepreneur, thought men and women had different strengths when it came to flirting. 'For women, it's knowing how to use their bodies and fulfil the guys fantasy. For men, it's intelligence and portraying confidence to the woman.' So, she should be a sexpot and he, someone from whom you'd buy life insurance.

Doug the dentist explained, 'A good flirt is good at making connections with people they have never met. It's the confidence to be able to walk up to someone and start talking.' We can't talk about New York flirting without mentioning the C-word...confidence. Confidence seemed to be an essential component of the New Yorkers flirting arsenal. Both men and women mentioned this key attribute, which encompassed both being social and having the ability to converse with anyone. When asked, 'What are you looking for when you flirt with someone?' Dana, the pretty, brunette, analyst replied, 'Status', but after realising that might sound a bit superficial, she quickly changed it to 'confidence'. It seems many New York women were looking for confident, outgoing, high-earning men.

Alexis, the research assistant agreed, 'Who you are with is a status symbol. Everything speaks about who you are, your house, your partner, rather than just "being".'

Corey, the fire-fighter and actor, had the New York women's number, 'Women like somebody who is outgoing and buys them drinks'.
He's quite right, according to these New York women. They liked men who:
 '...can think on the spot to keep the conversation going'; men who have '...confidence, it's the way they walk and carry themselves.'

Alesha, the broadcast journalist, agreed, 'I like extroverts, guys who are approachable and have something to say, are fun to talk to, social guys.' They don't call them fast talkers for nothing, Dana the business analyst was also turned on by a man who '...is smart and can maintain a conversation'.

It seemed especially important to both genders that men displayed confidence. Possibly, because it was his responsibility to do the initiating, approaching and wooing. And, because New York women are so capable, strong and independent, they want to make sure that the men are at least at their same level as them.

PARIS
Traditional gender roles govern Parisian flirting behaviour. Both sexes thought that the other wanted to feel like a man or woman. Parisian men thought the women wanted to feel attractive, without appearing too aggressive. The women thought the last thing the men wanted was for them to be too available. Perhaps that's why the men have to try so many times a day!

Because Parisian men flirt constantly, to stand a chance, they have to continually up their game. The men interviewed mentioned two main things they felt the women of Paris wanted '…the originality to be approached in a new way,' and, for this to be done with honesty. Antoine, the debonair 35-year-old banker, identified that women want, '…honesty, but not too honest because it has to be credible.' It seems that in a game which is carefully calculated, the best players are the ones that make it look natural. Although, even when you are acting natural, others suspect it's a game. Dishy Mathieu, the art director with the chiselled jaw said, 'It must not look like flirting. It must look like a pleasant moment. If it's obviously a flirt, they will turn their backs. They like to be charmed but not to be victimised.'

The men also noted that women need to feel that they are not merely a sexual conquest. Jean-Luc, the chain-smoking Parisian native, was blunt. 'They don't like men who just want to have sex'. They like to '…feel special and not like he is going around with everybody'. They want to '…feel they're attractive, that the guy is interested in anything other than their ass'. Frederique, the 28-year-old sales manager, put it this way: 'The theory is women want a 'romantic commando' sometimes romantic, sometimes tough'.

In another nod to sexual stereotypes, the men thought that women like them to be in the driving seat. Nicolas, the matter-of-fact project manager, said that women want to ' …have confidence in the man. A woman likes to know that a man can drive at the beginning'. They like a man to '…take care of the woman but still act like a man', agreed gallant Guilliame, the book seller. Sure enough, the women of Paris are looking for men who are genuine; who make them feel special and who assume the manly role.

Like their male counterparts, Parisian women knew exactly what the men liked – after all, it was in her job description as an intelligent, charming, mysterious, sexy Parisian female to know so. French men like women '…to let them act like a man,' and '…to flatter his power,' they said. Martine, the logistics coordinator, explained men like, '…reinforcement of his manhood and virility. They like to feel they are likeable, capable of seduction, desirable; they are better than their mates.'

Juliette, the social worker, thought that men liked '…the girl teasing him, as in "You're such a bad boy, you are such a naughty boy".' Such coquettish lines are reminiscent of some of the New York women's comments on the same subject.
'They like sexy girls to boost their ego in public. The game has to be subtle and clever. To be sexy is a sense of acting,' explained sophisticated Stephanie the business analyst. The men of Paris don't like easy conquests, as Stephanie went on to say. 'They like to know you are not too easy to get, to give a bit of resistance, but not too much because then they get bored and leave.' 'Men like the woman to be quite feminine, mysterious, and withdrawn,' said Charlotte, the 32-year-old editor, 'The image of femininity in France is still old fashioned. A woman in Paris must be intelligent, and there must be a question mark at the end.' Keep him guessing, girls! PhD student Veronique, knows exactly what attracts Parisian men. She is the perfect, silent woman. 'I like to see men desire me. Men often like my mystère'. She went on to describe her modus operandi. 'I don't verbalise, I smile. I don't ask questions or if I do I ask very few.' Juliette, the wide-eyed social worker, gave this advice. 'Ignore them with a hint that you're not really ignoring them. Don't express your opinions, or if you do, do so very gently.' Sophie, a 34-year-old primary school teacher, employs similar tactics. 'Pay a little attention and then act like you don't care.' It seems that the women deliberately act in accordance with the men's preferences. However, not all women played this game. Sandrine, the director's assistant, threw up her hands in despair

and said, 'I am extreme because I don't know how to do it. I am too straightforward for men my age. After an hour of talking I will say, I like you.'

LONDON

The women of London really don't get what men want. The men say they want an assertive woman, but the women think differently. And the men, while they seem to understand what women want, possibly don't really know what they want for themselves. The women think the men like '...sexy girls to boost their ego in public'. Are we in New York? Or, alternatively, a woman who is ladylike and demure. Wait, perhaps Paris? Yet, the men say they like strong, confident women. Take Sam the erudite website designer. He said, 'I like a woman who talks about something that matters; has an opinion about something; is engaged and not passive, and who doesn't act coy or prim as an act'.

When asked what the men liked, an interesting pattern became apparent in the women's answers. It seems as if the women humour the men. According to many of the female interviewees, men want to have their egos massaged. They crave '...attention from women regardless of who the woman is'. They like women to '...listen to what they have to say' and be '...interested in them because they love talking about themselves'. They want women to '...ask them questions and then remember their answers', and they like '...girls laughing loudly at their jokes even if they're not funny'. London women thought that men want:

- '...to think they are the only ones'
- '...to be flattered'
- '...to be found amusing'
- '...to feel important'
- '...to tell you about how good they are so you will say yes, yes, yes! '

If you go by this litany of self-interest, the women of London seem to see the men as indiscriminate, self-important, egomaniacs. Yet, going by the London men's responses, they proved to be sensitive, enlightened and liberated.

When asked, 'What do you think a man likes when it comes to flirting?' Jane, who works in the financial industry, said, 'Men like subtlety.' Claire, the red-headed accountant, gave this advice, 'You could look across the room, but don't be too eager or too cold.' Rachel, the children's book illustrator said, 'A man doesn't like you to be too full on, but would like to know they are in with a chance. They need to know they won't be rejected. They like coyness, head flicks, and giggling.'
'Men like women to draw attention to their femininity' was a common refrain. Yasmin, a PR consultant said, 'They like it when girls use their girly-ness.'

The women thought that the men '...like to feel manly in an emasculated world; for you to bring out their alpha male without sounding sycophantic', as Emma, the bubbly presenter, said. Georgina, the 28-year-old secretary, put it this way: 'They like demure and petite women, someone who plays up to the men and lets them feel they are in charge.' Even Anoushka, the level-headed solicitor, agreed with this assessment: 'They like you to be ladylike and presentable, the sort of girl they can take back to their mum.'

The men, however, did not mention these feminine attributes. Nor did any of them speak about their need to feel 'manly'. While the women of London were off the mark, the men were more insightful. Some said that women like men to be funny and attentive, which is exactly what the women said they liked.

Simon, the witty PR exec, was off to a good start when he said that women like 'Humour and champagne!' 'A sense of humour, sincerity, compliments. They know what the end result could be but they don't want it spelled out,' said Daniel, who manages a bar.

Alex, in import/export, was clear about the most effective approach: 'Ask questions about her. Put her as the centre of attention.'

'Women like humour and to be listened to. They like people to make them feel attractive and pay compliments about their physical appearance and their remarks,' agreed Samuel, the charming cabinet maker. The men were all on the same page. James the optician was of the view that women '…want to be stimulated…at a physical and mental level. Holding their attention, listening to them and adding humour is important. Flirting is two-way.' Time and again the men emphasised the importance of attentiveness and communication to women. Duncan the journalist said 'She likes it if you pay her attention, make good conversation. She wants a sense of connection with the person she's talking to. It's about finding something in common, a deeper involvement.' Alistair the broadcast journalist said, 'Girls want to be hit on without knowing they are being hit on, the suggestion has to come from the woman that there might be something more.' 'Women can spot a bullshitter straight away,' said Adrian, the fast-talking real estate agent, 'They like compliments. Girls like to talk about themselves. The occasional touch is good, not too much. They like to be in control and in command.' Max, the music publisher, with his sensitive insights, could never have spent a Saturday night alone at home, He said, 'The flattery comes from being able to listen to what they are saying and remark appropriately. They like to be valued.'

While the men were amazingly accurate about what the London women liked, some refused to generalise about all women and said things such as:

- 'It depends on the women. Some want a shy guy and others want a confident bastard.'
- 'They are all individuals, you have to treat them differently.'
- 'They like being regarded as individuals. They are not just objects.'
- 'All are different. Some might like more physical contact. They like you noticing things about them. Others are more upfront. The most difficult thing is recognising each girl's boundaries.'

It seems the two sexes are following different rules. Such discrepancies could arise for a number of reasons. If the women are playing by the traditional roles, then the men are not keeping up their end of the bargain. It seems the main reason the women aren't breaking free from their stereotypical roles and being more assertive is because they think the men wouldn't like it. And, while the men say they are quite happy to be pursued, perhaps the women are more attune with what the men really like than the men are themselves. Are the men talking the talk, but not walking the walk…across the bar to where the women are?

STOCKHOLM

The Stockholm men appeared to be as perceptive as the London men. After they espoused the usual, 'Men and women aren't different' and 'They like the same thing as me', Stockholm men showed that they know what women want:

Here's Per, the virile Viking on the subject. 'Women like to be talked to in a special way, get compliments, be made to feel special in the way you talk to them. They like you to remember the details in what they say. Like-minded Mattias thought that women like '...flattering comments about clothes or hair but not too pushy or offensive, be a bit subtle, don't make it too clear that you are flirting. Listen and give interesting comments to what she has to say instead of just talking about yourself.' Like their London counterparts, Stockholm men pointed out that you can't generalise about women. Henrik the banker spoke about 'recognising them as individuals,' and said that what women like '...depends on the woman. Some might like compliments and others might think it's sleazy'.

The men recognised that to have any sort of chance, it has to be all about her. Hugo a 30-year-old accounts manager explained, 'They like compliments on hair, clothes, shoes, but it's more about tactics than what they like. It's not trying to impress her with what I am good at but rather making her feel special. They like to feel like they are in control.' But it was Andreas the personal trainer who may have just stumbled upon the holy grail of flirting. 'Women', he said, '...like to feel that we had a connection that couldn't have happened with the others.'

Stockholm men would never dare to come on too strong. 33-year-old Stefan gave us the benefit of his experience. 'If you don't know people it's more formal. To break the barrier is the trick.' And, obviously, this must be done subtly. Why? Because that's how the women like it! Henrik the banker explained, 'You would have to be more subtle with someone you didn't know. You would want to portray yourself as funny, easy-going and without any problems. You don't want to look like you work too hard and would downplay that you work in the city. You wouldn't say that you work 12 hours a day. In Sweden we work 8 to 5 and don't work more because women don't want that.' Andreas the personal trainer said it was all about '...being polite when you approach. Use humour to show you are interested in them, but not too much', he advised. The men know they are dealing with some smart women. Bjorn, a PhD student said, 'They like genuine compliments. Women are intelligent they can spot what is fake or real.' Per agreed the first step is to get past a woman's barriers. He said, 'You have to let the woman discover you without being too obvious'.

Are the men also fans of subtlety? Some women didn't think so. Johanna is an opera singer. 'Guys like it when girls take the action. Then they don't have to do all the work.' Several London women had made similar observations.

Jenny the PhD student in biology insisted, 'They like it when girls are assertive and take charge in flirting,' she said. 'Being forward works for me' said confident Katarina, the florist who is as fetching as her flowers. However, other women had different perspectives: Kristina is a global HR manager. Men '...want to be in charge a little bit. They like the assertiveness but are not used to it', she said. Eva the press officer agreed, 'They like a bit pushy, to you to show you are interested, but the guy still wants to control the pace.' It appears that the question of who makes the first move is a thorny one, regardless of gender dynamics. Because of her important job, men expected Clare, the air traffic controller, to be the one to land the plane. She said, 'Many men get intimidated when they hear I am an air traffic controller. They might say "Why didn't you come over to me?" However, she still feels reluctant to make the first move, 'But the thing is, if I did that, I wouldn't do it right or the way they wanted me to.'

It's clear the Stockholmers are trying to forge a truce in the battle of the sexes and are challenging traditional roles of what is expected for men and women. However, it seems a person's preference for assertive or not, depends more on individual choice, than genetics. In the same way that the men insisted that you can't generalise about women, Maria, a 33-year-old project manager said, 'It depends on the man and where you go to flirt. Some men like women who show a bit of initiative. They like the spark of a woman to show she is attracted, but not too full on.' Annika, a pretty, petite nurse, agreed, 'He likes to be the one in charge and who says, "Go ahead". If he has a strong personality, than he wants to decide. If he's softer, than he likes the woman to decide.'

Swedish men bear the burden of many expectations: they must be polite, friendly, and not too flirty. The men seem to like it when the women take charge. However, how much of this is due to gender equality and how much of this is due to the fact that the women don't like to be approached? Perhaps one reason the guys are so willing to have the women do the initiating is because it doesn't go over very well when they do it. An often, thankless task, but someone has to do it!

CONCLUSION

London and Stockholm men regard women as individuals and seem well-versed in what women like. Similarly, a few astute Parisian men pointed out that women were different. However, their reasons were self-serving. If they were aware of a woman's individual preferences, they could manipulate the situation more thoroughly and gain an advantage in 'the game'. Both Stockholm men and women maintained that their tastes were the same. And they were right. Stockholm men know what women want: to be given compliments, to be made to feel special and to have it her way. The Stockholm women, almost unanimously, thought the men liked assertive women who take charge. Just as well that the men seemed to have a preference for assertive women. Stockholm men want a candlelit dinner and flowers before they put out. They too want compliments, and to be made to feel special. New York men felt that women wanted to be found sexually desirable. In truth, this may indicate that it was really the men who were partial to women with sex appeal. The New York women focused more on their desire to have the man take care of them. In a nod to conventional gender roles, the women thought the men enjoyed having their egos stroked in front of their friends. The men, obviously, made no mention of such things.

The Parisians were on the same page when it came to gender preferences in the dating game. The women knew that the men preferred women to play hard-to-get and the men confirmed that assertive women didn't do it for them. Both men and women liked being approached in a unique way; they liked provocative, intelligent discussions and were insistent that the men act like men and the women behave like women.

Conversely, in London it seemed as if the men and women were flirting with people in other countries, so different were their responses. The men knew exactly what the women wanted: humour, attention, compliments and to be made to feel special. The men said they liked strong, assertive, confident women with opinions, with whom they could banter. However, the women thought the men were looking for coy, ultra-feminine women and raised the subject with astonishing regularity. The London women seemed to think that the men liked to have their egos stroked. Yet, the men were the ones that showed an understanding that it takes two to tango…and to flirt. So while London men are in tune with what women want, the women don't seem to have a clue about what men want. The unanswered question is, why not?

FLIRT FILE

Here's a general rule of thumb: As there is no guessing what someone might like, being upfront and obvious is useful. They will just tell you! What men like women to do:

- Have something interesting to say
- Be open and up for fun
- Be well presented, not overly made-up or dressed overtly sexually
- Give him attention, interest, and make him feel good.

What women like men to do:

- Listen to them
- Make them feel sexually attractive, but not like you're only interested in sex.
- Make them laugh

Chapter 20: What They Don't Like
TURN-OFFS ABHORRENT ANTICS

While New York men are expected to be assertive, Stockholm men are left out in the cold if they come on too strong. Yet men who talk about themselves too much are shooting themselves in the foot in New York. A common turn-off in all the cities was women who are too clingy and men and women who are too sexually aggressive. Some cities, like Paris, were appreciative of feminine women while in London girliness and gossip will get you exactly nowhere. Generally speaking, the men and women interviewed knew what the other did not like – hopefully, not because they had been guilty of such behaviour themselves! The only exception was the Londoners. The women mistakenly believed that the men didn't like sexual assertiveness.

NEW YORK
Although New Yorkers thought that being confident was important, especially for men, some strayed over the line, from confidence into arrogance. This was a big no-no. If you want to impress a New Yorker, being sensitive to the difference is essential. In the capital of capitalism, people look for the middle ground. Women should be neither too fat nor too thin. Men shouldn't be too arrogant or too supplicating. Women shouldn't be too aggressive, yet they should show keen interest. New York women were just as likely as the men to adopt a 'take no prisoners' approach to flirting. Yet they were aware that men found this unappealing.

The cardinal sin in New York is failing to read the signals that someone isn't interested. A big turn-off for both men and women was 'Not getting the signals that I'm not interested.' Men don't like it when '…he says he is not interested and she keeps going; not responsive to his cues,' said Lisa, the credit card executive. Sarah, the fashion buyer, agreed, 'Not understanding that he is not into it is a big turn-off.' A majority of the men interviewed also recognised that, 'Women don't like somebody who just doesn't get the hint'; somebody who is '…too aggressive, not getting signals they are not interested'.

The women interviewed thought other turn-offs for men were:
- 'being seen as desperate'
- 'being too obvious about it, it's not good to border on desperation'
- 'being too clingy too quickly'
- 'being too flirty, too trashy'
- 'sloppy, over-the-top flirting, perceived as being trashy'
- 'too drunk, all over them, touching them too much'.
- 'having attitude.' Men don't like a '…snotty, bitchy, complaining, attitude.'

However, Rebecca in recruitment took a more even-handed view. 'Men are different, some like bitchiness; others don't'.

When asked what they thought were turn-offs for women, some perceptive New York men said:

- 'The man talking too much about himself'.

- 'Being self-absorbed, talking about things you have accomplished, conversation revolving around the man'.
- 'Talk too much about self and don't listen'.
- 'Not asking them questions'.
- 'Thinking more about themselves than the person they are talking to'.

The men were quite right, it seems. Unemployed Marie said, 'I do not like the ones with an attitude'. Dana, the brunette business analyst, likes men to be, '…a little self deprecating, not full of himself.' Stacey, the make-up artist, said much the same thing. 'Not bragging, being down to earth.'

It was equally important to New Yorkers to feel unique. As Dana quipped, 'Everyone in New York has attention deficit disorder because they are constantly being distracted by what else is on offer'. The men were aware that looking at other women is a major turn-off for the ladies. David, the confident, 28-year-old, architect acknowledged that 'Women don't like it when another girl walks by and you look at them.' He was spot-on. Alesha, the striking broadcast journalist, agreed, 'I don't want him to act like a Lothario or be too aggressive; flattering but not fawning. Just flirting with me and not everyone'. 'Men need to realise it's not a one-size-fits-all kind of thing,' said Alexis, the sharp-witted research assistant. Listen up, guys. Don't expect to use the same old tired line and pull the same lame moves on New York women and think it's going to work.

While being too aggressive or arrogant won't get you far in the dating game, it is just as bad, if not worse, for a man to be too passive. New York women are self-confident and independent, yet they are still looking for the man to 'take care of them'. Thus, weaklings are a turn-off. The men are very aware of this. According to Chris, the 30-year-old environmental engineer, 'Women don't want to constantly lead. It's a push/pull kind of thing.' He thought that women were looking for men who are '…not boring and being a little difficult'.

Joel the entrepreneur rattled off a long list of turn-offs. 'Women don't like it when men are too aggressive, obnoxious, being too intrusive, not getting signals, or too passive.'

New York women are looking for a guy who is assertive, but not aggressive, is aware, but not a wimp – and the men know it. In another example of the superficial gender equality that New Yorkers seem to have achieved, the men are also looking for women to behave in that middle ground between aggressive and passive. Unemployed Marie thought that, 'Men don't like aggression or the woman having too much dominance'. She explained that men don't like it when women are '…too all over them'. 'There are so many beautiful women out there, guys don't like it when you cramp their style.' Andrea, who works for a charity, put it plainly, 'They don't want you to come on too strong'. Stacey, the make-up artist of Puerto Rican descent gave an example: 'They don't like it when women call them out. For example, saying, "You think you are so slick."' And whatever you do, don't be a smart Alec, or in this case, a smart Alexis. Astute Alexis, the research assistant, warned, 'Being too serious isn't good, the revelation of whether or not intelligence is appreciated.' Her insights would be better appreciated in Paris.

PARIS

When asked 'What turns men off?' the Parisian women seemed to think... 'A lot.'

They gave a litany of what not to do.
- Don't be too easy to get.
- Don't be too mysterious and withdrawn.
- Don't be too loud.
- Don't be too quiet.
- Don't be too aggressive.
- It's OK to be shy... just not, you guessed it, too shy.
- And, whatever you do, do not be obvious!

Charlotte, the 32-year-old editor, explained, 'Being too loud or energetic will look stupid.' But, is there a place for humour in Parisian flirting? Let's see, a New Yorker, a Parisian and a Londoner walk into a bar... 'No! Being funny doesn't work,' says one Parisian woman. Why? 'Because a girl shouldn't try to capture everyone's attention.' Ah, so funny girls are seen as attention seekers. Mirth is too much.

Like their New York sisters, the Parisian women also thought that being too obvious that they were looking for a relationship was a major turn-off for men – presumably because, mostly, they were. Martine, the logistics coordinator, said, 'Men like women to not think about the future, but only the moment.' Sophisticated Stefanie, the business analyst, agreed, 'Guys don't like it when you make him think you are looking for a long-term relationship.' 'Complicated women' and 'Women who don't know what they want' were also cited as turn-offs. The common perception was that men didn't like women straying out of their prescribed gender roles. Men don't like women:

- '...acting like guys'
- 'not being feminine or being too direct'
- 'being vulgar or too loud in her opinion'.

However, those women that did wear too much make-up, or laughed too loudly or wore their miniskirt too short, would qualify for a one-night stand. Parisian women are well-versed in what is expected of them – to be feminine without being a floozy.

Top turn-offs for women, according to Paris men, include coming on too strong and being too arrogant, (or not confident enough), not showing them respect, being rude to them, or mistreating them. The list of offences, as outlined by the male interviewees included being: '...too pushy, vulgar, talks about sex too quickly' and being '...too arrogant, too confident. 'Women don't like men who just want to have sex', observed Greg, the communication student, who is obviously no dummy. Eccentric Olivier was also not born yesterday. He said, 'Women don't like explicit sexual offers, being rude, naughty talking. "Hey baby do you want to shag?" They wouldn't want to be touched too quickly or in an oppressing manner. Physical contact too soon is bad'. While the men seemed aware that Paris women didn't like men to come on too strong, the men seemed incapable of a different approach. Many women complained about how forcefully the men came on and how persistently. Francine, the petite publisher, said, 'Guys just speak and don't even care if we are interested.'

LONDON

Both the London men and women interviewed were aware of the fine line between overt and covert sexual attention. No one wants to be too bold. However, if you are too subtle, you face being banished to the fallow fields of friendship or taking up citizenship in 'what could have been' land! While Englishmen wanted women to be more obvious, more assertive, and to have opinions, the women thought the men wanted the opposite. 'Men don't like you to be too forward, too full on, or too suggestive,' insisted Sophia, the lithe dancer. When asked 'What don't Englishmen like when it comes to flirting?' the women of London said:

- 'You shouldn't come on too strong.'
- 'You shouldn't be overtly keen. Men want to chase.'
- 'Avoid too much invasion of personal space, otherwise men feel like they are the prey.'
- 'In the end men want to win.'

In truth, London men said they wanted women to express their interest more overtly. Yet, the women were convinced that: 'Flirting is a subtle art so men don't like it to be too overt,' said Annette the jazz singer. 'Men don't like you to have too many opinions, a bit of banter is all right, but not too much. They don't like you to come on too strong,' said another. Anoushka the sexy solicitor, gave her professional opinion, 'Don't be too forward – be polite when flirting, but not too full on because it scares them'. Rachel the illustrator agreed, 'Men wouldn't like to be blatantly chatted up.' Jane who works in the financial industry put it this way, 'Men don't like you cheapening yourself to flirt.' The ladies seem to have a point. Take Charlie, for example. For this 30-year-old, floppy-haired entrepreneur, his turn-offs '…start with the three B's: Bad shoes, bad breath, and being brash.'

The women were also aware that London men also do not care for superficial attempts at femininity. They said men dislike:

- 'talking about subjects which are irrelevant to boys, such as celeb gossip, and wearing too much makeup'
- 'talking about inane subjects such as lipstick and things'
- 'shovelling on the makeup and putting on lipstick in front of them'
- 'being all crap and girly'.

The women got this right, at least. Most London men aren't interested in having women play traditional roles. Take Duncan the journalist, for example: 'I like it if a woman talks about something that matters, has an opinion about something. It's about being engaged and not passive, not acting coy or prim as an act.'

London men were singular in their emphasis on women as real people. The men don't believe that women possess certain characteristics simply because of their biological make-up. Many men pointed out how different each woman is. 'They don't like not being regarded as individuals. They are not just objects.' observed Chris, the ex-military man.

The men also cited 'coming on too strong' as a major turn-off for women.

New York men's penchant for physical contact would not go over well with the London women. Samuel, the 38-year-old cabinetmaker, was well aware that women don't like men '…staring at their breasts, boasting, or talking more about themselves than them.' Many men used the word 'lech' – an abbreviated form of 'lechery' – when describing what women did not like. They also mentioned coming on strong as a major turn-off. Alex, who works in import/export, summed up the fine line between assertiveness and aggression, 'If a guy is bold, he can be successful, he cannot, however, be crass'. Perhaps this was one of the reasons that held the men back from approaching women. Sam, the website designer, said, 'Women don't like too much lecchiness or being too forward. Women want to feel like they have been chatted to and talked to and listened too rather than aggressive flirting.'

Yet, what to talk about? Some men were of the opinion that women don't like you to be too serious too soon. Adrian, the real estate agent, said, 'You can't be too serious, or bring up anything that might be baggage, not serious emotions too soon, because when you are flirting you are supposed to forget about your problems and just have fun. You want to show the other person "If you are with me, you will be laughing all the time; come into my world".'

STOCKHOLM

What do the men and women of Stockholm think are turn-offs for the opposite sex? Unsurprisingly, coming from a culture that gets social with the help of alcohol, being too drunk was the biggest turn-off for everyone! Yet, on this question, the men and women had markedly different preferences. The interviewees constantly referred to a Swedish concept called 'jantelagen', meaning 'Don't think you are better than everyone else'. In Stockholm, unlike New York, if you strut your stuff, the object of your interest is sure to saunter away. The men knew they could not be too obvious they were flirting, they certainly couldn't skip to the sexual part too quickly and whatever they did, they could not be overconfident. And, while the men might not admit it, the women knew they had better not be seen flirting with lots of guys.

A major turn-off for the women, according to the men, was looking like you were flirting in the first place. 33-year-old Stefan said, 'You've got to be smooth. My best flirting encounters are when they think I don't want anything.' Henrik the banker agreed, 'The initial pick up is hard because you have to think of something clever to say that's not too obvious.' The Stockholm men knew that playing the macho man would not get them far. Showing confidence, talking about himself and perhaps even bragging were not an effective strategy for attracting the opposite sex – add to this being drunk, looking scruffy, smelling bad, being rude, undressing her with your eyes and making her feel like a piece of meat.

'Swedish women don't like guys who show they are only after sex,' said Henrik, the banker. Frederik, the 28-year-old student, had reached the same conclusion, 'They don't like obvious sexual invites because it's skipping a lot of steps in between.' Andreas, the personal trainer said, 'You can't be too sexually direct; can't move too fast; can't go up to her girl and grab her'. Or even worse, 'Being drunk and putting hands on boob'. His Viking ancestors must be rocking in their watery graves.

Jenny is a PhD student in Biology. In reply to the question, 'What don't men like when it comes to flirting?' she replied, 'Nothing, they are just happy if girls talk to them'. However, not all her Stockholm sisters shared her sanguine assessment. Many women said that men didn't appreciate inebriated women. Eva, the press officer, was adamant that men don't like it if you are, 'Too drunk, and flirting with lots of people at the same time'. Apparently, a few drinks are a good thing; a few bottles, not so good. The women also said that the men didn't like girls who wear too much make-up, or are too sleazy, vulgar, unhygienic or 'smelly'. Well, who would?

Even worse than being unkempt, according to the women, is behaving like a bonobo – a matriarchal primate species known for its promiscuity. Clare, the 30-year-old air traffic controller said, 'They don't like it when you are showing lots of boys attention', or '… flirting with lots of people', as Katarina the florist pointed out put it. We heard a similar refrain in New York.

Yet, unlike the capricious New Yorkers, the Stockholmers are expected to choose a partner and stick with them. As Kristina, the global HR manager explained, 'If you flirt, you had better choose wisely because you have to stay and suffer the consequences.' If you've just chatted up a dud, other guys will have seen you operating and they don't like it if you flirt with lots of guys.

The women also thought the men weren't fond of women who were 'too forward' or 'too clingy'. Clare the 30-year-old air traffic controller, said, 'Swedish men don't want a woman to depend on him. They want an intelligent girlfriend who is an equal'. Just make sure she isn't more than equal. Guys get scared of women who are too independent. They don't know how to handle it,' agreed Johanna the opera singer. As Kristina, the global HR manager, said, 'They don't like too intelligent. They like intelligent women but not more than them. If they feel less equal, they will disappear.'

CONCLUSION
New York men know the women expect them to be assertive. There's no room for reticence in this fast-paced city. They also know that talking about themselves is not going to get them very far with the ladies, but whether that stops them is another matter. Similarly, the men of Paris recognise that women do not appreciate a guy who is too arrogant, or too overtly sexual. However, this does not seem to change their behaviour, either.

The women of New York are aware that the men like them to fulfil their fantasies without being trashy – something of a tall order. It sounds like the Parisian women could share some of their secrets with them. This holds true too in Stockholm, where according to the women of Stockholm, their menfolk don't like women who are vulgar or sexually aggressive. London women also thought that their men did not like to be obviously chatted up. Yet this perception that men didn't like a woman who was sexually suggestive was not borne out by the men's responses. Almost without exception the London men interviewed echoed David the recruitment consultant's sentiment: 'I like it when she comes on strong.'

The Parisian women had a long list of things that men would not like. Top of the list was trying to be funny, being too loud or energetic. The women also thought that being too obvious about wanting to be in a relationship would work against them.. The Stockholm women know they must make a choice and stick to it when it comes to choosing a flirting partner because the men did not like a woman who hedged her bets. One thing was for sure, if you were any of the following: too drunk, too sexual, too confident, too slovenly, or too bold, the women of Stockholm would not be talking to you! Nor would the men.

FLIRT FILE

What men don't like:
- Overtly sexual or aggressive women
- Boring or uninteresting women, even if you are attractive!
- Women who are too coy or aloof.

What women don't like:
- To feel like they are just a number, one of many
- A man who talks to much about himself
- A man who is too arrogant, or too passive

Chapter 21: Who Approaches
WHO MAKES THE MOVES?

Women are proactive in all other areas of life; job hunting, flat hunting, friendship hunting. Why is it, when it comes to the most important area of life, our relationships, women sit back and wait? Women have long been conditioned to be patient and pliant prey, consistent with the traditional gender stereotypes of men as active and women as passive. But, why should the man always have to be the one to approach? And, why should the women only get to 'choose' from the limited selection of guys bold, drunk, or cocky enough to approach her?

When it comes to the amorous approach, New York is about spark, Paris fire, London the slow burn and Stockholm a gentle sizzle. New York women prefer him to do it, but his tardiness certainly isn't going to stop her from acting! Parisian women would never dream of making the first move. London lasses don't like to do the luring, but give them a few drinks and you just might get what you came for, while in Stockholm, she is more likely, than he, to approach.

The men of New York know that he who hesitates is lost, while for Parisian men making the first move is practically noblesse oblige. The London males understand that it's the women who call the shots, but they'd like to do so from their chairs, while the Stockholmers can't agree on who actually does the initiating and approaching. Are the men doing it as much as they say they are, or are the women simply not giving them enough credit? So who makes the moves, the bedroom eyes, the beguiling smiles, and body language that shouts 'available'? And who moves first, physically crossing the room, to initiate a flirtatious interaction?

Dr. Monica Moore, an associate professor in the Department of Behavioural and Social Sciences at Webster University in St. Louis, spent over 1 000 hours in singles bars watching flirting behaviour. She identified over 52 flirtatious approachability signals that women give out to men. These signals ranged from the more obvious: hair flip, the lip lick, the pout and the coy smile, to the more subtle, like displays of the palms or neck. Tim Perper, an independent researcher, estimated that two-thirds of all approaches are initiated by women. However, when Tim later asked, 'Who made the first move', the men most often thought that they were the ones who instigated the interactions.
The approach is one of the roles most commonly assigned to men in flirting interactions. Thus, who makes the first move reveals how closely a culture is tied to traditional gender roles. The interviewees were asked three questions: who was most likely to initiate the flirting, who was most likely to actually physically approach the other person, and, if they thought it was better to choose or be chosen.

NEW YORK
New Yorkers are not usually ones to leave things in the hands of destiny. Half of the New Yorkers interviewed in this study agreed that both men and women were equally likely to initiate an encounter. In addition, 65% of the men interviewed preferred to be the ones choosing the object of interest, although some New York men admitted it was easier to be chosen. Of the women interviewed, only 40% said they like to make the choice. This

reflects a popularly held belief of New York women that men are the prime movers and shakers in natural selection.

A third of the women believed that men mostly come on to them first. Marie, 28, and currently unemployed, observed, 'Men are quicker to notice women as they are more predatory.' However, when it comes to physically approaching the object of interest, almost every New York woman interviewed said that the men were most likely to come over first. Alesha, the striking broadcast journalist said, 'Women in New York are more aggressive than most women. Traditionally it's the man who does the approaching.' Some even felt that it was the man's 'duty', and that men, by nature, are less shy or intimidated than women. Over two-thirds of the men interviewed agreed. As Mike McDreamy, the buff banker, explained, 'There is the old expectation in culture that the man will be the one do to it.'

When it came to those 'come-hither' signals, half of the New York women thought that men and women were equally likely to initiate flirting, a third of the women thought that it was solely the men's turf, and only a few women thought it was the women who did it exclusively. When it came to actually walking over, the women thought that it was the men's domain, almost exclusively. There appeared to be two main reasons why women thought it was the men who initiated and approached. The first reason: it was their 'duty' to do so; the second: men don't mind rejection.

When New York women were asked, 'Do you approach men?' 56% said 'Yes' because they had nothing to lose. As for the other half who didn't approach men, their reasons were 'I don't have to' or 'You don't have to wait very long for a man to approach you.' Alesha, the striking broadcast journalist, said 'It's no big deal. You have nothing to lose'. 38 year-old Dana, the pretty brunette analyst, agreed, 'You have nothing to lose so if you see a guy you like, you might as well try'.

Sarah, the smart and sassy fashion buyer, echoed the general consensus, 'There is nothing to lose. My generation approaches men'. Entertaining Alexis, a sharp-witted research assistant, confidently asserted, 'With a couple of drinks and if there is enough of a signal, I would definitely approach a guy'. 'I will approach a guy if I want to talk and I am attracted, said Lisa, the high-powered credit card executive, 'But I will usually try and 'bait' first with eye contact'.

On the other end of the spectrum, the women who declined to make the first move did feel they had something to lose. Gina, the Chinese occupational therapist, said, 'If we do approach a guy, then he will have more power and think we are easy'. She explained, 'It was the way I was brought up'.

Stacey, the 28-year-old make-up artist of Puerto Rican descent justified her thinking thus: 'It's okay for a woman to manoeuvre her way over but not to directly approach.' As was found throughout the research into the New York flirting scene, the women who were third generation immigrants, and still had strong ties to their own heritage, were more conservative in their flirting views.

In the minds of many New York women, it is the men who are supposed to take the long walk across the room. Andrea works for a charity. 'I prefer to be approached,' she said.

'It's a sign of being valued or held in esteem'. She expressed dissatisfaction with men who departed from the script. 'Nowadays, men expect women to do the approaching.' Rebecca, who is in recruitment, simply said, 'I like being chased'. However, she was prepared to make an exception. 'I'd only approach a guy if I wanted a cigarette'. It seemed that some New York women felt it acceptable to approach a guy if you want something. Susan, the budding journalist, said, 'I'll approach a guy if I want a drink and they intrigue me', she said. Her birthplace, Ohio, seemed a million miles away

The women of New York are as assertive as the men at every turn. The reason they think that the men are the ones most likely to initiate and approach is because that is their role in the gender role game. But, like any good game, you can change the rules, to ensure that you win! So New York women like the men to do the chasing but if he proves to be slow on the uptake, she will assume the role of huntress.

Sarah, the fashion buyer, said, 'I'd like for them to ask me for my number. If they don't have the smarts to ask, then I … make sure they get the message.' Lisa, the credit card exec, explained, 'The most successful interaction is when the man closes the deal by doing something. He asks for her number. Or the woman is clear in her intention and what she wants and he responds'. This technique ensures that the man feels in control but really it's the woman pulling the strings. As Stacey, the make-up artist, said, 'Men are more aggressive. They are more likely to approach you but not necessarily date you. The guys want to be the pursuers and we know how to work them.'

Although New York women take on the men in most aspects of their lives, when it comes to the dating game, they play their prescribed passive role – to a point. Some New York women do not want to approach the man because they feel it's his responsibility while others simply don't get the opportunity. It appears that many New York men are so aggressive that the women don't get the chance to initiate flirtatious encounters. Both genders mentioned that New York women need to be 'hard' because of the constant attention from men. The attention was tenfold if you were 'hot'. Andrew, the 34-year-old attorney, estimated, 'A good-looking girl in the city can be approached hundreds of times a night.' Here's the Catch 22. The women can't afford to let down their guard because the men are in perpetual hot pursuit. Yet it is only the persistent male who will break through New York women's hard facades. 38-year-old Dana, the business analyst, empathised with the men's plight, 'New York women will say "No" more often than "Yes". So many women look like bitches in this city that it has to be intimidating for men.' Not only did the women feel that the man's proper role is the hunter, they also cast him as a Superman immune to rejection. Andrea, who works for a charity, was convinced that 'Men are less intimidated by groups'. Gina, a 33-year-old occupational therapist of Chinese descent, insisted that 'Women are more afraid of rejection'.

A little over half of the New York men interviewed believed both genders were equally likely to signal their interest. However, when it came to who makes the actual approach, two-thirds of the men believed that that was their job. Whatever the woman did behind the scenes to get him there was up to her. The men were also divided on whether they preferred women to approach them.

Who moves first?

When asked, 'Do you approach women?' 64% of the males said they did. The reasons they give were:

- 'I'll talk to anyone'.
- 'I want to get laid.'
- 'I like meeting new people and making new friends.'
- 'I don't care what happens.'
- 'I'm not afraid of rejection'.
- 'I am curious.'

How do the men feel about women approaching them? Almost all the men were in favour, although some had reservations.

Literary agent Justin said, 'I would be suspicious but I would like it'. David, the architect, said, 'If it's not a challenge, then it's not interesting. But it's hard for guys to take the first step, so anything the woman can do to help is great.' Many said it would depend on whether he was attracted to her. Jason, a high-school science teacher, was indecisive, 'I think I would like it but I am not sure I would like it. It would depend on the particular woman. If I am attracted great; if not, not so great.'

Then, there were some men who were just as interested in maintaining the gender roles as the women. Bryan, the aspiring musician, was of the opinion that it 'Depends how they do it. Sometimes I can be put off because it almost feels emasculating'. Corey, the smokin' hot fire-fighter and actor admitted, 'It feels weird. Guys like to be the aggressor and don't want to be perceived in the feminine role'.

PARIS

In Paris, the men make the moves and the women decide if the men's advances are successful or not. Veronique, the PhD student in French literature, explained, 'Women don't flirt. The guys try to flirt with the girls. She decides if she is interested. She could say, "Go away". Women like to make men wait to test their intentions.' The men like the women to wait too. Most men showed a strong preference for initiating – they liked to be the hunter. Frederique, the 28-year-old sales manager, revealed, 'I don't like her to rush into things and make it too obvious she is into me. I like to make the first move. If a women makes the first move then she takes herself off the pedestal where I have put her.' These are ideals held up by men. The women either become expert seductresses or risk life in a convent. The savvy women will play the game. Geraldine the jewellery maker said 'Sometimes the best way to catch a guy is to ignore him. If I like him, I make him wait for my attention.' Others struggle with the 'playing hard to get' game. 30 year-old Sandrine, the director's assistant, said, 'I had drinks with a guy who was dying to see me before he left for a trip. We kissed, and, after that, he didn't have time to see me anymore.' Maybe they should take some tips from the New York women who kiss a different guy to 'take the edge off' while they are waiting out the 'three-to-five-date rule until you can have sex' with the guy they like. With all these self-imposed flirting regulations it's fair to say that the Parisians, especially the men, like a challenge.

Like their New York counterparts, the Parisian men – some 62% of them – like to select the women with whom they chose to flirt. In stark contrast, only 33% of the Parisian women interviewed, elected to make that choice. Martine, the logistics coordinator with flowing brown hair, explained her preference for being chosen by saying, 'I wouldn't want to lead the person into something. It stems from their choice. It's very French, an old fashioned value.' Let's roll that clip again. Martine has just said that men should have the choice, without any interference from women. It doesn't get any more passive than that. She then defends her position by saying it is very French – a.k.a. not something an outsider would understand – and that it was an age-old tradition. Martine, like many other French women, was philosophical, 'It's always been this way,' she said.

Unlike New York men who, on the whole, seemed happy for women to be assertive, not many Parisian men appreciated such forthrightness. Initially, they all thought it would be fine for a woman to make the first move, 'If she were pretty', although she would most likely be put into the 'girl for the night' category if she were so forward. But, after they thought about it some more, most echoed this man's sentiment. Shy Laurent, the architect, said 'I wouldn't think she would really want to talk to me, it could be a trap.' In a culture beset with rules and game playing, wariness is par for the course. Said Jean-Luc, 'Sometimes she might do it just to see if she has seduction.' Many men thought that if a queen of hearts approached him, he would end up looking like the joker.

The Parisians interviewed in this study bore out Perper's findings that men tend to think that they take the initiative, far more than they do. When asked who was most likely to initiate the flirting, the Parisian women's answers were very similar to their New York sisters. Half of them thought both genders initiated flirting, a third of them thought it was men only, and 20% thought it was a female-only domain. Sophie, the primary school teacher, said, 'Men start with the compliments, not the women.' Veronique, the PhD student said, 'I do nothing. He does everything, but he will recognise the invitation.' Thus the women make their approachability clear and the men respond accordingly. Take Guilliame, the bookseller, for example. 'Women give me a look, an opening to approach them. If you send me one sign, I will take it. She gives you the opportunity to show you know how to appreciate a woman.' Thus, French men think that they initiate flirting encounters far more than the women give them credit for. Are French women such smooth operators that the men don't know they've been reeled in like a game fish?

However, there was little argument about who approaches first. Almost all the Parisians interviewed, both men and women, felt that it was the men. All women, except one, thought that approaching was exclusively a male domain. Only a handful (11%) of men thought 'times are changing' with both men and women being free to make the initial approach.

While Parisian women like to think that they are as likely to initiate a flirting encounter as the men, Parisian men are convinced that both the come-on and the 'come on over' are their prerogative. When asked 'Do you approach women?' 75% of the Parisian men interviewed said they did. This was even more than the confident New York males. (64%). The reasons they gave were:

- 'I like her'.
- 'I'm attracted to her'.

- 'Just for fun'.

Of all the men interviewed, Parisian men were the largest group to lay claim to approaching women. To them, a woman who is audacious enough to make a play would only rate a one-night stand. Thus, girls play hard to get and guys are over the top to try and compensate,' explained Charlotte, the 32-year-old editor. Greg, the communications student, admitted, 'Every man shows desire for every woman, so it's hard to get the first kiss'. Monique, the 28-year-old sales rep, compared French men to their British brothers. 'In France, guys stare too much. 'You have to ignore someone. Guys flirt so over the top and cheesy! If you don't ignore them, you can't get rid of them!' 'In the UK, guys are more respectful. They don't stare as much. If you ignore them, they won't come over'.

The good news is that some Parisian men understand how the women must feel. Eccentric Olivier really got to the bottom of things: 'They have to see if guys are interested in anything other than their asses.'

The few Parisian men who said they didn't approach women were, 'too shy', 'afraid of rejection' and 'didn't want to be seen as 'that guy'. Shy Laurent, a 30-year-old architect, spoke for his fellows, 'If you're just a regular guy, women ignore you because they think you are like those guys'. There is a difference between 'drague' and flirting,' explained handsome Mathieu, an artistic director. Trying not to be mistaken as 'that guy' made some Parisian men very cautious. Bespectacled and chain-smoking Jean-Luc said, 'I only talk to people I know or have been introduced to'. Greg, the communication student, said, 'I can't get in contact with people I don't know. I am shy. Usually we meet if we both know the same person.'

The two main reasons that women gave for not approaching men was because they were 'too shy', and, in a city full of assertive men, they said, 'There was no need to'. Juliette, the social worker, said, 'I have been told I look cold, but it's just that I want to protect myself because it's so easy to have sex.' For Geraldine, the jewellery maker, 'It's not that we don't want to talk to them, we're just not brave enough to do it.' And then, almost as if she was apologising for daring to think outside the gender box, she said, 'Besides, some women like the tradition of guys coming to them.'

But the Parisian women is not a wholly passive participant in proceedings. It is the Parisian woman's responsibility to control the pace of the flirtation. She must, in her subtle way, be the enforcer of the limits. However, it is not always easy. Monique, the sales rep, said, 'I force myself to slow down.' Sophie, the primary school teacher, agreed, 'If he texts or e-mails, you have to make him wait, but it's hard!' Quite a few of the women confessed to finding this difficult.

'It is not so easy to do,' said Charlotte, the editor. 'I don't impose limits, I always take the flirt too far.'

Perhaps it's advisable to follow the lead of Lorraine the author, and let what will be, be. She said, 'It's hard to control the rhythm of a good flirt. It's beyond the sum of the parties.'

LONDON

London men believe that the flirting power lies in the hands of the women. David, the recruitment consultant, maintained that 'Women are very much in control in terms of dating situations'. 'Men are the supplicants,' confirmed Duncan the journalist, who had a reliable source. Both men and women agreed that initial contact was the women's domain. 43% of the women interviewed thought that 'both' men and women do the initiating. 35% , that 'women' are most likely to initiate, which means the women were involved in initiating 78% of the time. This was completely on par with the men's observations. A common sentiment was: 'There is more chance of success if it's the woman who makes the first move.'

So, she signals that she wouldn't mind being approached. However, once she has indicated her interest, she certainly isn't expected to follow through. This is when it is the men's turn to step up. Two-thirds of both men and women interviewed believed that making the approach was almost entirely the domain of the men. Tradition was usually the explanation, as Max, the music publisher, made clear.

'When men do approach it's most often because that is what is traditionally known', he said. Alex works in import/export. 'Men know they've got to (approach) and think women expect it'. He's right, according to Anoushka the sexy solicitor. 'This whole 'boys' idea stemmed from my parents. Most of my friends are the same. Wanting to be proposed to, and have a boy ask your father for your hand in marriage. Everything else in our lives is so modern, this side we want to keep. It's being modest. If you want to be treated like a lady, you have to behave like one.' True to their English rose roots, a whopping 69% of the London women interviewed wanted to be chosen. Genial Gemma, the producer of a morning breakfast show, said, 'The ideal is to be chosen by the guy you like. You secretly choose and they reciprocate.'

The responses from the London men were more varied. 33% wanted to choose, 33% wanted to be chosen, and 33% created their own category of 'mutual choosing'. This 'mutual choosing' category was the first such response among all the people interviewed in the different cities, reinforcing the impression that London men like both people to be involved in the interaction – flirting is not a power struggle for these sensitive New Age guys. However, lack of confidence also seemed to play a large part in their preference for being the prey rather than the predator . Daniel, who manages a bar, admitted, 'It's due to a lack of self-confidence, thinking 'why would they be attracted to me? I've decided since my mid 20's to just assume that she is interested in me.' James the optician said, 'I don't know. I just don't think the woman would actually see me in that light. Sometimes when a woman says hello to me on the street, I think it's because they feel sorry for me because they think I am old.'

Anthony, the guy who makes geek chic, said, 'I wouldn't want to be so confident that I could choose. It's nice to have someone interested in you. It's nice to feel wanted.' One man asserted, with a stiff upper lip, 'With choosing comes responsibility. Some people could do it without using their moral responsibilities.' Shhh, don't tell the Queen!

In London, who makes the first move in the dating game is governed by unwritten rules of etiquette, many of which are about respecting the personal space and privacy of others. It's understandable then that approaching someone – in essence doing all the things which English society disapproves of – is not a practice that is carelessly embraced. It appears

London males are especially sensitive to these implicit rules. Were they simply law-abiding lads? Or, were they using the rules as an excuse to not have to talk to women…?

Just over half (52%) of the men interviewed believed that women always initiated the flirting. 20% believed that both men and women were likely to initiate flirting.
In other words, women were involved in initiating the flirtation 72% of the time.
These men believed that 'Women have the control. Women are more subtle. They 'engineer' the man approaching'. Simon in PR said, 'Women will be the passive part of the process, even before the process is underway'. Alex, who works in import/export, said, 'Women give the signals and men are more proactive,' – the men react to these signals and approach. This is the New York woman's ideal!

Of the London males interviewed, 72% said they approached women, which is just as well, as it was expected of them. However, while English men may be expected to approach women, they don't embrace the job with much enthusiasm.

James the optician does make the move, '…but I always hate doing it. I think, "Oh god, what just happened there?" I don't feel like it's the real me approaching. I am more into the slow burn.' Some men stressed it had to be natural:

Duncan the journalist said, 'I guess I do approach, but I would never engineer it. It has to be natural.' Anthony, the IT guy, took umbrage at the word, 'Not approach, but naturally chat. I am getting better.' James pointed out there was no safety net if you approached, 'There is a lack of plausible deniability when approaching. You can't pretend it could or couldn't happen because you've just walked over to them.' Sam, the website designer, said, 'I don't do it as much as I think I should. I usually get to know women because there is a reason. Because of the city and so many people, men don't always know how things are going to go. Sometimes it's a surprise when you approach. One girl just looked at me and said, 'No'.'

The average London male is aware that his approach may not be well received. After all, the London female has been influenced by the same rules that he has! No talking to strangers, don't intrude, respect peoples' privacy. As one man pointed out, 'With British women there are rules of engagement.'

The men of London often do nothing for fear of offending. Samuel, a charming, 38-year-old cabinetmaker said that he would never speak to a woman who is on her own in a bar. 'I assume she either wants to be on her own, or she is waiting for someone. Either way, I'm not going to intrude.' Daniel, who manages a bar, said, 'You show a certain amount of respect by not going up to her even if you want to. She might be busy.' Perhaps behind the 'respectful' man hides a reluctant, apprehensive, even fearful one. James, the optician, said, 'I wouldn't want to intrude or interrupt.' This was a sentiment many of the men expressed. Now, if, he is thinking, 'I will respect her by not intruding on her space' and she is thinking, 'If he likes me, he'll come over and talk to me and if he doesn't, he won't', what you get is a stalemate.

Therefore, the majority of men said they would love to be approached by a woman. Charlie, the floppy-haired entrepreneur said, 'I'd love it. I like confident women.' Alistair, the broadcast journalist, shared similar tastes. 'I like a woman to be assertive. She might have come up to me, but that doesn't mean she is caught.' Adrian, the real estate agent echoed, 'I like them making the first move. The initial icebreaker is the hardest part. If a guy knows a woman is interested, he will be happy.' This is a far cry from Paris where women who take centre stage are harshly judged.

However, while they may say they like this assertiveness in theory, for some London lads there is a fine line between women taking the initiative and making them spill their lager in surprise. 'If they were really pushy it would be too much,' said Max the music publisher. 'I like to know a woman is interested but not coming on too strong. I like to chase, but you need to know she's in it,' said Christopher, the 32-year-old ex-military man. No one seemed sure of the line between coyness, confidence and cockiness. Alex in import/export said 'Some guys would be happy with cleavage and a phone number, but they don't want the girl to come too easy, but do want to know they have a chance. They want the carrot. Coyness is good, but not ice queen.' Simon, who is in PR, said that if a woman were to approach him, 'I'd find it unusual. I wouldn't want to feel hunted.' However, most guys agreed that if they were attracted to the woman, than such forthrightness would be just fine, thank you very much.

Soft-spoken Anthony, who works in IT said, 'It would depend on the person and it I found them attractive. A few girls asked me out and they were more into me than I was into them. If you get on well with the person who comes up to you, then it's great.'

Some guys really weren't sure if they'd like it if women approached them, but it was often because they felt they would be caught off guard, not because they would feel suspicious of her, like the Parisian men. Anthony admitted, 'I'd feel startled but there is a certain degree of flattery.' It seems the feelings of being startled, can also be interchanged with being scared, and even affronted!

Simon said, 'I'd be slightly scared. I might feel slightly affronted and might feel she is a player.' Adrian, the real estate agent said, 'I would like it, but I wouldn't like it over the top. I might feel like a rabbit in the headlights.'

While they say they are all for confident women, ladies, don't be put off by their initial startled expression. Give them a few seconds to register that they've just been approached by a fair damsel, and then, let the games begin.

As we have seen, London men are not natural hunters, and some might need either a prod or a pint to get the ball rolling. The women act within their limiting gender roles and are mostly passive in flirting encounters. Thus, problems arise.

Layla is 30 years old and own a boutique. She is the perfect modern 'Londoner' – half-Turkish, half-Bulgarian, and has lived in London for over a decade.

Layla relayed the following story in exasperation. She was alone at a restaurant in Picadilly Circus. It was late afternoon and she was having a cup of coffee. The handsome Englishman across from her kept peering over his copy of the Daily Telegraph to catch a sneaky glimpse at her. He'd then quickly look down and pretend to read. She really wanted to chat to him, and so was returning the meaningful looks. Yet, the interaction never went any further. 'Why didn't he come over and talk to me?' she asked, frustrated. Well, if the guy doesn't get the hint, take action. You must first change your proximity, and get closer to him. Slowly walk by him with a smile. Create the opportunity for a conversation to arise. She looked aghast. 'What would he think of me? What would everyone in the restaurant think of me?' And so Layla and the handsome Englishman went home alone and probably didn't live happily ever after.

Many of the women used the word 'approaching' as a euphemism for engineering the flirting encounter. Thus, 61% of London females say they approach men, although, as we've seen, the physical act of walking over, seems to be left up to the men. So how do the London ladies fare in taking the bull by the horns? There were three different approaches, evenly split between the three groups. .

Some women are traditionalists:

- 29-year-old Rachel, the illustrator: 'I still have the old fashioned element. I like the men to approach.'
- Mousy Mary, the astute 28-year-old PA: 'I've never gone out and tried. I will wait for the men to make the first move.'
- 28 year-old Georgina, the Manchurian secretary: 'I don't approach men. I wouldn't want to come across too pushy. I am old fashioned. I would want to be approached.'

Then there's your modern madams:

- Liz the account manager for a big advertising agency: 'I've approached guys and they've loved it!'
- Jennifer, the down-to-earth finance analyst: 'Men like confidence. I'm quite forward but in a funny over-the-top way.' Obvious flirting is OK as long as it is done with humour.
- Catherine in IT: 'It depends on time. I can't always wait for him. I know some men are intimidated by me so I will go up to them.'

And then there are the sirens. These women are the queens of 'come hither'.

- Emma the smiley presenter: 'He would have to come to me but I would make it as easy as possible.'
- Alice, the glossy haired investment banker: 'I would approach him, but I wouldn't get out of my chair.'

STOCKHOLM

The usually like-minded men and women of Stockholm were divided in their responses to this question. Like the Parisians, the majority of Stockholm men thought that they initiated the come-on and made the first move. Most of the women, however, thought men and women were equally likely to both communicate interest and act on it. In theory, the women would like to think that they are unconventional enough to approach men, but when it comes to a practical application of the theory, they still don't do it. Often, because they simply don't feel like it.

The majority of men said that it was they initiated a flirtatious encounter. Yet, just over half of the men interviewed that said they wanted to choose whom to chat up. Compare this to 87% of the women interviewed, who said they liked to choose. Stockholm women, clearly like to take the initiative. Henrik the banker didn't seem to mind. He said, "I like to be chosen, then have the choice whether to accept or not'. Perhaps he was a Parisian woman in a previous life? One popular guy never even got to chance to exercise his choice. Frederik the law student said, 'I would like to choose, but most of the time it's me being chosen'. However, not all Stockholm women are beating down the men's doors. Mia the gallery owner knew the power was in the choice and said, 'I would like to say 'chose' but I think 'to be chosen'. It's easier to say 'no'. It's safer.' This is a culture of caution, after all, except during the weekend hours of 11pm to 2am and the seasons of Spring and Summer.

Two-thirds of the Stockholm males interviewed (63%) thought that it was the men who initiated the flirting. 28-year-old Mattias said, 'Men do most of the initiating, but I only start it if I am really physically attracted to her.' And, when it came to approaching, the men thought they did even more of the hard work. A sizeable 81% of men thought it was they who most often took that long walk across the room. In Stockholm there is no stigma attached to assertive women, and in a society that prides itself on its gender equality, you would think that the women would make the move more frequently than they do. As it turns out, unlike Paris, it's not that they are not encouraged to, but it's because they don't have to. Per the virile Viking said, 'Men do the work and the women choose. They are always in control.' As another example of how Stockholm culture differs from other cities, enterprising Eric, the cool café owner explained, 'Guys are most likely to start looking at a girl and girls are most likely to follow it up if they are interested.' However, Kristina, the global HR manager, thought it was the other way round, 'Men are most likely to approach,, but not until they have gotten the signal from us, but it's hard to make them go away in a nice way'.

Two-thirds of Stockholm males said they approached women, but with reservations. Henrik the banker said, 'Yes, but I am quite careful. I would gauge if she were looking at me. I need to know she is not going to reject me immediately'. Frederik, the 28-year-old law student, said, 'Yes, I make contact with them. I am not sure how, but I don't directly approach them. I try to bump into them in a natural way'. There's a hot tip on how to get ahead with Swedish girls. Don't look them directly in the eye or make any sudden movements. Bjorn is a 31-year-old doctoral student, said, 'Yes, I do, but sometimes I don't like going up to girls. I feel stupid'. 33 year-old Stefan, the bicycle shop owner also said, 'I do, but rarely with the consciousness of flirting, but more about having the urge to say something like "I like your shirt".' Methinks he doth protest too much.

Almost three-quarters of the women (73%) thought that both sexes were as likely as the other to begin the flirting. Mia, who works in a gallery, helped to explain why men think they initiate more than the women, more than the women think they do. She said, 'We are good at making them feel as if they have started it.'

The women were split 50/50 in their thinking as to who was most likely to approach, the men or the women. Those women who said that men were more likely to approach, said they did so because the men were more 'desperate' for a relationship or because the woman had made her will known. This contrasts with Paris and New York where the men make the moves because the women expect them to fulfil a masculine role. Katarina, the gorgeous florist, said, 'Men are more likely to approach because they are looking for relationships. They need a woman to fulfil their lives, but women don't, they have already achieved it (fulfilment).' In another example of Stockholm's proficiency at role reversal, it's not necessarily the women who looking for relationships.

Two-thirds of the women interviewed said that they had no compunction approaching men who appealed to them. Jenny, a PhD student in biology, approaches men because 'I want their attention or want something from them.' They felt that it was empowering. Johanna the opera singer, said, 'If they are interesting and inviting, why not?' For Eva, the press officer, 'It's the only way to get things going.' Kristina, the confident, global HR manager, is a role model for her gender. 'Initially, I send out gentle approachability signals. But after the approach I back off a bit because I don't want to appear pushy. I was exchanging glances with a guy at a restaurant. Before I left I tore out a piece of newspaper with the band that we were going to and said, "If you don't have anything going on now, you should join us".' Of the women who didn't make the move, they were either too shy or weren't looking for sex, a relationship, a cigarette or free drinks. Eva, the press officer said, 'I don't get attracted to guys I don't know.' Emile, the cautious accountant, unsurprisingly said, 'I prefer to let them approach me. I'm too shy. I think they don't want to talk to me.' Clare, the air-traffic controller, said simply, 'I am not looking for anything.'

CONCLUSION
When it comes to initiating the flirting encounter and making the approach, Paris and New York seem to abide by traditional gender roles. A big difference between Parisian and New York culture is that a woman in New York could also be the one to initiate a flirtatious encounter. This wasn't strictly the man's prerogative, as it was in Paris. In Paris, both the men and women accept that the men do most of the initiating and all the approaching. However, in New York, it is mostly the women who prefer to bait the hook, and expect the men to reel themselves in. The Londoners, both male and female, accept that the women will make her choice evident by giving out approachability signals, and the men will be expected to respond to those signals. Whether they have the courage to do the necessary is another story. Most of the cities' male and female inhabitants had pretty similar answers to each other. However, in Stockholm the men and women differed completely in one of the few instances they weren't completely in sync. The men say they do much more work in the flirting game than the women, but the women are convinced it's equal. Are the women giving themselves credit that they don't really deserve?

In cultures where the status quo is for the men to approach the women, the most popular school of thought that goes like this: If he really likes me, then he will come over and talk to me. Therefore, if he doesn't come up to me, he must not like me. However, this doesn't take into consideration that he might be shy, doesn't want to disturb you or doesn't think that you are interested in him.

The guy a woman really wants to meet probably isn't the one approaching her. After all, if he's approached you, how many others has he also approached? Feeling special yet? The one you want to be approaching is that guy over there – the one in the corner who, while having fun with his friends, is aware of you but is too shy to break the ice. If you're doing the choosing, you'll have a much greater chance of finding a compatible match with more banter and less banality. Get off your stool, girl. You'll thank me later.

FLIRT FILE

How to break the ice:
- Think of things in your vicinity as your 'props' which enable you to start the conversation
- Use situational questions which fit in with the context of your immediate surroundings such as:
- At the supermarket: 'Have you tried this brand before?'
- At a bus stop: 'Has the 31 bus been by recently?'
- At the gym: 'Do you know how to use this machine?'
- At the bookshop: Have you read anything by this author?'
- At the gallery: What do you think of this painting?
- This method can be employed anywhere; allows you to be proactive by being able to choose who you approach and the risk of losing face is eradicated.
- While you have specifically chosen to approach the person because you are attracted to or interested in them, they don't know that. As far as they're concerned you are merely seeking an answer to your question.
- However, a word of caution. As an opening gambit, asking for a cigarette is only effective if you are in a country where the habit is cheap. Do not use this technique in London.
- The chances of making a good match are much higher if you do the choosing
- For women, the power is in being able to choose amongst the entire pool of men, not just amongst the small percentage of men who approach you.

Chapter 22: One-Night Stands
THE MORNING AFTER

Having sex with someone whom you've had minimal time to get acquainted with and, where both parties have probably imbibed alcohol, is usually called a 'one-night stand'. Having a one-night stand is a personal decision, but it's helpful to know how it works in different cultures. You might think a one-night stand with a Swede a novel way of warding off the cold. He or she, on the other hand, could interpret it as the first night of many, in a meaningful relationship. You might be planning your wedding while having sex with the hot New Yorker. But beware! In New York, one-night stands last only a night. In Paris, if you get to first base you'll probably score a home run, but, whatever you do, don't tell anyone. In London, it would be impolite not to see whether casual sex leads to anything more permanent and in Stockholm, if you have an itch, scratch it!

New Yorkers want a modern, commitment-free, fun-filled, and liberating sex life, but deep down they also want tradition and a wedding ring. Casual sex is disapproved of in Paris. The woman who has a reputation for being easy won't be seen as a suitable candidate for a long-term relationship. Compare the attitudes of Parisians and Stockholmers towards one-night stands and it becomes apparent that in a culture where gender equality is greater, so are both a woman's and a man's choices when it comes to the question of whether or not to engage in casual sex. In societies where there is less of a taboo attached to one-night stands, women are more likely to have them.

The issue of one-night stands is a much bigger one than the act of sex. In traditional gender models, recreational sex is typically reserved for men because they view it as their genetic birthright. Thus, a woman's ability to choose to have sex without the confines of reproduction, and in a pair-bond only scenario is a factor related to both freedom and power. So, can a night of 'ooo-ing' and 'ahh-ing' ever end in 'I do'-ing? Can the morning after ever end in 'happily ever after', or do you both call it a day?

NEW YORK
Trying to find consensus on the attitude to one-night stands in New York is like trying to find a 'typical' New Yorker. Justin, the 38-year-old literary agent, said 'Everything has changed since Sex and the City,… Britney Spears, Paris Hilton. But again, it depends. You can find people who will judge. You can find people who won't. There is no way to generalise something like this because it depends on who you are talking about. Are you talking about a church-going grandmother from the Upper East Side? Or are you talking about gay guys from Chelsea?'

Yet, if you believe everything you've heard about New York City, you'd think having a one-night stand was as common as technical problems on the L-train. Mike, a tall, handsome banker, with the confidence to match, explained the attraction of having a one-night stand in New York. 'Here today, gone tomorrow is the mentality. Because you will never see the person again, it's much easier to be bold than in smaller cities. In New York it's easier to find quantity than quality. Everyone flirts to hook up. There are 8 million people, you can flirt, hook up, bang em', and never see them again. Guys are like dogs, they will look at any girl who gives them attention back. The girl gives the 'okay' back. Guys are always on for flirting; always looking for the next "bang".' Corey, a wannabe actor with leading guy looks moonlights as a fire-fighter – or is that the other way round? He was pragmatic. 'It is common in every culture. Always has been and always will be'.

Some New Yorkers, it is true, are fully on board with the 'sex on tap' mentality. David, the 28-year-old architect, said 'We're young, we're single, we're financially stable, let's have fun!' Stacey is also 28, a make-up artist of Puerto Rican descent. She may not share David's outlook but she recognises the mindset. 'Having sex with loads of guys in my Manolo Blahniks is not my lifestyle. But a lot of women aspire to this lifestyle'. But, despite all the sexual innuendoes and references, the openness, and the fact that New York is a 'sexual town,' one-night stands seem to be something of an urban legend in New York. People said that everyone was 'hooking up', although when asked what percentage of their friends were doing it, they would say 30%. It seems like the idea is being sold that having sex whenever you want, with whomever you want, is liberating, even modern. However, only a small percentage of women are buying it. Alexis, the sharp-witted research assistant said, 'You sure hear about it and read about it but I don't know who these people are'. Andrea, who works for a charity, echoed this sentiment, 'The line we're told is "It's not a big deal", but I don't believe it. You've skipped too many phases too soon'.

While the women of New York take on the men at their own game, they are traditional at heart. Marie, who is currently unemployed, is '…not interested in one-time things. I would rather have something regular. I think everyone will do it at some point in their lives, but if she (a friend) does it a lot you think, why are you so afraid of commitment?' Even with its liberated shop front window, the New Yorkers are still being sold 'happily ever after'. In New York, while men and women are on an equal footing in many superficial respects, there was a constant and pervasive harkening back to more traditional ideals—especially when it came to the one-night stand.

The jury was divided on whether there was a stigma attached to women who indulge in one-night stands. Lisa, a high-powered New York woman, works for a large credit card company. In her view '…it depends on your friends, your job, and your religion in New York City. I have really conservative friends that wouldn't approve, especially of the woman being casual, but most of my friends are pretty laid back about the whole thing.' Alexis, the research assistant agreed, 'There is '…not as much of a stigma as there used to be. In New York men and women know they are independent.' 'Women aren't judged,' concurred Alesha, a striking broadcast journalist. It's a pretty open culture. In fact, women pride themselves on it. It's a quest to see how many guys you can hook up with in the bathroom. They would go in with the mindset of one-night stand but might want more, truthfully.'

Red-head Rebecca in recruitment thought differently. 'Women are judged more harshly.' 'But my first question is, "Was it good?" and then "Were you safe?".' When women feel free to talk about sex and make known some truth about their desire and bodily pleasures, they challenge deeply-held taboos. In Paris, women can't admit to their friends they had a one night stand, let alone ask about the level of sexual pleasure. Joel, the 33-year-old entrepreneur, admitted, 'Women are always judged and men aren't.' Said Bryan, the lanky aspiring musician, 'If I was doing it, I wouldn't judge her. But you have lower standards for one-night stand. A girl I'd have sex with, wouldn't necessarily be a girl I'd go out with.' He continued beating the same drum, 'Women are looked down upon but not men. Generally, if the man does one nighters, he's a player, if the woman does, she's a slut, and nobody wants to marry a slut.' Then, there's the morning after. 'We call it 'the walk of shame', said David the architect. 'Girls are all dressed up like they are going clubbing and it's 6 am.' Gina, the 33-year-old occupational therapist of Chinese descent, was well aware of the double standards. 'For guys it's like 'I just got laid!' For girls, they lose respect.'

Thus, many women seem to buy into the idea that you have to wait at least three to five dates before sleeping with the guy you really like. This is a view that the men share. Corey, the actor/fire-fighter, said, 'I think it's a bad idea for a woman to have sex with a guy she likes in the first three to five dates.' This pretence seems to be mostly so he won't categorise her, rather than her necessarily wanting to wait. Alexis, the research assistant, knows the rules. 'I refuse to be a notch on a guy's belt. I expect him to call me and take me out at least five, six times. If I sleep with him he is going to think I am a slut.'

She isn't necessarily waiting to have sex because she wants to, but rather so he won't think ill of her. This attitude echoes the confusion expressed by many other female interviewees, who openly admitted that feminism and liberation had 'messed them up.' On the one hand she's supposed to get an education, a great job, earn her keep, and be equal to the man. On the other, it's still not OK for her to sleep with whomever she chooses, when she so chooses. So, what's a girl to do? Become successful and then struggle to find a man who is, at least, her equal in terms of education or income? Or struggle to find a man who won't shy away from, or feel emasculated by her independence? 'Liberated Slut!' or 'Dependent Prude?' Tough call, that one.

Women are confused as to whether having sex is liberating or slutty. Not only did some women adhere to the double standards themselves, but they looked down on those women who chose to follow their own libidos. The conservative attitude towards one-night stands, and the traditional ideals of how sexuality is played out, is more pronounced amongst the native New Yorkers and the second and third generation Asians and Latinos, than the more recent internal migrants. Stacey, the make-up artist of Puerto Rican descent, was frank, 'My friends are getting sluttier by the day'.

Like the men, the women have different standards for short-term relationships and long-term ones. The general sense amongst interviewees was that when it came to one-night stands, men were quite happy to lower their standards. Yes, they'd go for the '6, or 12-beer girl, the one who isn't so attractive, but are willing to take home after a multitude of beer ' or the easy 'second hottest of the group, who is insecure due to her hotter friend.' The New York woman isn't quite so willing - unless of course he's a hot bartender and she needs to get laid.

Despite the pressure to postpone a sexual encounter with someone you really like, the women of New York are not, necessarily, going without sex. They simply have sex with guys who they know they won't want to see again. The men share this perception. Russell, the 28-year-old graphic designer, said, 'A lot of women will have sex with you if they don't think it will go further. You don't want to be seen as promiscuous with someone you like.' This way, the women of New York get to have sex, yet aren't considered a 'slut' by the guy they are 'saving' themselves for. As a bonus, they get to relieve some pent up horniness they have no doubt acquired while waiting for Mr. Perfect's allotted number of date rules.

It's the perfect win-win scenario.

Like the men, New York females know what they want, and go after it. And, sometimes, what they want is sex! Susan, the journalist, didn't mince her words or reveal her sources, 'Sometimes, a girl's just gotta get laid!' While not so fervent a fan of the one-night stand, Rebecca, in recruitment, admitted, ' I might not respect myself. I might think 'I could do better than that', unless, that is, I just needed to get laid.' So, one-night stands are not OK, unless you 'just need them.' New York women are 'traditional' up to a point. If the male doesn't eventually get the point, then she will make sure he does. Or have sex with the hot guy at the salsa club just because she feels like it. So, not so traditional then…

The men of New York face their own conundrums when it comes to the one-night-stand. They too want to get laid. That's the nature of the beast. However, the guys know they have to be careful in not treating their 'prey' like a one-night stand while still trying to ensure one. 'A guy knows that his challenge is to get some "sexual action" out of a woman, without making her feel tarty for doing it', explained Chris, the environmental engineer. High-school science teacher Jason shared this insight. Women '…want to earn your first kiss. They want to attract the opposite sex, but they don't want to feel like a slut.'

At least, in New York, everybody understands the unwritten rules. If you go home with someone on the first night, the chances of it turning into a relationship are next to nil. Most guys interviewed didn't take one-night stands for more than just a night of sex. They also realised that if a woman goes home with them, she's probably equally not interested in something more. She knows the rules, too. 'One-night stands usually don't turn into relationships because we just let it be what it is, ' said Dana, the pretty brunette analyst.

It was a common perception among both the men and women interviewed that one-night stands couldn't possibly lead to a genuine relationship. When asked if many relationships are formed off the back of a one-night stand, Doug the dentist answered, 'Probably not any functional ones'. The implication being that two people couldn't possibly have a healthy relationship if it started with sex. This is a quite different mentality from Stockholm and London where, oftentimes, this is how relationships start.

The reasons are multiple: Firstly, the fact that many of these casual encounters are borne out of beer goggles; secondly, because the hunt is too easily won. Joel, the entrepreneur said, 'People want to be challenged. If it's too easy people don't like it.' Men often said they would think she was probably having casual sexual encounters with other people too, and they wanted to feel special. Chris, the environmental engineer, said, 'A girl you hook up with the first night doesn't last because it was too easy. If I just met her and we already had sex, chances are she is with everyone else as well.'

The men want to show off their money and their arm candy and prove themselves the leader of the pack by taking the most beautiful woman home. If she doesn't sleep with him, he has wasted a lot of time and money, and if she does…it's a no-win situation because then she's a slut. That is, he's not that special any more. As Russell, the graphic designer explained, 'If a girl had a one-night stand, it would be regarded as a non-relationship. The guy would over think it. They wouldn't think they were special and chosen, but rather some random dude.'

However, this is not the mentality of all guys:
Jason, the high-school science teacher, was less judgemental. 'I don't think it's wrong to hook up. If we had a one-night stand and connected I would definitely want to see her again.' Doug the dentist agreed, 'I wouldn't stop having a relationship with someone if we had a one-night stand. If you have chemistry with someone, why wait for formalities? I wouldn't judge her or think she is a slut.'

On the subject of casual sex, New Yorkers' double standards stab you in the back with a stiletto heel. The New Yorkers know the rules: have sex, have fun, but just don't do it with someone whom you'd want to see again. Despite the seeming 'equality' between the sexes in New York, the virgin and whore stereotypes that prevail in Paris, are alive and well in the Big Apple too.

PARIS
It seems the only thing holding Parisian men back from having more one-night stands are the Parisian women. Yet, the main reason Parisian women aren't having more one-night stands is the attitude of Parisian men towards women who have one-night stands. Confused yet?

One-night stands are often for one purpose and one purpose alone, that of having sex. Antoine the banker admitted that he would have a one-night stand if he needed to sleep with a woman. To satisfy one's primal urges, bespectacled and smouldering Jean-Luc observed, 'There are always women of low morality around'. Antoine went on to compare Paris with London, saying, 'In the UK, women act much more like men. Girls on the street talk about one-night stands. They are much more open in London. If they want sex then they have it. Women in Paris might want it, but they would be much more worried about what other people think.' Shy Laurent, the 30-year-old architect, made a similar observation, 'In Paris girls take more time before having sex. It can take several months for a girl to take her boyfriend to bed. The women are more conservative in this way.' Frederique, the 28-year-old sales manager, summed up the Parisian woman's typical response, 'I want to, but I can't.' Sophie, the primary school teacher has lived in both London and Paris. She explained the difference in the attitude towards casual sex by saying, 'A one-night stand in the UK may turn into a relationship because they have less inhibitions and judgement. In London, everything is available. In Paris, it's structured. Most women think if they have sex the first night they won't be well thought of.' She's probably right. Nicolas, the matter-of-fact project manager, wasn't the only man to admit, 'I wouldn't respect her if we had sex.'

Parisian women are cautious about having one-night stands because they know they will be harshly judged for doing so. The social consequences of a night of fun are just too severe. If she has sex, she is 'only a girl for the night' and if she dutifully waits, then she is a 'girl for life'. Guilliame spoke for the majority, 'Men don't want the one-night stand woman long-term. She was just physically attractive and nothing more. For a long-term relationship, he would want a natural girl.' There seem to be two contrasting views of femininity, and the two categories are equally unattainable. French philosopher and social theorist Micheal Foucault contends that far from being 'natural' sex is 'a regulatory construct produced by regimes of power'. Thus, we get the virgin/whore stereotype where women who find pleasure in sex are perverse while women with no desire are virtuous. Parisian women are trying to live up to an impossible ideal.

So, in Paris, a woman's sexual desires and choices must be strictly concealed. Many of the women interviewed said if they did have a one-night stand they would keep quiet about it. 'One-night stands don't happen often in French culture. Men don't like that. If you have the reputation for doing that, they won't consider you for long term. If you do it, you don't tell anyone,' said Juliette, the social worker. It's not only the men who judge women ruthlessly if they have a one-night stand. Women are equally prone to patrolling themselves – sometimes its other women who are the harshest critics! Martine the logistics coordinator, said, 'If a woman had a one-night stand she would be treated as a neurotic nymphomaniac. She wouldn't tell her friends. She would keep it as her dirty little secret.'
Where does this attitude come from? Catholicism was referenced many times when people tried to explain modern-day Parisian flirting.

Charlotte, the 32-year-old editor, said, 'The kind of guys we know, educated, strong families, Catholic, will always try for it, but might actually prefer to hear "No".' Again, it's the woman's job to keep the man in line. She must resist temptation and be strong for both of them. If she gives in to her desires then she is a nymphomaniac with skeletons in her closet and no hope of ever landing a husband.

Parisian women place importance on relationships. If not in one, they have no value or esteem, and the only other role available is that of mistress. 'For girls it's usually not for a one-night stand, it's to try for a relationship,' said Martine, the logistics coordinator. Veronique, the PhD student further clarified why one shouldn't have sex with someone one likes. 'Guys like mystery so you have to keep them going. After they've gotten what they want, they would call you back again, but just for sex.'

Thus, Parisian women appear to believe that it's in their best interests to act the 'virgin' role in order to secure a long-term relationship. But none questioned the fact that by wielding the virgin and whore stereotypes so effectively; men maintain a great deal of power in the relationship sphere. Instead of demanding that men become more open in their thinking, Parisian women seem to spend a lot of time and energy trying to become a 'significant other'. Unsurprisingly, men spend a lot of time trying to take advantage of this aspiration in order to attain their own desires. Yet casual sex just doesn't fit with the men's conception of the ideal wife and mother.

But this doesn't mean that Parisians don't ever have one-night stands. They do, but, they're a form of currency – or perhaps, more accurately, something which women will gamble on once they have run out of other tactics to make a man commit. One woman explained how this works. Sophisticated Stefanie, the business analyst, said, 'A woman would only have a one-night stand to please a man in the hopes he would like her better and it would lead to a relationship.'
Isabelle, the librarian, admitted, 'I will try to turn it into something more.'
There is a great deal of role-playing, mask-wearing, and subtext and strategic planning that goes into the carefully contrived pas de deux of the Parisian mating dance. Greg, the communication student observed, 'Parisian women are always thinking, 'If I do this, then he will do that.'

---

6   Foucalt, Michel. The History of Sexuality, Vol. 1: An Introduction. London : Vintage, 1990.

Sophisticated Stefanie the business analyst, lived in London so she knows what she is talking about. 'One-night stands are much more common in London. In Paris, they make you wait because it's a woman's way of showing she is more than a sexual object.' Her comment is telling because it implies that first of all, women are using sex because it is their main and, perhaps only, form of power. The fact is that she holds the power only while she 'makes him wait': giving in, then, means giving away her only bargaining chip. Her statement also implies that a woman's default mode is as sexual object, and only time will prove that she's more than that. By contrast, she implies, in London, women are viewed as fully human, more than just sexual objects: they don't have to make the guys wait.

Imagine the frustration involved in all this. If a man and a woman have sex – because both of them want to – the woman is unfavourably judged; if they don't, the man can easily go elsewhere for gratification. Do it, or don't do it, the woman still loses out. In the high stakes of Parisian sexual politics, women just can't seem to win. This isn't going to change, though, until women reject the stereotypes that make everyone so miserable. But first, they must admit that there needs to be a change. Even in the face of this extraordinary social manipulation, women insist that it is they who are calling the shots. In an attempt to assert that it's women who have the power, Juliette, the social worker, proclaimed, 'Parisian women demand a lot and are very proud,' 'Women deny men sex because men actually want to be made to wait,' she said.

Yet, while it's initially hard to make contact with a Parisian girl, if you get to first base, you will probably hit a home run. As 35-year-old Francine, who works in publishing, put it, 'It's harder to make contact with French girls, but once you kiss, you can have sex.' But to sum up the Parisians' attitudes to one-night stands, nobody said it better than 28-year-old sales rep, Monique. Women, '… have a different relation with the body. They don't want to give it up so easy. Every man shows desire for every woman, so it's hard to get the first kiss, but once you do, you will get the sex too. If the girl has a different guy each night she is like a highway. If she doesn't seem interested then it's better. Make him work hard for the kiss, then it's OK to have sex.'

LONDON
Perhaps it is the Londoners' reserved natures – it took courage to have a one-night stand in the first place, so might as well stick with the one you've got? Perhaps it is the Londoners' tendency to want to explore what might lie beyond the morning after? Perhaps it is that there is less stigma attached to women who have one-night stands? Whatever the reasons, Londoners are having sex with strangers. One-night stands are apparently common amongst both men and women in London, any stigma is likely to be attached to the man's account and having a relationship afterward seems like a logical step in the process.

Stefanie the Parisian business analyst compared Parisians to Londoners saying, '…if we kiss, it will go further. In the UK a kiss means nothing.' So does a kiss mean nothing in London? Picture the scene. A liberated London woman has made her interest obvious by kissing the face off one of London's eligible but inhibited bachelors. The pair somehow manage to make it back to either one of their places, without being arrested for indecent exposure in the back of the cab, with the bar on their inhibitions set so low it'd take a professional limbo dancer to get under it. And so the scene fades to black and we assume the two enjoy a night of bliss. What happens the next morning?

For a seemingly reserved culture, the Brits are refreshingly open-minded about their sexual antics. 'Half of my friends have slept with their partners on the first night,' revealed Christopher, a former soldier, lowering his voice and shutting the door, just in case the neighbours overheard. Sex with strangers might be fine, but airing one's dirty laundry in public is not. Similarly, 32-year-old Gemma, a producer, confessed, 'Of course, I racked up a lot of shagging.' 'People here are not ashamed about having one-night stands. There isn't the stigma or idea to be ashamed,' explained Catherine, who may be in IT, but is far from geeky. Annette, the sultry-voiced jazz singer with curves to rival J Lo, said, 'We can talk openly about having one-night stands. We are not embarrassed about it. We drink loads and alcohol is a big factor of casual sex.'

Alcohol plays a large part in the London flirting scene, especially when it comes to one-night stands. This should come as no surprise. We're not talking about the tee-tippling Parisians here. In this culture, where the men are shy and reserved and the women are hesitant to make a move lest they scare them off, is it any wonder that a drop of the old social lubricant is necessary to help ease the slow and creaking wheels of the flirting machine? How else would the Londoners ever get it together? Jane works in the financial industry. She said, 'One-night stands stem from being pissed. The second date, when you are sober, is to check to see if there is anything else.'

So why is it so common to have a one-night stand and see the other person again?

Some of the interviewees answered this question with typical British self-deprecation. Samuel, the charming, 38-year-old furniture maker said, 'Brits are insecure. They had it once and think, 'what if I never have it again? It was good once with this person, it can be good again.' 29-year-old Rachel the illustrator blamed it on British reserve. 'Maybe we are so grateful to find someone who wants to go to bed with us, given our reserved nature, we want to keep it. Maybe because it takes so long to actually be with someone like that and remove the barriers, that you are more open.' 'If you wake up in the morning and it still feels good, why not continue it into a relationship,' said Sam, the 30-year-old website designer. Simon in PR reasoned thus, 'In order to have gotten there that quickly there has to have been a fairly strong attraction. There is a reasonable chance it will persist.' Liz, the accounts manager for a big advertising agency, agreed, 'If we shagged, then it would be important, so let's make sure to see if it's not something more.' These two London lads summed it up: 'Better the devil you know than the devil you don't,' and 'If it's nice, do it twice.'

The English national character is one of reserve and thus flirting is not undertaken lightly. Anthony, who is in IT, compared the Brits to the outspoken Yanks. 'Sex is a greater part of everyday interaction in the US. In the UK, because we are reserved, we are less likely to entertain casual sex if there's nothing behind it. It could be a hangover from our Victorian values. We are more subtle. Americans are much more in your face, more tactical.'

The nearly unanimous response was that Londoners don't go out looking for sex; they go out looking for relationships. As James the optician said of the one-night stand, 'It happens with the aim of having a relationship, not just the aim of having sex.' 'In the UK a one-night stand could end in a relationship,' said Samuel, the furniture maker. If there is a genuine bond there, it's not going to be broken as easily as that', agreed Claire, the red-headed accountant.

While their Big Apple brothers go out looking specifically for sex, the London males stressed that this wasn't how it worked for them.

Charlie, the 30-year-old entrepreneur, said, 'People don't set out to have a one-night stand. You tend to go out and meet someone and get on well, one thing leads to another and you end up in bed. But people don't set out just to have sex.'

'Sex is simply a natural part of deciding if someone is right for you, but not necessarily the aim. We're not that obsessed with sex so it's not part of the social rules. If I sleep with a girl on the first night it's because I really like her. You're better off first testing out if the sex is good,' said Alistair, a 32-year-old, broadcast journalist with a voice for radio and a face for TV. Daniel manages a bar. Speaking for his London brothers, he said, 'We are serious with our flirting and one-night stands. You would only bother with someone in whom you are interested and not just do it for fun.' So it's less about lust and more about love? Yes, according to Max the music publisher. 'A lot of one-night stands have ended up in marriage and kids.'

This was the general theme for the men. They're looking for relationships, unlike New York men, and therefore they're only likely to have sex with someone they really like. And, ultimately, women who 'do' and those who 'don't' aren't put into separate categories. David, the recruitment consultant, drew this comparison with American dating culture, 'In the States there are two boxes, either to have a one-night stand or to get married. Everything is black and white.' Alex, who works in import/export, put it this way, 'Americans are more criteria-based than personality based'. The Londoners constantly reinforced the idea that their dating culture was much more relaxed and less absolute than their neighbours across the pond! So relaxed, in fact, that spending the night with someone could also double as a money-saving technique. Anna, the voice-over artist, elaborated, 'The dating culture is more regimented in the States. The English are known for being promiscuous and it's not looked down upon to pull. In London, the distances are quite far and cabs are expensive. It's just easier and cheaper to spend the night.' Budgeting with a bang!

Just to be clear, not all the women in London are making a hasty run for the last tube to Sexville-on-Thames. Mary, the 28-year-old PA with sensible shoes, said, 'If I wanted a relationship with a guy, I wouldn't give it all away. Equally, for a relationship, I wouldn't want to be with a guy who has one-night stands.' Claire, a red-headed accountant, agreed. 'In the UK, by the second date you are a boyfriend. I wouldn't go out with a guy who was dating two other people as well.'

Unlike Paris, in London, the men are the ones who are most likely to be judged for having one-night stands. They quickly earn themselves a reputation for playing the field and are stigmatised by the women. James the optician was aware of having to deal with the consequences of such intemperate actions. 'People in London go to the same places so you are more likely to see them again and will feel guilty every time you see them. People talk. You can get a reputation of just using people.' Simon in PR pointed out the drawbacks of living in a small place when he said 'The UK is small geographically. You will most likely see people again. You just stick it through because you don't want people to get a bad impression of you.' Anoushka, the matter-of-fact solicitor, with gorgeous curls, described just that kind of impression. 'Sometimes you can meet someone and see them again. If you get the idea this person has one-night stands, you wouldn't want him as boyfriend material. You want to think it's special.' Claire, the red-headed accountant, said, 'I'd feel insulted if we had a connection, a one-night stand and then he never wanted to see me again. If it was in the circle of friends, we would inevitably see each other again. It could get awkward.'

While the men are wary of getting a reputation for using people, if you're a London female it's just good manners to carry on after your one-night stand.

As 28-year-old Georgina, the secretary, explained, 'It's less rude to date them than blank them.' Yes, even when it comes to one-night stands the English are mindful of being polite! Georgina wasn't alone.

'I've never had a one-night stand and then not seen them again. It's about manners,' said Gemma, the 32-year-old producer.

So, if all you take away with from this chapter is this, remember, in London, sex with a stranger is OK, so long as you say please, thank you and don't dismiss them afterwards.

STOCKHOLM
What happens in a secular, egalitarian society in which women have equal economic power? S.E.X., lots of it, and no stigma attached to those who have it.

Bjorn, a 31-year-old doctoral student, explained, 'One-night stands are really common in Swedish culture. The culture is quite liberal and not particularly religious. It's probably due to the combination of equal rights for women and early sex education in schools. Since people have goals other than to raise a family, it changes the purpose of sex. It becomes a need. Modern society is drifting away from the evolutionary mechanism. Women choose careers over families or don't have kids until their late 30s, which is riskier for child bearing from an evolutionary perspective.' Kristina, the global HR manager, said much the same thing. 'In our society, we want everything to happen so fast and want to be productive all the time. Women have more freedom and men don't judge those women who do have one-night stands. Maybe we don't attach love and emotion to sex. Church and state are separated and don't have much influence.'

Affable Mattias, the MD of a soft drink company, compared the difference in attitudes towards women in the Sweden and the United States, 'In the States, there are so many rules girls have to follow and they can be easily judged. In Sweden, girls can be as they want, because it's accepted to have casual sex and no one judges you.' Unlike a Parisian woman, who might have sex as a last resort to entice the guy into a relationship, or, even a New York women who would only have a one-night stand with someone in whom she wasn't interested, the women of Stockholm have the freedom to engage in sex as they choose.

Frederik, the 28-year-old-student said, 'One-night stands are very common. It's not a big deal to have sex, but it's not easy to pick up. Girls always think I am just talking to them because I want to have sex, but that's not always my intention. Actually, it's more common for women to go out and say "Let's meet a guy tonight" than it is for men.' Eva, the press officer, gave the women's perspective, 'It's a different way of looking at sex. There aren't any moral issues surrounding it.' Maria the project manager summed up the city's attitude to sex. 'It's an open culture with lots of single people. More and more people are living alone in Stockholm. People are afraid of commitment and love living by themselves. Swedish people love their own space; almost everyone has their own flat. If you want sex you have to have an one-night stand. It's common to have sex several times and that's it. People need sex but don't want a boyfriend. Massage parlours and saunas do well because people need physical contact.'

Yet, when you combine independent people, who live alone and who are not interested in having a relationship, loneliness is bound to creep in. Jenny, the biology student, said as much. 'Loneliness is severe in Stockholm. Around 57 to 65% of people are single.' Mattias, the MD, agreed, 'The houses are designed for single people. We call it 'living alone together'. There is a downside to Swedish women's liberation. Mia, the elegant art buyer for a gallery, described that downside, 'Swedish women feel they have to be independent for a public face which differs from what their heart feels.' So, if you want to play with the big boys, you have to leave your softness and vulnerabilities at the door. What is a lonely Stockholmer to do, especially if they are allergic to cats? It was often mentioned that friends will have sex to try and fill the need of companionship, which still allows them to retain independence. Jenny, a PhD student in biology, explained, 'You know he's not dangerous and you know what you got. If you're not in love, it's okay to have sex.' Per, the hot Viking, agreed, 'It's better to have fuck friends than a one-night stand with strangers.' However, Bjorn was more cautious. 'It's more practical to have sex with friends, but it gets complicated. There is a point in every male/female relationship where the guy will think about having sex with the girl. She will decide what happens from there. If she accepts, they start as friends who have sex and it can get very strange.' Sounds like he's talking from personal experience. The Stockholmers admit that friends who have sex might seem like a practical solution for a rampant libido, but they know it's not a perfect one, as Mia, the elegant art buyer said, most eloquently, 'Two people coming together for self-fulfilment, without taking it to a deeper level, is like being alone with another person.'

In Stockholm one-night stands don't have to end in marriage as one woman pointed out, 'It depends on what you want. Sometimes you only want him for one night.' Stockholm women make active choices in their relationships, as well sometimes deciding that all they really want is sex. Katarina the florist was frank. 'One guy didn't want to have sex on the first date. He wanted to get to know me better first, but I didn't want to see him again after that.' Makes sense. She had wanted sex and since he hadn't been obliging, there was no need to see him again. Unlike the New York and Parisian females, who had marriage in their sights, the Stockholm women interviewed were not forced to rely on marriage to give them social legitimacy or economic security. Thus, Stockholm women don't have to care whether one-night stand sex leads to a relationship or not. Her sexual choices are her own.

The women of Stockholm aren't necessarily anti-relationships; they just didn't feel the pressure to be attached. Not for them the belief that their whole existence depends on heterosexual pair bonding. But, just in case you think every Swedish women is jumping into bed with every man they meet, there were a few exceptions: Clare, a 30 year old air traffic controller said, 'I don't have one-night stands, but it's not a moral thing. I just don't get attracted to people in that way. My friends do though.' 32-year-old Annika, the pretty, petite nurse agreed 'For me sex should be love and private and personal. Couldn't share it with whomever.'

But can a one-night stand lead to a relationship? The Swedes had a similar view to the Londoners. Often the relationship starts with the sex. As 33-year-old Johanna, the opera singer, said, 'Relationships start with sex. That's what everyone wants in the end. We don't have a dating culture. We have sex and then start the relationship.' Maria, the press officer, echoed this when she said, 'This is a common way relationships start. First you have sex, then you get to know them.'

The men were in complete agreement. Stefan said, 'For me it always does, so it's more like sex on the first date. If I'm not interested in the person than I won't have sex with her.' He added ruefully, 'It's usually the other way around as well, girls usually don't want me for my body.' Per, the virile Viking, said it best. 'It can start with a one-night stand and turn into a relationship. It's more likely you just keep having sex with the same person rather than a relationship.' But, 'I don't separate the two. No unwritten law you have to wait to have sex. I want to know what I am getting into. We are liberal and horny.' As in London, the men of Stockholm men were also looking for more than just a hot night of passion. Henrik the banker wanted '...more than just an orgasm. I am looking for short or long term.' However, more nights of hot passion were not discounted. Frederik, a 28-year-old student, said, 'You get a connection with someone when you have sex. You want more.'

Stockholm inhabitants, once again, showed that gender roles are not derived from biology alone. Stockholm is an exciting example of what happens when traditional gender roles undergo a paradigm shift. Given Sweden's pole position in the global gender equality stakes it seems that women's strong positioning in the public sphere translates into more fun for everyone in private. However, Stockholmers seem to be trying to figure out how to satisfy their libidos while still satisfying their hearts.

CONCLUSION

In New York, people kiss as a recreational pastime. Thus, they have more room to manoeuvre in the awkward space between flirting and fornication. In London a kiss means little. A one-night stand, however, may well be the first step in a relationship. In Paris once you kiss, sex is probably on the cards. For Stockholm residents a kiss is just a kiss, and a fuck is fun if you both want it.

Where do these differences stem from? The list is long: Catholicism, history, economic power, but ultimately, it boils down to a woman's standing in the society. Without the repressive demands of men on her sexuality, a woman has the choice and freedom to engage in sex as she chooses. While Parisian women have to bide their time, and wait for the man to choose her and then make his move, London women make active choices about who they will or won't date, as do Stockholm women. The image-conscious society of New York portrays women as having sexual freedom. However, looking more closely, it doesn't seem to be the case. Much like the Parisian women, women are still judged, and double standards are rife. This does not seem to be the case for Londoners, who are less likely to have sex just for the sake of it. Alcohol plays a big role and it's often necessary to meet again sober 'just to make sure there's something there'. Also, you're very likely to run into the person again and this is a culture of impeccable decorum. It's all about manners, darling. In Stockholm, it's all about equal opportunity orgasms. And the men know exactly on which side their bread is buttered. As Per, the virile Viking, said, 'We are equal here so women don't get the label they are easy. Swedish men aren't so stupid to judge women for having one-night stands. Then we know it won't happen anymore.' Words to live by.

FLIRT FILE

- In Paris, cover your body to avoid the drageuers.
- In New York, the length of the skirt, is the length of the relationship.
- In London, wear what you want. He's too polite to tell you if he doesn't like it.
- In Stockholm, just wear something warm. You get to choose, anyway.

LIQUID LUBRICATION

Flirting and alcohol go together like Anthony and Cleopatra – and like the famous lovers, the combination may result in either transcendence or tragedy. Thus, one can't study flirting thoroughly without addressing the part that alcohol plays. In some cultures alcohol seems to add to the fun. In other cultures, people drink because they think it will lead to fun. In more reserved cultures, alcohol helps to boost confidence. Whatever the reason, the effect of alcohol inevitably helps lessen or even remove inhibitions. A word of warning, however. Those couple of drinks meant to help you unwind often leads to a couple more, and before you know it, you're not so much unwound, as entirely undone.

NEW YORK
In New York, alcohol features prominently in the flirting scene. A common response to 'Where is the best place to flirt?' was 'Anywhere with alcohol.' For a New Yorker, flirting without alcohol is like ordering a plain, black coffee at Starbucks. While New Yorkers are the first to follow the 'anytime, anyone, anywhere' motto, most of the serious flirting happens in bars and clubs, after the witching hour, and with a drink in hand. Marie, who is currently unemployed, summed up the flirting scene in the Big Apple in three succinct phrases: 'Louder, more obnoxious, getting bombed.'

New Yorkers don't have much of a chance to be sober when it comes to flirting.

Most of their flirting happens in the presence of alcohol. And, one of the major rituals for getting to know someone new is for him to buy a drink for her. Yes, it's always him buying for her! In New York, the women drink just as hard as the men, and there are no hard and fast rules about who makes the first move. One woman admitted that, 'with the help of alcohol' her friends would approach men.

While sassy, independent, New York women bait the hook, booze and bonk with the best of them, they never buy the drinks. They see it as the man's duty, as part of his role as provider. A man's willingness to buy a woman a drink not only helps these women get their buzz on, but it also gives some insight into his income. In New York, a mint julep takes on a different meaning. Out-of-work Marie explained: 'Guys have more money, power and stature; if they want to keep that they should earn it by paying for everything. It's chivalry.' Lisa, the credit card exec, highlighted the flip side of that coin. 'American guys are the worse. They come off as crass and self-important. If they buy you a drink, they think you owe them something.'

The idea seems to be that if a man can drop $20 on a drink for a woman he just met, and her friend too, chances are he is able to buy her more than drinks. He is also expected to continue buying drinks all night in order to continue enjoying her company. Kristin is a cool, eloquent, 35 year-old pharmaceutical rep. She described a date she had been on. After their fourth round of drinks, the guy looked at her pointedly and said, 'Are you going to get this one?' She smiled and made a quick exit – and complained that he had been too cheap to buy dinner in the first place. Sarah, the fashion buyer who oozed style, and has probably never bought a drink in her life, concurred, 'Guys should buy more drinks. I expect the guy to buy drinks. If he doesn't, then I don't want to talk to him. It's a compliment if the guy buys and besides they make more money so they should give more. Guys suck you in, "Hey what's up, do you need a drink? Let me take care of you." Men like to have the upper hand of supporting the women. My guy friends try and make a lot of money so they can support the girl. They say how am I going to get a girl if I don't make any money.'

In a place where being extroverted and social is very important, drinking helps people overcome that last barrier between themselves and the object of their attraction. David, the 28 year-old architect, admitted that the more drunk he is, the less choosy. 'There are "6 beer girls" and then there are "12 beer girls", the ones for whom you lower your standards'. Is beauty, then, in the eye of the beer-holder?

Alcohol helps those fun-loving New Yorkers become even more gregarious. And if you get rejected? Simply blame it on the drink. New Yorkers acknowledge that drinking to excess will most likely feature in their nights out, although not always with complete acceptance. When asked, 'Do you have any intentions when you go out?' one man answered, 'To have a good time, and try not to drink.'

When speaking about going home with someone, which seemed to be a common bedfellow to extensive drinking, Dana, the high-powered New Yorker who works as a business analyst on Wall Street, revealed, 'There would be more shame that I was too drunk than that I had sex with somebody.'

PARIS
Despite the reputation of their wine, Parisians don't drink much. If they did, they might find that they would be more likely to let down their guards. Unlike the New Yorkers, Parisians simply don't let things get messy. Ever. The French don't rely on excessive drinking when flirting. Mostly, because the art of conversation is held in such high esteem and, let's face it, drunken people are not the most stimulating or articulate conversationalists. More than a couple of drinks is frowned upon in Parisian flirting circles. So while the Gaelic language makes the word 'wine' sound like liquid sex, and France produces in the region of seven to eight billion bottles of wine a year, the Parisians aren't over-imbibers.

In Paris, extreme drunkenness is disapproved of. While drunken men are also looked down upon, the rules are even stricter for women and Parisian men are repelled by women not being able to hold their drink. Antoine, the 35 year-old banker explained that alcohol cheapens the interactions. 'Because you are never flirting alone, there is always someone with you on your wavelength. When you are completely drunk you talk to anyone, they are not necessarily on your wavelength. That's not flirting.' Crinkly-haired Jean-Luc said, between puffs of his cigarette: 'It's not elegant for a Parisian woman to drink...maybe one or two glasses. If she drinks all night, I won't flirt with her.'

As well as seeing alcohol as an obstacle to intelligent conversation and the harbinger of possible projectile vomiting, Parisians are also very concerned with what others think of them; with being 'politically correct', and behaving appropriately in public. However, this special brand of political correctness is actually Parisian correctness, how a Parisian should appear to others while in the public sphere. Antoine declared, with no small measure of gravity: 'It's a culture of respect. You can have one or two glasses, max, to be more relaxed. With alcohol you will forget all the rules of political correctness.' Another reason alcohol is frowned upon is because the dishevelled, drunken look is just a bit too 1993. So drinking is outmoded and a real no-no for women. The Brits call women who emulate laddish behaviour and drink like men, 'ladettes'. While the word has a French ring to it, you won't find any of them on the streets of Paris.

The women themselves acknowledge this view and accept the unwritten rule. 'To flirt you must use your mind and you can't be too drunk.' 'It's not elegant,' says Charlotte, the 32 year-old editor. 'If you throw up in Paris and he is not your boyfriend, then you have no chance with him. This is much worse than having a one-night stand …You have one glass to put you in a good mood. We like to stay tipsy. If you want to flirt, you can't be drunk.' Sophie, the teacher, said that moderation was a social norm very much held in place by men. 'Men don't like women to be drunk…two or three glasses to be relaxed and then stop.' Monique, the 28 year-old sales rep admitted that she secretly wanted more to drink. 'Guys don't let me drink, but I want to drink,' she complained.

But who buys the drinks? In Paris, as in New York, the man always buys, but perhaps for different reasons. It seems that this social norm is embedded in their DNA. It's his duty and both the men and women know it.

LONDON
Single Londoners socialise at certain times and in certain places; Friday or Saturday night, at a pub or club, and usually after more than three drinks. That probably explains this Parisian's opinion of flirting across the Channel. 'In the UK they only flirt in bars and at parties, half drunk, screaming in your ear, trying to get laid.' In contrast to the abstemious one-pint Parisians, London men and women don't acknowledge any such restrictions. In a culture where people are not supposed to intrude on others' space, be over-familiar with strangers, and are known for being reserved, is it any surprise that drinking is an important social lubricant?

'Drinking is quite central to one's world view,' asserted Alistair, the 32 year-old, broadcast journalist. In fact, it seems it's almost impossible for the English to flirt without copious quantities of 'do-it-fluid' inside them. This is especially true in the case of English men – possibly because most of the pressure in the flirting game is on them. They are the ones who are expected to make the moves. As Jane, a lovely brunette, who worked in finance confirmed, 'It's easier for girls. If a guy came up to me and started flirting I could say, "No, sorry". But me and my friends could go up to most guys and they would all happily talk to us.'

When men were asked what they observed their friends doing when they flirted, alcohol almost always featured. Charlie, the 30 year-old, floppy-haired, entrepreneur said, 'They would look at women but pretend they weren't. They would get very drunk and hope for the best. We drink more for alcohol courage.' Sam, the 30 year-old website designer, said this about his friend: 'He'd get drunk first, want to go and talk to her and then say "No, I'm not ready yet" and have another drink.' And, if all else fails, just do what one guy recommends, 'Get drunk and lunge.'

Buying drinks was the number one thing the men said they did in order to achieve flirting success. In New York, drink buying was often a quick and easy way for men to display their wealth and for women to assess it. When a guy orders a jeroboam of Krug there's no mistaking the fact that the bulge in his pants is his wallet. However, a London man, for the most part, buys drinks to be chivalrous and gentlemanly. And, let's face it, a few drinks helps to melt away any reserve. Buying drinks isn't just the male's domain. Unlike New York females, who feel it's a man's duty to pay for the drinks, London females often buy a round. In fact, most women would feel very uncomfortable if it was a completely one-sided arrangement. While traditional gender roles apply in the initial stages of the dating game, drink-buying is far more egalitarian. London women are more liberated in this respect than their trans-Atlantic cousins. Jane, who works in finance admitted, 'Sure, it's nice if a guy buys me a drink, but I would certainly feel very uncomfortable if it remained so one-sided the whole evening. I would definitely buy him a drink back.'

STOCKHOLM
Like London, alcohol is an essential component in the otherwise quite timid, Stockholm flirting scene. And like Londoners, the residents of Stockholm are quite retiring… most of the time. Between the hours of 7am and 11pm the shy Swedes might throw a brief blink in the direction of someone to signal interest. From 11pm onwards, once they've had sufficient lubrication, pawing to the point of mauling ensues. However, because of the prohibitive cost of alcohol, much of the Stockholm social scene takes place at pre-parties. Drinking at home is less expensive. Pre-parties are usually single-sex affairs, and then, from about 11pm to 1am everyone meets at a bar and proceeds to get thoroughly plastered. Once again, much like London's bravest, this has the desired effect.

Stockholm's men '…are a bit shy, but they can approach you after a few drinks,' said Bjorn, a 31 year-old PhD student. Mattias, the 28-year-old managing director of a soft drinks company, confirmed this modus operandi. 'The men have to be drunk in order to approach. When we get drunk we get social.' However, Mattias admitted, 'Maybe some aren't good at judging how many drinks it takes.' Henrik is a banker who has been living in London for the last two years. He said, 'We have a cocktail culture in Stockholm. It would take longer, and with more alcohol, to get to the flirting stage.' Andreas, the personal trainer, best summed it up: 'Swedish flirting; get drunk and then paw'.

However, in Stockholm, a man could get into trouble for offering to buy a woman a drink. Katarina the florist said: 'It's considered pushy by Swedish women to have a drink bought for them.' Clare, a 30 year-old, air-traffic controller explained the female perspective. 'Some girls don't like it when guys pay. They want to be equal. It's all about economics. The women don't need the men to pay because they have their own money.'

Anders, the sales rep agreed, 'In Sweden if you asked if you could buy a girl a drink she would say, "No, let me pay half" and then you would say "No, it's on me." We are supposed to be very equal.' Nonetheless, Stefan, who owned a bicycle shop, said he liked it when Swedish women bought him a drink. 'Swedish women are good at that.' Yet, in this icy land of pricy tipple, Frederik, the law student was revealing: 'Buying a drink really means something. It means you want to have contact.'

CONCLUSION

In Stockholm, they drink to loosen up but buying a Swedish woman a drink could bring the night to a premature end. The approach most favoured by English men is to get very drunk and hope for the best. The London lass who can match a lad pint-for-pint is regaled, but the Parisian mademoiselle who tipples too much is reviled. And in New York, equal opportunity drinking is the rule but it's the men who are expected to foot the bill.

FLIRT FILE

- Watch the interactions around you. Who is buying the drinks? What are they ordering? How much are they drinking?
- Ask the bartender, the most knowledgeable person in the place, as to the correct protocol.
- When in doubt, don't have the next drink. Conversation can go from charming to cheesy in one vodka tonic.

Chapter 24: Daytime Flirting
ARE THOSE MELONS RIPE?

Some prefer the light of day in which to dazzle their dreamboats, catching them off guard with witty repartee. Others like to hide behind the cover of night, taking advantage of the fact that people expect flirting to happen in bars and nightclubs. The reactions were mixed as to which was preferable. Let's not forget one of the places where our singletons were sure to spend the majority of their days: the office. Was flirting in the workplace taboo, or was it a sure-fire way to make sure your papers were the first out of the copy machine? Where is the best place to flirt?' elicited some unexpected responses. However, this is not to be confused with 'Where is the most unusual place you've found yourself flirting?' Answers ranged from 'underwater' to 'the dentist', to a funeral.

NEW YORK
'Where is the best place to flirt in the city?' elicited answers such as: the laundromat, art gallery openings, coffee shops, book stores, the subway and the park on weekends. Asking where the best place is to flirt in New York is like asking where the best place is to breathe. It can – and should – be done anywhere. This observation summed up the majority response. 'It depends on the other person, if they are open to meeting people, anywhere'. This New Yorker spelled out the wealth of potential pickup joints in her city. 'Anywhere there are lots of people and your guard is down is good – somewhere relaxed. Parks, clubs, the street, the library, day-to-day places are where you meet the high quality people'. A common response was, 'It depends on the neighbourhood. They're aggressive in Jersey, in Manhattan, less aggressive.' Gina, the 33-year-old occupational therapist disagreed, 'In Brooklyn and Queens, guys want a relationship. Outside of the city, in Manhattan, no one wants a commitment.' Lisa, the high-powered credit card exec had it all laid out, 'It depends on what kind of guys you are trying to meet – dive bars for frat guys; business men go to Wall Street and rooftop terraces; Alphabet City for the artistic guys'. So, where's the best place to meet a New Yorker? It depends.

Here's a hot tip from one New York woman. She identified the tennis courts in Central Park as one of the few places in the city where you are guaranteed to find straight men. One wise guy suggested that the best flirting goes on in his bedroom. And, because this was New York and women were just as likely to have high flying jobs, one woman said the best flirting takes place when 'travelling for business, in a hotel bar.'

Bars and clubs were mentioned repeatedly, but had their pros and cons as worthwhile flirting venues. As one woman suggested, the best time and place for a flirtatious encounter is, 'Happy hour between 5 and 8.' As New Yorkers expressly go to bars to flirt, rich pickings are to be had. However, this didn't mean they were necessarily the best places to get lucky. Women don't trust the men's motives in these watering holes and are wary – with good reason. David, a 28-year-old architect, admitted, 'If you are at a bar, you didn't go there to be friendly. Guys are sluts.'

The drawbacks of bars and clubs as fertile hunting grounds included:

- Superficial experiences: 'In bars it is easy to flirt, but it's not very real, it's more transient', said Sarah, the smart and sassy fashion buyer.
- A lethal combination of expectation and pressure from friends, prying eyes, and even oneself: 'In a bar there is more pressure. I put too much significance on what happens', said Doug the Dentist.
- Lots of competition: 'Bars are good, but women are constantly getting approached, so you have to make yourself extra special in order to stand out', said Corey, the actor/fire-fighter.
- Women with their guards up: 'Bars, restaurants, clubs. There is lots of opportunity but there is a trust issue', said Russell a 28-year-old graphic designer

The issue of trust was why some people brought up the 'V factor'. This meant that a friend 'vouched for' you. Many mentioned friends' parties as a great place to flirt because they have the 'V factor'. One man said, 'A friend's party is always good, where the initial barriers are broken for you.' Another male echoed the importance of someone giving them credibility or acting as a reference. 'The best flirting is done wherever there is a loose association with someone, a place where people can give you cred'. Another pointed out the element of time as an important factor. 'On the street on a nice evening is good, any place that gives you a common purpose, friends' gigs, friends' parties, anywhere where people have time'.

Do the New Yorkers flirt over the photocopier? Of course they do! Almost 90% of them said yes. However, they were definitely aware of boundaries. Russell, the graphic designer said, 'I flirt, but not to start anything, just for fun.' Andrew, the 34-year-old attorney, confessed, 'I do, but it's really restrained and mellow.'

Jason, the high-school science teacher, admitted, 'Only with someone at work who I know well, as it has gotten me into trouble in the past.' Curly-haired Chris, the environmental engineer, said 'I do, but with older women, so it's not misconstrued.'

The women were just as cautious:
Amusing Alexis, the sharp-witted research assistant said, 'It's safe there because I always try and keep a boundary.' Lisa, who works for a large credit card company, said, 'I do flirt, but just too smooth things over, not seriously.' Attractive Alesha, the broadcast journalist said, 'Yes, but just for fun, for a little flirtation. I try to keep it just a work thing.'

Many New Yorkers mentioned that flirting during the day was preferred. Susan, a journalist said, 'It makes doing mundane tasks more interesting'. At night, New Yorkers go out to see, be seen, and score. It seems with 'daytime flirting' the pressure to attract the bold and the beautiful is off. People are able to flirt more 'generously'. Rather than trying to appear the biggest, best and most successful, people can flirt for the fun of it. Joel, the 33-year-old entrepreneur, said engagingly, 'The greatest buzz is making someone smile and laugh no matter what she looks like.' Justin the literary agent thought that, 'Daytime flirting feels more above board and friendly. No stigma or perceived expectations.' Rebecca, the 35-year-old recruitment consultant said, 'It's better because it's unplanned, spontaneous.' The New Yorkers felt daytime flirting was more relaxed, less pressurised, and a fun way to pass the time. Ah yes, and you weren't drunk. 'Day flirting is good because it's not alcohol-infused. It happens more naturally, but only if I am in a good mood,' said Dana, the pretty brunette analyst. Andrea, who works for a charity said, 'If you go to a bar you accept there will be some flirting going on. In day-to-day it's a slower process. You have to first set up a mutual flirting space because you're not automatically set up for it.' In the debate over whether night or day was the best time for flirting, one woman summed it up, 'The difference between day and night flirting is whether you want a friendly buzz or a boyfriend.'

Those who were skeptical of dalliances at the drugstore said, 'Everyday flirting doesn't go anywhere. When I am at the grocery store I am just concentrating on getting my cornflakes.' Bryan, the lanky aspiring musician, said, 'It would be less expected at the supermarket as people aren't used to it, they are too in the zone.'

Alesha, the broadcast journalist concurred, 'I don't think about day flirting. I just want to take care of my transactions'.

Andrew, the blonde attorney with slick-backed hair, was vehemently against daytime flirting, 'It's not good to do; it's just bad etiquette. People have their guard up and are unapproachable. People are on the move and going somewhere'. Jason, the high-school science teacher agreed, 'I don't like to interrupt people – shouldn't stop their flow'. This is New York after all. Time is money, honey!

PARIS

French men regard themselves as natural flirts. Therefore, as Antoine, the debonair banker, pointed out, 'We don't go to a certain place, at a certain time, and start flirting, it's just our natural state.' Moreover, alcohol is not an integral part of the Parisians' flirting scene either. Alexandre, who works in business tourism, pointed out, 'It can be done anywhere and you don't need alcohol to flirt.' Try telling that to the Swedes!

For the Parisians, somewhere that is too noisy isn't ideal for getting to know someone. While in New York, bars and clubs are regarded as fertile flirting ground. In Paris, the general consensus was, 'Not in a nightclub, you can't speak, and flirting involves talking'.

The interviewees all emphatically emphasised this point, perhaps because of the great importance they put on the dying art of conversation. One woman's response to the best place to flirt was, 'When you know the person, a café. You have to be able to hear. Otherwise, something between a pub and a disco.' Despite their great love of dancing, Parisians were much more likely to mention 'dinner' and 'cafes' as good places for after-dark flirting. The Parisians also thought that friends' parties were the best places to flirt and like Jona Lewie, you'll probably find them in the kitchen. One Parisian male identified his home as the best place to flirt. There's always one!

Parisians continually referred to flirting with people whom they already knew. It didn't seem very common to socialise with strangers. 35-year-old Francine who works in publishing said, 'If it's a friend of a friend than I give him a chance, but not a stranger on the street.' Juliette the social worker explained her reluctance by saying, 'We use more provocation in the big city. You are more yourself with someone you really like.'

So, did the Parisians expect to pick up more than their dry cleaning on a Saturday afternoon? The Parisians, especially the men, seemed to be up for some daytime flirting.

Although they acknowledged that nothing would ever come out of it; it was purely for entertainment. Nicolas, the pragmatic project manager, said, 'You know 90% of it won't go anywhere; you have less to lose.' Shy Laurent, the 30-year-old architect said, 'Daytime flirting is just for a short period of time. I never think I could start something serious in a public place. On the metro we could look at each other and that is all that will ever happen.' Veronique, a PhD student, concurred that eye contact is as far as daytime flirting goes, 'It's not speaking, but with the eyes.' Parisians, like many New Yorkers, also saw daytime flirting as a fun way to pass the time. Matthieu the dishy artistic director said 'It's more difficult, but more rewarding, because everyday locations are a bit boring and people like it when something out of the ordinary happens.'

Eccentric Olivier, with the lightly tanned skin was another fan of daytime flirting. He said, 'It's the best place, you have a good flirt and then let her go.' And this Casanova finds daylight a distraction: 'I fall in love with girls I see on the street every five minutes.'

Not all the Parisian men interviewed were fans of daytime flirting. Antoine the banker explained why he doesn't flirt during the day, 'I'm not in the mood. At every hour in the day I am focused on something else. My time for flirting is 8pm to midnight.' A descendant of Cinderella, perhaps?

The women were much less likely than the men to say they flirted in daytime settings. While New Yorkers found that nightclubs and bars offered less meaningful encounters, Parisian women felt the same about daytime flirting. Sandrine, the director's assistant said, 'The supermarket checkout is not real because of the short amount of time. You can't discover the other person.'

Sophisticated Stefanie, the business analyst outlined her ground rules, 'No flirting in the street or in the metro. You are like prey.' She has a point. One man admitted he used daytime flirting with strangers to hone his seduction skills. 'My main motive for everyday flirting is to prepare for when I meet someone I really do fancy.' This woman, however, was content to fantasise about her daytime dalliance. 'You can imagine you'd be with him after.'

When it comes to flirting at work, the genders were divided. More than half of the men interviewed said they flirted at work, while less than half of the women said they did. Alexandre works in business tourism. He commented on the differences in expectation of behaviour when operating in the outside world, 'In my private sphere I can be myself and not PC. In the public sphere, I must be polite and PC.' The Parisian women seemed to be very cautious about flirting at work. Martine, the logistics coordinator said, 'I want to be known for my work, not for whom I'm dating.' Monique, the sales rep agreed, 'In the office, if you are new, it's like, "Which one of us will get her first?"'.

LONDON

Unlike the tee totalling Parisians, alcohol plays a large part in the London flirting scene. Thus, the best place to flirt is 'Anywhere there is alcohol', or as Alistair, the broadcast journalist put it, 'At the bottom of three or four pints of Guinness.' The women agreed, 'A pub, a bar, a jazz club. A glass of wine relaxes you. Alcohol is a part of it'. Other places mentioned were house parties and horse jumping. We are in England, after all. And a place where flirting is verboten is the beach, according to one shy guy, 'Not at the beach because people are too naked.'

So, if alcohol and flirting are a natural pairing, do Londoners flirt much in their day-to-day activities? It seems that they are more likely to than the Parisians, but less likely than the New Yorkers. The men are slightly more likely than the women to flirt in daylight hours. And, of course, the women will only admit to being 'charming'. Apparently, it's only after dark – and with the help of a gin and tonic – that the London ladies truly get their flirt on. Well, there were exceptions.

Anoushka, the sexy solicitor said, 'I would as part of communication, but there are different agendas going on there. It's easier because of lack of expectation. It's more fun, not as a means to an end.' Annette, the shapely jazz singer said, 'It depends if you have the time, attraction and mood. I like my own space though.' To one man, flirting during the day and flirting after dark, was like, well, night and day, Simon, the PR exec said, 'There is more at stake with someone I am attracted to. You want to see them again so you are more cautious, reticent; rather err on the side of caution.' We are not trying to capture a poisonous snake here. Do these London ladies have more venom that we thought?

Interestingly, both men and women were much more likely to flirt at work, than during their daily activities. Almost every Londoner, both male and female, said they flirted at work. As Jane, who works in the financial industry said, 'Flirting at work makes life happier for both sides.' Sam, the website designer agreed, 'It just makes things easier.'

Georgina the secretary thought that with office flirting, you were 'More likely to get what you want.' This could be due to the Little Red Riding Hood principle that prevails in these parts: 'Don't talk to strangers'. While work colleagues may be annoying; may gossip behind your back; may sniff when they should blow, they are not strangers and hence fair game.

STOCKHOLM

In theory, Stockholmers love the idea of flirting in daylight hours, but it seems that, in reality, flirting only happens under very specific conditions: late at night on spring and summer weekends, with several shots of schnapps under the hood.

Swedes don't like to stand out from the crowd and Stockholm women, in particular, don't appreciate 'obvious' flirting. Thus, most people did not mention the usual bar or club in answer to the question, 'Where is the best place to flirt?' Everyone knows that people go to such places expressly to flirt. Per the virile Viking said, 'Bars are the most common, but not the best. The library is good for flirting, the subway; anywhere there is a lot of people and they don't move around a lot and are able to focus on someone.' To Frederik the '…worst place is a club. The best is work and everyday places, places where people act themselves.' Hugo, with the sketchy beard and slight paunch, is an accounts manager. He pointed out that good places to flirt were, '…trains, libraries, friends' parties, work. A place that's not very obvious that you have to flirt. There is no filter that says "I have to flirt now". Places where there is no pressure.' Annika the nurse with the bewitching bedside manner said, 'Anywhere people are in a relaxed environment. Not a bar, maybe school or the workplace'. Clare, the air traffic controller said, 'Anywhere that people can meet, a café or a course.' But, are courses the best way to break the ice? 'At university it took three sessions before we started saying hi to each other.'

Unlike the New York night owls, Stockholmers claimed to prefer daytime flirting and 88% of both men and women interviewed admitted to flirting at work. Bear in mind, though, that in Stockholm 'Pass the stapler' most likely counts as a pass. Stefan, when not riding his bicycle thought the best places for flirting were 'On the train, and everyday situations'. He then added, 'But you have to be subtle.' 70% of both males and females said they flirted in day-to-day places, although evidence for this flirting frenzy was lacking, perhaps because of all that subtlety.

The benefits of everyday flirting ranged from '…more innocent, and can ease tension' to '…the time span is shorter so it's mainly for getting acknowledgement and feeling better about self, or to get something'. However, Bjorn the PhD student, who was not a proponent of everyday flirting, said, 'I feel I lose energy making contact with people I don't know'. Frederik, the erudite law student said that with daytime flirting, 'You have to be brave.' He probably was referring to the fact that one had to flirt without any alcohol in their system!

Stockholmers are not known for their daring. Their responses to 'Where is the most unusual place you have found yourself flirting,' weren't exactly astounding: 'McDonalds at 4am', 'a pedestrian crossing' and 'at a private party where I didn't know anyone besides my friend'. How audacious! Speaking for her fellow citizens, Mia, the buyer for an art gallery, declared, 'You wouldn't dare flirt without alcohol!' Thus, despite their stated preference for daytime flirting, the real business is done late Friday night at a pub. Explaining the etiquette, Eva the press officer said, 'People drink too much and then start talking.' As most Stockholmers don't go out on week nights, they have to cram it all into a short time period. Clare, the air-traffic controller said, 'People work hard and then go to extremes during the weekend. They don't know how to balance. I go out during the weekdays and it's more relaxed.' So, in reality, the only place where a Stockholmer is guaranteed to get his or her flirt on is on a Friday or Saturday night, between the hours of 11pm and 3am. Maria, the project manager, agreed, '7pm on a Friday night is different from 3am. People are nice and you can talk. At 3am, it's "Come home with me".'

For the Stockholmers, the issue was less about where to flirt and more about what time of year to flirt! 33-year-old Johanna the opera singer, explained, 'In Sweden we're not good at communication, maybe because of the climate. Summer is short. We are learning how to communicate on the internet.' For flaxen-haired Katarina the best time for flirting was, 'Spring time when you can be outdoors and there is sunlight and warmth.' Annika agreed, 'In the summer, and somewhere there is alcohol. People are shy and need something to come out of their shells.' Frederik the law student offered an explanation, 'Our families sat in cabins in the woods, alone, being quiet, and drinking. Then all of a sudden summer comes and we are supposed to be social?' Banker Henrik elucidated, 'Spring and summer are 100% better for flirting. After a small bit of sunshine, everyone is outside eating and drinking. In winter, people stick to their friends and stay home.' Flirting in a parka, with 20 layers underneath, isn't very titillating. As Andreas, the personal trainer said, 'Everyone dresses for warmth so physically it represents an emotional barrier.' However, affable Mattias, the soft drinks MD protested, 'It's the weather that is cold, not us!'

CONCLUSION

In New York, no place was out of bounds for flirting, while night time flirting had its pros and cons. The Parisians were up for flirting all the time, but continually stressed that nothing would ever come of daytime flirting because there wasn't enough time to get to know the person. Londoners seemed to only seriously get their flirt on in the evening, but they warmed up during the day at work. It was the polite thing to do, after all. While the Stockholmers seemed to like the idea of daytime flirting, in a reserved culture that doesn't encourage talking to strangers, and with no alcohol involved, it was no surprise that it didn't really seem to happen.

FLIRT FILE

- After 7pm, having had a few drinks, at a bar, is not the only opportunity to meet someone.
- Day flirting perks include: People not having their guards up, no competition, it's free – you don't have to buy drinks.
- Best venues for day flirting: Bookstore, cafe, supermarket, library, class, and your neighbourhood where your chances increase of running into like-minded people – your neighbours

Chapter 25: Flirting Alone or With Friends?
HUNTING IN PACKS

The infamous book 'The Game' made 'wingman' a household term. The original definition of wingman was used by the US Air Force. It referred to a pilot whose plane is positioned behind and outside the leader in a formation of flying aircraft. Today, it's not happening in the skies, but in pubs and clubs, and the target is not other planes, it's women. According to the Urban dictionary, 'a wingman is a guy you bring along with you on singles outings that helps you out with the women. The wingman's main duty will always be to occupy the least attractive girl of the pair so that you may engage with the "hotty".' So when it comes to flirting, do people prefer to act as a lone wolves, wingmen – or wingwomen? Or do they hunt in packs?

NEW YORK
In this sociable city, looking like you're having fun is key. Standing alone in a corner – bad. Being at the centre of a laughing throng of people – good.

In New York if you are alone, people assume it is because you have no friends. Andrew, a 34-year-old attorney, makes a point not to flirt with a woman on her own. 'I don't flirt with someone alone because they are alone for a reason; either waiting for someone or has no friends.'

New Yorkers mostly go out in single or mixed-sex groups of two or three people – too many people in the group impedes the ability to mix and mingle. Some reasons for mixed groups are practical. Clubs and bars like to keep the ratio of male to females even, for a conducive amorous atmosphere and because an overdose of testosterone can lead to trouble. Russell, a 28-year-old graphic designer complained, 'You can't get in anywhere with a group of guys.'

Not a single New York male said they preferred flirting alone. If you're male, it's especially important to have a friend with you when flirting. Joel, a 33-year-old entrepreneur said, 'It's easier to approach if you are with a friend. It shows that you are not a lone stalker and you have a way of showcasing your socialising abilities.' Corey, the actor/fire-fighter, added his voice to the chorus. 'Groups of two, single-sex, is the best combo for going out, or have a platonic girl friend with you so the girls trust you and think you are a good guy.' Joel the entrepreneur agreed, 'If I am with girls who are just friends it's easier. The perception is you're more approachable and not just out to hook up.' Russell, the graphic designer, echoed the popular approach, 'If you are a guy it's best to have two others with you. It's more helpful if you are in a mixed group because they think you are nice and safe. They might think you are dating one of the girls and that is an added bonus.' And you thought the possibility of someone already being taken was an impediment. This is New York. Unless you have a ring on it, there is no such thing as being off the market. It fact, Russell would be considered even more desirable, as he has been vetted by another female and passed the test.

Chris, the 30-year-old environmental engineer, was philosophical about the question.

'Same numbers as her is good. She is with a friend and I am with a friend. But after a few beers, nothing matters.'

Despite the men's careful calculations, the women were aware of the 'wingman' phenomena, and weren't impressed. Susan, the budding journalist, was more receptive to solo operators, 'If he were alone than he is probably being more himself, and not just impressing friends.' The New York males will blatantly vie for the women's attentions with no qualms about usurping their friends in what is a highly competitive environment. Actually they prefer flirting in full view of their buddies, as this is the perfect way to showcase their own sociability, give them credibility, and help them earn 'who da' man?' points.

The women interviewed were split on the issue of whether they preferred to flirt alone or in the company of friends. New York women are equally competitive and some felt it best not to put themselves in the situation where they would have to 'fight' over a man with their friend. 'If I'm with friend this complicated thing about allegiances arises; deciding which one of us gets the guy. There is a hierarchy for competition,' admitted 38-year-old Dana, the pretty, brunette analyst.

New Yorkers are in a conundrum; they don't like flirting alone, but small groups mean more competition. Perhaps this is why so many interviewees, both male and female, emphasised that they liked to be singled out and made to feel special and look good in front of their friends.

PARIS
Both men and women were equally divided on the question of whether they preferred to flirt alone or with a friend. Many said it didn't matter. Thus, they have more flexibility in the flirting stakes. The Parisians go out in large, mixed-sex groups, which may even include married couples. They deliberately avoid going out in small, single-sex groups for fear of being seen to be 'out for one thing only'.
Opinion differed when it came to whether or not people would mix outside of their groups. Some stuck to their groups:

- 'We socialise in our groups, but we don't mix.'
- 'It can be complicated to flirt with people outside of the group. Usually I only flirt if I have been introduced by a friend.'
- 'We get together in mixed gender groups, and usually just flirt within that group. It's hard to mix outside.'
- Others said that mixing outside the group was easy:
- 'We go out in mixed groups, but we don't always stick to our groups. In Paris 50% of people are single.'
- 'We go out in mixed groups, but it's not hard to flirt outside group.'
- 'We go out in mixed groups. We would flirt in our group or with friends of friends, mixed gender, but it's easy to flirt outside the group. A male friend could point something out you didn't see.'

Were these people flirting on the same planet, let alone the same city? Or, perhaps, this is another Parisian paradox?

In Paris it's rare for women to go out without the accompaniment of men. If they do, the Parisian view is that they are sexually available. Lucy, an Englishwoman who was living in Paris made this observation, 'It's not like in England, where I go out on my own all the time with no trouble. If I do the same here in Paris, all the Parisian men think that I'm up for it.' As Charlotte, the book editor explained 'You don't go out in Paris unless it's in mixed groups. If you are just with girls then you are more likely to attract the boys; if it's just boys, then it looks really seedy, like they are just going out to get girls.'

The men who preferred flirting solo gave reasons such as 'The friend might be watching me' and 'Flirting is a special/short relationship that happens with one person. I don't notice others around me.' This thoughtful soul preferred going it alone out of consideration for the woman, 'She might be embarrassed or pressurised to have two people approaching her and might not react naturally.' Alexandre, who works in business tourism, prefers to hunt alone to avoid competition. 'It depends on the friends. If they are better than me, I prefer to be alone. We talk before the party and we choose which ones we like and those girls are off limits to the other, but it doesn't always work out so well.' The men who preferred having a friend around said they felt more confident and comfortable with a wing-man.

LONDON

The Londoners expressed an overwhelming preference to flirt alone and, thereby, avoiding scrutiny by their friends. While they both agreed strongly on this, the women had a plethora of different reasons, while the men just didn't want to lose face.

In a culture which takes its privacy seriously, it's no surprise that Londoners much prefer flirting solo, rather than in front of others. However, as Londoners usually go out with a group of friends, flirting tends to happen with people they already know and who could, potentially, tease them! The Londoners are forced to gauge interest in a group context. And, to avoid being busted by their friends for flirting, they must do so discerningly. One way to tell this is to compare themselves to others in the group. They learn to tell when someone is flirting with them when the conversation is

- '…more directed to just one person.'
- 'You are the person in the group that gets told the interesting story.'
- 'It depends which direction the person is facing, or in group conversations if the conversation is directed at you.'

To meet someone new usually entails approaching their group, a rather daunting exercise for both the men and women of London. Georgina the secretary admitted, 'I'd feel more confident flirting alone, like I was less likely to be laughed at. A group of blokes can be scary.' The men find groups of women equally intimidating.

Unlike the New York males, who see approaching groups of women as proof of their manhood, London men would rather take a dip in the Serpentine Lake in January than attempt such a feat of daring. One said, 'There is nothing scarier than a gaggle of girls.'

Charlie, the entrepreneur, still scarred from an experience he had with a group of girls, 20 years ago! 'Groups of females can be quite intimidating,' he said. 'When I was 10, I walked by a bunch of girls and they started laughing. Maybe they weren't even referring to me, but it was scary! I will never put myself in that situation again.'

Alex, who works in import/export for a well known beer company, felt the same way, 'Groups of girls are often out for the craic and you could become the craic!' 'I would never approach a whole group of girls. You would have to be an entertainer,' ventured Simon, who works in public relations. Samuel, the furniture maker, used a similar metaphor, 'With a group of girls, you need to be able to capture and hold their attention, which is almost impossible to do unless you are a magician.' Take heart, gents. You don't have to be David Copperfield to approach women. Nor will you have to saw anyone in half. Buying her a drink is less labour intensive and much less risky.

Women liked flying solo because they didn't want to be evaluated. 'I feel watched, like people are judging me.' Some wanted to keep their intentions and activities secret. 'I prefer to flirt on my own so my friends don't see what I am doing.' Others felt pressure from well-meaning mates. 'My friends are so desperate for me to find someone if they catch a whisper of me with anyone, they get excited.' Being 'socially aware' was another reason for favouring the solo flirt. Liz is an account manager for a big advertising agency. 'Since you focus attention on one person you will either be excluding people or sickening people.' Some preferred flirting alone for reasons of privacy. Jennifer, a down-to-earth finance analyst said, 'On your own you have the freedom. You don't feel like you are being exposed. When you are first flirting you are only giving part of yourself. In front of a friend they might let on to something that you didn't want to tell.' Sometimes the decision to flirt alone was part of a strategy. 32-year-old Gemma, a morning breakfast show producer said, 'This is how I appear to one person rather than him and his mate. You know more of what your effect is when it's one to one. There are less variables.' Some London women expressed a preference for the men they were flirting with to be equally discreet. 'I like it subtle, for them to let you know they are flirting but not so everyone can see, ' said Catherine, who is in IT. 29-year-old Rachel, the illustrator, agreed, 'Not coming on too strong. I like a sly, cheeky flirt, so no one else knows.'

For the men, it was of paramount importance to flirt solo in order to avoid being mercilessly teased by their friends. The males felt self-conscious and embarrassed at 'being busted' for flirting by their friends. 'If you cop on that your friend is flirting he gets embarrassed. His demeanour changes. He becomes more serious,' said Adrian, the real estate agent with the shiny shoes. Like the women, the men also used the word 'freedom' in their preference for flirting alone. Soft-spoken Anthony in IT said, 'I prefer flirting alone because there's greater freedom. One's inhibitions are increased if there are friends around. The level of embarrassment is higher.' James the optician with the killer specs said, 'It's an ego thing. Being rejected in front of other people is bad.' Christopher, the former military man, confessed, 'If you are with your mate and there's a chance you'd get knocked back, you wouldn't do it. It's important to save face with your mates.' Although, this is not to say that he wouldn't do it at all. He continued, 'You'd do it when they're not looking.'

Such furtive flirting reflects the Londoners' code of conduct: Never be seen to want anything – or anyone – too badly; never be earnest, and always maintain a sense of irony. On those rare occasions that flirting in front of others happens, one London male praised his friend who would 'lie on a grenade' for him, meaning he would 'take' the uglier woman of the two. Ah, the sacrifices men make in war.

STOCKHOLM

While the inhabitants of some cities, might be as likely to go out on a Tuesday night, as they would on a Saturday night, the Stockholmers save it all up for the weekend. They only really go out on Friday and Saturday nights, although this practice is slowly changing, as the Swedes become more 'European'. The weekend starts with a 'pre-party' at someone's home to avoid the expensive drink prices. These are usually single-sex parties with a few mates. Then, everyone meets at the bars and clubs from about 11pm to 1am. For those still standing, the early morning morphs into mixed-sex 'post-parties'. When everyone is sozzled, the dynamics of solo vs. group tactics soon become irrelevant.

The Stockholm men didn't seem to have a clear preference for flirting alone or with friends. The ones that did have a preference for flirting alone, thought this way because of what their friends might think. 'It's less intimidating flirting alone' said Frederik, the 28-year-old law student. Stefan said, 'If I was with friends I would be thinking, "What would they think? Do they think she's stupid?".' Henrik, the Swedish banker who lives in London, prefers flirting with friends for the sake of his image, 'Definitely with a friend. On a Friday night if you were going out alone you would be a loser.'

Emelie, the cautious, 32-year-old accountant echoed this sentiment by saying, 'If you are alone men might think you are desperate.'

Unlike the men, who didn't show a strong preference for flirting alone or with a friend, the women preferred flirting alone. These are some seriously independent women! New York women who go out together have an understanding. If a cute guy wants to talk to your friend, you'll catch up with her later. Stockholm women have a different perspective. Thus, if they are in the market for a flirting encounter, they prefer to go out alone. As Eva, the press officer, explained, 'I don't want to alienate my friend. My attention would be on my friend if I go with her.' Johanna, the opera singer, agreed, 'I want to put my attention on one person, otherwise I will be talking with my friend.'

Stockholm women also preferred to approach men who were on their own. The reasons ranged from 'People are more themselves when they are alone,' to 'If they have a friend with them, you don't want to disturb them.' However, at least one male interviewee said that it would be more likely for a group of women than a group of men to go out and say, 'I want to get laid tonight'.

The Stockholm women like to hang with their homegirls, and are not interested in being disturbed, unless they so choose. If a Stockholm male wants to impress a woman, he must also impress her friends. And that, is not necessarily easy.

The men spoke of women being in close-knit groups. Andreas the brawny personal trainer said, 'If they are very tight in their group, you have to be special to approach them. Their friends will get bored and then want to go.' Bjorn, the doctoral student, also spoke of the perils of trying to break into a group of Stockholm women. 'If they are talking with their friends it puts more pressure on me because I have to compete and have an audience. It's more like a staged show. A lot of psychological things happen when you know you are being observed.' Hugo the accounts manager didn't seem to mind. He said, 'She will be more comfortable if she is with her friends and will feel that her friends are happy. If I like a girl,

I talk to her friends first.' And then, he makes his move. 'You have to be like a predator. Separate them from the flock.'

CONCLUSION

When on the prowl, New Yorkers mostly go out in single or mixed-sex groups, of two or three people, with the express interest of meeting new people. Parisians usually socialise with the same people with whom they went out. Mixing with strangers in Paris doesn't happen as a general rule, and when it does it's nowhere near as commonplace as in New York. In Paris, the groups are mixed sex to mask predatory intent. In fact, if a couple of guys were at a nightclub on their own, they would be viewed with suspicion. Unlike up-front New York, in Paris, if you have seduction in your sights, it's best you operate under-cover. The English also hunt in packs but they have a tendency to stick to those they know, either because their dance card is already full or they are too shy to make the first move.

This often adds to the level of difficulty when it comes to putting on the moves in London. Self-conscious Londoners prefer not to have any witnesses to their wooing yet because they go out in mixed-sex groups there's little chance of isolating their prey. The Stock-holmers' main prerequisite is that the object of their interest be alone because there is less pressure and it's less intimidating. For New York men, it's especially important to have a friend with you when flirting. Due to their competitive nature, the New York women weren't quite so convinced that flirting with friends around was a good idea. In Stockholm, it is common for girls to go out on their own as well as in groups of five to six women, just to enjoy each others' company, and if you want to impress, you'd better up your game!

FLIRT FILE

The benefits of flirting alone:
- Whether you prefer flirting alone or with a friend, the best scenario is realising the potential of both situations.
- Opportunities when you are alone are everywhere: an airport, at the supermarket, or even taking a stroll in the park is important.
- You can't have someone around all time acting as your security blanket, so start experimenting on your own.
- The good news is that when flirting around, there is no one to compete with, you are the smartest, funniest, and best looking!

The benefits of flirting with a friend:
- You don't have to worry about being regarded as Johnny no-mates.
- If you get nervous, your friend can fill in.
- You can swap objects of interest, if you find your original target is cuter from afar, and far from cute.

Who to go out flirting with?
- • Someone who is open and looking to meet others
- Preferably he/she is already in a happy relationship, so you get all the gold!
- Someone who is of your same attractiveness level, or even slightly less. If you are a mere mortal, don't be hanging out with models if you are trying to attract a man or woman.

How to conjure someone out of a group?

Method 1: (Used by an individual)
- Do not, I repeat, do not go up to the group on your own.
- The person will eventually have to leave the group to go to the bar, loo, etc. Use stealth and wait patiently for that moment.
- 'Magically' appear next to them.
- Use the contextual suggestions in the 'how to approach' section: i.e. Have you been served yet? Do you know where the restroom is?

Method 2: (Used by people in a group)
- Move your group in very close physical proximity to the other person's group
- When you are in close physical proximity to them, bump your chairs, hips, backs, etc. And say, 'I'm sorry, it's awfully crowded in here.' Follow up with another question or comment, 'Is it always so busy here? It's the first time I've been here.'
- Be close enough to jump into their conversation, if they look open and are having fun.

FRIENDS' FOLLIES

While people might not admit to employing certain flirting tactics themselves, they don't mind sharing their friends' follies. These different perspectives produced some interesting results. All the women interviewed described their friends in hot pursuit, shamelessly wielding their womanly wiles. Men described male behaviour ranging from effacing to downright offensive.

NEW YORK

Steve Martin wrote: 'In New York, one's sense of competition had to be practical: there was always someone doing better than you, always.' It should come as no surprise that New Yorkers didn't describe their friends' flirting in flattering terms. These kind of comments were typical. Men said they'd seen their friends:

'making an ass of themselves, overdoing it, not being subtle or relaxed', 'making fools of themselves'. The women, too, described their friends as 'making fools of themselves', 'making up stories to impress guys, 'hanging on every word', 'ignoring other friends' and 'becoming very good listeners' – as if they weren't before. Lisa, the credit card executive, summed up the New York attitude. When asked, 'What have you observed your friends doing while flirting?' she said, 'I've never looked at this. I think it's because I don't care. It's a big city and I am out for me.'

This is the land of 'bigger is better', the capital of capitalism. Here, the mating dance is exaggerated, magnified in a way which amplifies traditional gender roles. While the women of New York are as independent and competitive as the men, when it comes to attracting the opposite sex, the women fall back on their womanly wiles. Demure downcast looks, hair twirling and gentle touches on his shoulder are popular weapons in this charm offensive. They become very good listeners, expressing fascination with the other person. Their voices get higher, or deeper, and the talk more risqué. They smile and laugh more, giggling at a higher pitch in an excess of happiness. Emotions and body language are exaggerated. The women become more enthusiastic, more empathetic and more obvious that they are seeking attention. Femininity is also amplified. Alexis, the sharp-witted research assistant said of her friends, 'Some come on too aggressively to guys. There's a lot of physical contact and subliminal sexual actions'.

Smart and sassy Sarah, a fashion buyer, explained the thinking behind the strategy, 'Everyone is flattered by sexual attention, coyness, demureness.' These New York women channel Marilyn Monroe.

The men of New York also revert to their default alpha-male instincts, according to their friends' observations. Some said their friends would sit up tall and show off their size when trying to impress a girl. They '…sit up straight and thrust out their chests to enhance their size, make eye contact and hold it unblinkingly. They 'become more talkative and overeager', 'embellish stories, exaggerate, and show off". One woman, Rebecca in recruitment, said her friends' adopted a similar approach to the men and 'made up stories to impress guys'.

PARIS
According to their friends, some Parisian men seem to favour the romantic approach; others are pushy and direct, or manipulative. The women were provocative in their conversation and their body language, or demure and mysterious.

The Parisian men observed their friends, 'being very romantic', 'controlling the area, being protective of her'. Then there were those forceful men who didn't waste time or mince their words. Eccentric Olivier, who was unemployed and therefore could spend time working on his tan, said, 'My friends would be more direct. He would hit on her immediately.' Alexandre works in business tourism. He said of his friends, 'They try to force questions and make their way into conversation, try to converse, even following someone'. Greg, the communication student, admitted, 'Sometimes my friend could be 'heavy' and say 'Do you want sex''.

Parisian women described their friends:
- 'showing her best side and her best attributes, laughing, provoking the person'
- 'acting coy, physical contact and touching themselves, like tucking hair behind ear, touching self. Physical contact is a code someone likes you'.
- 'acting, feminine, glamorous, aware of their bodies, curves…shapes. Start playing with their bodies.'
- 'touching hair, wearing clothes which emphasise their best features'.

Like their Marilyn-Monroe-channelling New York sisters, when it comes to sexual attraction, Parisian women rely on the same old box of gender tricks. The touch hair, smile, pout, make eye contact, look shy, repeat as necessary, approach is strikingly similar to that employed by the women of New York to lure a man – the main difference being if the man doesn't get the hint in New York, the woman will walk right up to him and make sure he can't miss it!

Parisian women also channelled Greta Garbo. Unlike their New York sisters, Parisian women played mysterious and aloof. Charlotte, a 32-year-old editor described her observations, 'Some dance and look at the men. Especially when you are dancing and watching him, it's an invitation. French girls look discretely and wait.' Sandrine, 30, is a director's assistant with a sleek brown bob. She sees her friends 'Paying a little attention and then acting like they don't care.' Sometimes the women do such a good job at acting indifferent that even their friends find it difficult to tell whether they are interested in a particular man. As Isabelle the librarian said, 'My friends act shy, and wait for men to come up to them. I wouldn't be able to tell if she liked him back.'

LONDON
Without the aid of alcohol the London males described their friends as shy; also 'formal', 'not tactile' and 'less sexy'. Well, I guess they would know! Luckily, their wit and humour seems to make up for what they lack. And, if all else fails, just bump. When the London ladies fancy someone, they ignore their friends, act girly and demure, and 'get their boobs out' – with or without the aid of alcohol.

London women flirt with single-minded intent. 'They would separate themselves away from the group,' said Georgina, the secretary, about her friends. Claire, the red-headed accountant, observed her friends, '…shutting out everyone else and focusing on that one person they are after.' Annette the jazz singer said of her friends, 'They'd be zeroing in on the guy. Being elusive to everybody else and giving the guy all of their attention'.

London women rely on the same old bag of tricks as their Parisian and New York sisters. London lasses described their friends acting, 'bubbly, overtly flirty or demure.' They '…give shy and coy looks…' and '…flip their hair'. The women '…play up to the men and let them feel they are in charge.' Anoushka the solicitor, said, 'You can tell by the big eyes, smiles. They look up at the men, get all excited, and giggle a lot – quite suggestive, but innocently'. Once again, the clichés of femininity are exaggerated. Rachel, a 29-year-old illustrator described her friends, '…giggling, touching arm and knee, acting 'girly', flicking their hair and enhancing how they normally act.' Jane, who works in the financial industry, said of her friends, 'Their body language changes. They become coy and use their body more gracefully. They giggle a lot more, and laugh inanely at unfunny jokes. They tailor some of their answers so that they are more pleasing. They give answers that they think the guy would like to hear – answers from a lady.'

However, some of the women adopted a more direct approach. Mousy Mary the 28-year-old PA said, 'My more confident friends are quite full on…I know my friends are flirting when they use their bodies to their advantage'. She explained that when they did this it was a case of 'boobs out', 'move hips', 'show necks', and 'arch bodies'. Liz, an account manager for a big advertising agency, echoed these sentiments. She said her friend would, '…play with her hair, arching her body and showing the neck. We call her the shark because she goes up and talks to everybody'. Some women remarked on their friends' regressive behaviour when on the prowl. Rachel the illustrator has a friend, '…who is really rude to the one she fancies the most – like a teenager.' Emma, a gadgets presenter on late-night television described one of her friends '…hitting them like a teenager, sitting on lap'.

In their defence, London women often have to be direct, as the men are reluctant to reveal their interest. Like the Stockholm males, who don't want anyone to know what they are up to, the London lads also prefer to stay below the radar. If they don't, they never hear the end of it from their friends. Unlike the New York males who were most likely to put down their friends' efforts, the London men described their friends' attempts with typical English humour. However, that doesn't mean they wouldn't bust them for it! David, a recruitment consultant with a very expensive watch, said, 'My friends are self conscious about being busted for flirting.' Daniel, who manages a bar, agreed, 'If you cop on that your friend is flirting they get embarrassed'. Shyness engenders a formal approach, while alcohol suppresses inhibitions, and humour greases the wheels. Simon the PR exec said that it is one of two extremes with his friends, with alcohol as the differentiator. 'They are either forward and drunk, or quite reserved.'

The shy guys are at a bit of a loss. Take this friend of James the optician, for example. 'One of my pals stands next to the girl he is interested in, like a colonial discovering a hillside in Africa, and then doesn't do anything about it.' Anthony the chic IT geek acknowledged that 'Most of my mates are shy beasts. There'll be lots of furtive glances and not much action. Some take a stiff and formal approach.' Charlie the entrepreneur's friends are '…not emotional, not tactile. They have a reserved nature. They are less flamboyant, less sexy.' Sam the website designer has friends who '…will completely shut down and become shy.' Other friends adopt the full frontal attack: 'One friend routinely gets slapped because his idea of 'pulling' is to grab anything in sight'.

Some blokes use humour: Samuel the furniture maker said his friends '… would banter, use smiles, humour, self deprecation, wit'. Sam the website designer described his friends using: 'Physical playfulness. An edge to their humour. A certain degree of teasing. Christopher the ex-soldier used a martial metaphor: 'My friends would use humour – seek and destroy. They'd lock on to someone.'

Some London lads just get drunk and hope for the best. It works for this friend of Christopher's, the ex-military man: 'One of my friends would get completely pissed and stand in the middle of the dance floor hoping someone would take pity on him. It always worked. He slept with over 100 women.' Alistair the broadcast journalist has '…a friend who'll walk in the proximity of a girl. If she looks at him and says something he's in, if not, he can say, "I was just looking for something". This allows for a get out clause. Not worrying about being rejected or losing face.' And then there is the 'bump' technique. Duncan is a journalist: 'My mate bumps into someone to start a conversation. He offers drinks, cigarettes.' At least he bumps bearing gifts. James the optician also had friends who employed a similar technique. He would '…put his drink next to her and say, "Sorry, did I knock you?"' The 'bump' technique is also used, with less effect, on the dance floor. Contrary to popular belief, 'accidentally' bumping into a girl while she is dancing is not the best way to attract her interest.

Some London men seemed to have picked up their seduction skills from Mr Bean. Alex, who works in import/export, said 'A friend of mine has a special technique; he'll do something stupid in front of a woman. For example, he has burned a girl, spilled drinks, said silly things so she will think he is cute.' It seems there is a place for buffoonery in London flirting so faux clumsiness and daft comments may well warm a girl's heart but surely by burning her she is more likely to slap you than snog you?

STOCKHOLM
If you go off to buy a drink at the bar, come back, and find your friend is missing in action, the chances are he's flirting. Hugo, the 30-year-old accounts manager, said of one friend, 'He ignores me and disappears towards the woman.' Mattias, the MD, said 'He stops listening to me and watches her, especially during the spring in Stockholm,' which is presumably when the ladies emerge from winter's cocoon. Weather seems to play a role in the mating game in Stockholm. Annika, the pretty, petite nurse referred to her friends flirting, 'In the summer, maybe at a picnic'. Does this mean that her friends don't flirt for the other nine months of the year?

After first claiming they didn't do it, many Stockholm males said their friends were 'aggressive' flirters. Bjorn, the measured, PhD student, was a case in point. After insisting that he didn't indulge in 'aggressive flirting', he said, 'Most of my friends do... They walk right up to a woman they like and start talking'. This is the height of brashness in the sedate world of Scandinavian seduction. On the other side of the spectrum, Stefan admitted, 'I am shy. When I flirt I try to avoid eye contact.'

Like Stefan, most men were more subtle in their approach. Frederik, the 28 year-old student described his friend, '…moving closer to the subject, hanging around the vicinity. If it's too obvious what you are doing, you will fail'. So the men sidle up to the object of their affections. Stefan, the bicycle store owner, said, 'One friend stood next to a girl with his back turned to her, then turned around to begin talking.' Henrik the banker said of his friends, 'After speaking for awhile they'd give indirect compliments, such as, "But that wouldn't be a problem for you.".' Bjorn the student was particularly scathing about some of his friends' efforts. They do '…terrible, terrible things, like pretending they are interested in something really obscure, like she is, to try and get on her side. This is self-humiliation and lack of integrity. This is too obvious'. However, the problem with the subtle approach, as Per the virile Viking explained, is that 'Some get nervous or shy and people think they are stuck up. They also have the problem of thinking too much before they approach'.

Like the men, some of the women earn themselves the pushy label. Johanna, the opera singer said, 'Some of my friends are very straightforward. They go straight up to guys. They say. "There's an attractive guy, let's go talk to him".' Emile, the cautious accountant said, 'My friends are pushy. If they see someone they like they want to go over to him.'

Stockholm women, like their European and American counterparts, also employ the tender trap. Clare, the air-traffic controller, described her friends, '…acting more girly, not showing strong opinions, acting soft, not letting on what good jobs they have.'

Kristina, the global Human Resources manager said that her friends, '…accent their best side physically, like in the animal kingdom. They smile a lot, twist their bodies, use their bodies, giggle'. Mia is the buyer for a popular Stockholm gallery. She agreed, 'Women put out their breasts, act sweet and endearing, make him feel like he is the only guy in the room'. Eva, the press officer, said that her friends, '… throw their hair, act girly and female, seek his attention, pose using posture and body'.

CONCLUSION
In New York, a friend is not just a friend, but a potential competitor! The New Yorkers couldn't help but put their friends down. The picture they painted was of both men and women playing up traditional gender roles. The Parisian men said their buddies come on strong while the women said their girl friends provoke male desire with their body language. If that doesn't work, they simply ignore him. That ought to get his attention. London women can tell their friends were flirting if they employ feminine wiles and give their full attention to the guy. Like the women of Paris and London, Stockholm women also play up their girliness. The London males said their friends used a number of tactics, ranging from affability to annoyance. Max, the music publisher, described this diversity of approach, which '…ranges from ridiculous, macho, outrageous, exhibitionism to more sophisticated charmers'. However, London men don't want to be caught in the act.

FLIRT FILE

Your friends can help.

- Have your friend go up to the person you fancy and ask them to join your group. 'He likes you!' Yes, it worked when we were 10, and it still works now.
- If you are lacking in confidence, have your friend approach someone and ask the opening questions for you, 'Is it always this busy?' 'Do you know where the bar, cloakroom, restroom, is?'
- Have a pre-arranged signal with your friend so they can make themselves scarce if it's going well. And, you charmer, of course it will...

GETTING BOUNCED

It is impossible to study the human dynamics of flirting without exploring what underlies most flirting encounters – fear. Fear of rejection is often responsible for preventing flirting in the first place. While some people regard rejection as an efficient way of weeding out candidates unworthy of their affection, others feel that their self-worth depends on the approval of relative strangers. Eric, a Stockholm café owner, put it like this, 'If you are successful you have a higher market value. You feel more beautiful. If you fail, it means you are a loser and that hurts.' Is rejection an intensely crippling and emotionally draining experience, or is it just part of the flirting process?

How a person copes with rejection determines whether they are more or less likely to flirt in the first place. And, the more people flirt the more resilient they become to rejection. Because, after continually putting themselves in these situations to be rejected, they eventually realise a) they don't get rejected as much as they think they will b) yes, they were rejected, but it really didn't feel that bad. A whole in the earth didn't actually open up and swallow them whole. Peoples' motives for flirting also seem to affect attitudes towards rejection. Those who flirt to have fun, as a way to pass the time, or to make other people feel good, are less affected by rejection than those who flirt to find a partner, to feel attractive or to gain confidence. This is because in the case of the former, you are not trying to 'get' anything from the other person; they can't reject you if you haven't asked them for anything.

New Yorkers, Parisians, Londoners, and Stockholmers approach rejection differently. In cultures where people flirt as a matter of course, like New York and Paris, rejection doesn't seem much of a deterrent. Since the Parisians aren't really showing their real selves when flirting, but rather a constructed image, they don't regard rejection as a reflection on their self worth. In contrast, Stockholmers don't flirt much. Therefore, when they do, they take it seriously and rejection is more likely to affect them. This could be one reason why they have to drink before they make a move. Like the Stockholmers, fear of rejection grips Londoners like a rabbit in a car's headlights. As Alistair, the broadcast journalist, explained, 'English flirting traits are designed around not being rejected. You weren't rejected because you never tried.'

People with more self-confidence are more likely to flirt, because they don't let rejection affect them negatively. They attribute rejection to uncontrollable external factors rather than internal factors, for which they are responsible. Marie, a New Yorker, articulated this strategy, 'I blow if off. I will make an excuse for him like he has a girlfriend. Or I say it's his problem not mine.' Londoner Alex, one of the few London males who could effectively deal with rejection, summed it up with this attitude, 'If it's an external factor I keep trying, but if it's me, I walk away'.

The Londoners, Stockholmers and the Parisians most often said they would walk away if a flirtatious encounter was not proving fruitful. The majority (79%) of the New Yorkers, on the other hand, said they would keep trying.

NEW YORK

New Yorkers don't mince their words. They know what they want and they ask for it. This is a city where there is always something new around the corner, and it's very easy to strike up a conversation with someone else. This social fluidity and their coping mechanisms help New Yorkers deal with rejection. The New Yorkers have the advantage of being able to move on quickly. Since it's quite possible to speak to many people in an evening, they don't have to dwell on the one rejection. It is hard to get too depressed if, within the next ten minutes, you are happily chatting with someone new, who is more responsive.

Duncan the journalist, who spent time in the United States, observed, 'Americans are more persistent; they keep getting knocked back and try again. Round one, round two, etc. They are more ballsy, it's more of a game. They are more open. One group would go up to another group and say, "Excuse me ladies, but my friends over here bet me…" They have incredible self-confidence.'

And they need it. New York males expect to be rejected if they are trying to flirt with a beautiful woman, so they take it as par for the course.

New York men see beautiful women as a 'prize' to be pursued even though they realise that there's fierce competition and the threat of rejection high.

Mike, the good-looking banker, said 'Guys get blown out by the attractive women. The attention they constantly get must be mind blowing; the "How you doin'?" catcalls…'

It is also their competitive edge that helps New Yorkers brush off rejection as easily as a fake Gucci bag seller in Times Square. Nobody likes rejection but for New Yorkers 'Rejection is the same as losing. People have egos, emotions, desires, and by nature don't want to lose,' said Corey, the actor/fire-fighter who is as hot as the fires he fights. This explains why the New Yorkers are most likely to keep on trying, instead of walking away. Thus, in typical New York fashion they turn a loss into a win: 'Some people probably use that (rejection) as a tactic or game,' pointed out Chris, the environmental engineer. Andrew, the 34 year-old attorney, was one such person, 'I see it as a challenge. It sets you apart if you continue.'

In New York, the battle of the sexes is overtaken by the law of the jungle. In the concrete jungle, it is the strongest that prevail. As Lisa (33), who works for a large credit card company, explained, 'Whoever is the most resilient or who can get over being shut down quicker is the most powerful.' New York is ruled by the motto, 'If at first you don't succeed, pick yourself up and try again.' Actually, they don't ever have to pick themselves up because they don't ever let rejection get them down. One after another, they said they had nothing to lose. If they get a 'Yes', they get the ego boost and pass the personal test; if they get a 'No', they don't take it to heart, they simply don't hear it. They laugh it off, call the guy a jerk or the girl an idiot to their friends and then move on to the next victim. This, laugh, put-down, move-on formula was employed by both men and women. David the architect exemplified this optimistic persistence, 'I'll keep trying. When it's going red, you try and get back in the green zone.'

If his advances were not appreciated, entrepreneur Joel would 'Flirt with someone else.

Bash her to my friends by saying she was no good anyway.' In yet another instance of New York women employing the same tactics as the men, Dana, the pretty brunette analyst, responded, 'I will call him a jerk to my friends. There are other guys.'

New Yorkers take a philosophical approach to rejection; never give up on sex or your self-worth! Try these for size.

- 'If they don't like you, it's not the end of the world.'
- 'I tell a friend and give myself credit for trying
- 'Find someone who won't reject you.'
- 'There are plenty of fish in the sea. Don't take it personally. You have done it to others.'
- 'Next.'

PARIS

In Paris, where flirting is regarded as a game, people are more likely to flirt. Because they are not personally invested in this game, but rather playing prescribed roles, Parisian men are anything but thin-skinned when it comes to rejection. Parisian women decide whether the men's advances are welcome and thus are rarely in a position to be turned down themselves. Rejection is not a major factor in the Parisian flirting scene, it would seem.

The Parisian men love women. They love looking at women, talking to women, and being around women. Since they have the sole duty of approaching women, they have a lot of experience in the field of rejection. Fortunately, like the New York males, they also have coping mechanisms. Sartre would be proud.

- It's impossible to succeed each time.'
- 'I'm sad, but I say, "There will be another."'
- 'You just go for another woman. It's the Latin way'.
- 'Things happen as they should happen, and it they don't, that's life.'

Greg, a communication student, explained his philosophy, 'I've been rejected at clubs and bars. I'll say "Hey, how's it going?" They say, "I'm not interested". It's not a defeat because I did something nice, which people normally don't do. I give myself credit for trying.'

Mathieu, the hunky artistic director, takes a pragmatic approach to being rebuffed. 'I think at least it makes things clear. I move on to the next. It helps me to get over her because I don't become obsessed with women who don't want me.' Some Parisian men shrug off rejection; others simply avoid it. Alexandre works in business tourism. He said, 'I think I've been rejected, but I never let it get that far. If I feel it's not right from the start, I don't insist'. Laurent, the architect, also followed this line, 'It's because I stop at the first signs that it's not a flirt'.

Then there were the Parisian men for whom rejection was an exceptional occurrence. Nicolas, the project manager, recalled a singular instance, 'Once, a woman didn't want to give me her number, but I am not rejected normally.'

Likewise, Olivier, the out-of-work graphic designer, said, 'She told me "No", but it doesn't happen often.'

In Paris the men make the advances and the women decide the outcome. Thus, rejection didn't seem to be much of a concern for Parisian women. 'I haven't put myself in the position to be rejected,' said Sophie, a 34-year-old primary school teacher. 'I don't go first. I just give the signals', said Isabelle the librarian. Veronique, the PhD student agreed, 'They come to me, I don't go to them'.

But, since flirting in the Parisian mind is only a game, it is easier to not get personally attached to the outcome. As Martine, the logistics coordinator, mused, 'It depends if you look at flirting as a game or not. If it's only about trying to seduce someone, than it doesn't matter.'

LONDON

The idea of rejection was so intertwined with flirting that many London males listed one of the traits of a good flirt as 'not taking rejection seriously'. The London men didn't seem to have any coping mechanism other than wanting to be consumed by a black hole. They took negative responses very personally, and the feeling of rejection even overshadowed their ability to see the positive spin offs of putting themselves out there. 'I'll sometimes not do anything to avoid being rejected,' said Anthony, the IT guy. 'Rejection destroys the backbone of who you are. Your self concept can be challenged and destroyed in one comment', said Sam, the website designer, with dramatic flair. James the optician also takes these things hard. 'Rejection hurts; it's an inadequacy. That's me on the floor down there.' Lads, ease up! You are taking this way too seriously. This 'soul-destroying' rhetoric is a far cry from the New Yorkers' shrugging their shoulders and moving on.

Even when the men are getting positive signals, they still don't truly believe it.

Samuel, the furniture maker, said 'I can see that she is flirting, but I still don't entirely believe it.' 'Sometimes when a woman says nice things to me, I think it's because she feels sorry for me that I am old,' said James the optician, plucking on a very small violin. With attitudes like these, it is no wonder that the London males don't like to put themselves into flirty situations. They are so unsure of women's signals, that it is evident why London males like a woman to be obvious in her interest.

Another reason London males are so affected by rejection is the amount of emotional energy they expend in the act of walking up to someone. Rather than looking at approaching women like going to the shop and buying a pint of milk, to them, it's akin to trekking across the Himalayas on broken crutches.
Daniel the bar manager's response was symptomatic. 'You feel like you are risking a lot, you put yourself on the line.' David the recruitment consultant spoke with feeling, 'No one likes to be turned down. It hurts. It takes so much guts and determination to do it, to have someone turn around and say "No" is quite painful.'

This aversion to rejection seems directly proportional to the amount of importance London males place on strangers' opinions when determining their own self-worth.

Samuel, the cabinetmaker, said 'I don't want to be disliked by someone, especially by someone who doesn't even know me.'

'Rejection is not nice, agreed Sam the website designer. 'It knocks your confidence so it makes it harder next time. It's even worse if it's a stranger because you don't know them.' Conversely, 'It's the biggest compliment when someone whom you don't know, who has only known you for ten minutes, likes you. It's an indication you are doing something right,' said James the optician.

Shouldn't the fact that someone doesn't know you, mean it is easier not to be affected by their opinion?

The women were equally wary of rejection. They preferred the man to put his neck on the line. However, the women seemed better than the men at dealing with the cold shoulder. Many London women admitted they had never even been in a situation where they could, potentially, be rejected. Take Rachel, the children's book illustrator, for example. 'I am not normally on the aggressive side so it doesn't happen often.' She wasn't alone. Mary, the personal assistant, confessed, 'I've never gone out and tried. I will wait for them to make the first move.'

Alice, the investment banker, was equally wary, 'I am cautious and would only make an effort if I knew I would be successful.' 'I don't think I have ever taken that risk,' admitted Georgina the secretary.

However, there were women who did put themselves out there, and thus they have had to learn to deal with rejection. Strategies include sanguinity, equanimity and civility. Here's jolly Gemma, the television producer. 'I don't know why so many people are afraid of being rejected, because it doesn't bother me in a flirting situation. Flirting is supposed to be fun, after all.' Annette, the jazz singer, does not sing the blues. 'For many people their self worth is measured against others' appreciation of them. I found out it's not me that is the problem, it's their own insecurities.' In typical English fashion, Claire, the red-headed accountant, avoids rejection with the utmost courtesy. 'If something jars and I feel we're not on the same wave length, I will keep trying for politeness, but I will slowly back off'.

Not having had much experience in rejection herself, Emma, a bubbly presenter, explained the 'polite' way to do the rejecting. 'If someone is too interested in you, you have to use different techniques. In order to save face you have to continue to flirt but tone it down so they think you are just being charming and not really flirting. You have to back down gradually'. This pretty much sums up how Londoners flirt – or, rather, don't!

STOCKHOLM

To Stockholmers, rejection is even worse than 20 hours of darkness a day. At least they can turn a light on to dispel the wintry gloom. Bjorn, the 31-year-old doctoral student, explained, 'People are afraid to get depressed in Sweden. Sweden has one of the highest suicide rates. We all walk around with a protective shell and when it's penetrated, it hurts.' Henrik, the Stockholm banker living in London, used a fruit metaphor to explain the difference in national character, 'Swedish people are like coconuts, hard on the outside and soft on the inside. Americans are like peaches, soft on the inside with a hard centre.' While New Yorkers chalk up an unsuccessful encounter to good flirting practice, the Stockholmers don't take rejection so lightly. Clare, the air-traffic controller, was despondent, 'Every time someone rejects you, another piece of your self-esteem leaves,' while Johanna, the opera singer, was more pragmatic. 'You have to be open to flirt. If you are open there is a chance you will be hurt.'

Why are the Stockholmers so afraid of rejection? One reason could be because of the serious nature of both displaying and disdaining interest. Mia, the buyer for a gallery, said, 'Everyone wants to be loved. Since flirting is more serious in Sweden, it's a big deal if you are rejected.' The Swedish expression 'Jantelagen' forms the foundation of the Swedish national character. You must not think you are better than anyone else, may not stick out from the crowd or wear your heart on your sleeve. According to Frederik, the 28-year-old law student, this 'we are all the same' attitude could even mean that if one person doesn't like you, than no one will! 'I think, "Maybe if one girl hates me, then everyone else will too".'

Another reason why the men are so afraid of rejection is that some of the women of Stockholm can be quite caustic in spurning male advances. Personal trainer, Andreas the Buff, said, 'The rejections can be very harsh. It depends where you go in Stockholm, but some girls can be really severe'. Swedish women can be very straightforward', agreed Henrik the banker. 'They might even say "Go away" or "I'm with my friends. Do you mind?" According to Stefan, the 33-year-old bicycle store owner, 'It could be "Go away you stupid fuck." Rejection is very severe in Stockholm, especially by the ones who have grown up here. There's a social code that the girls should dis the guys who come up to them.'

Unsurprisingly, the women have a different explanation for spurning male attention. Their story, to which they were sticking, is that they reject men because they come on too strong. Said Jenny, the PhD student in biology, 'I can take "No" for an answer, but some guys can't, so rejecting becomes a self-defence mechanism for women'. They're not rejecting you. They just care about your feelings. 'It's hard to make them go away in a nice way,' admitted Kristina, the global HR manager. Eva, the press officer, revealed the secret to success, 'We have a lot of strong women and boys haven't figured out how to approach in the right way, which is to be a man and at the same time be a gentleman.'

So how to reconcile the impression that men are so fearful of rejection that they don't dare make a move with these descriptions of unrelenting pursuit? Perhaps a major culprit is alcohol. Hugo, an accounts manager, conceded, 'Sometimes I have been rejected if I am drinking too much.' This, clearly, had also happened to Frederik the law student. 'When you are drunk she gets nasty and puts you off.'

It's not only inebriated men who get the brush-off. When asked if she'd ever been rejected, Katarina the florist, answered, 'You mean like if their girlfriend comes over? Once his girlfriend came along, and a couple times I was too drunk, but I was rejected in a good manner.'

CONCLUSION
While the New Yorkers look at a rejection as a missed opportunity to shout, 'I'm number one' to the world, the Swedes view it as a long walk off a short plank. The Stockholmers don't take rejection – or seduction – so lightly. It seems one way to get enough courage in the first place, and to take the sting out of a potential rebuff, is to drink heavily. The Parisians are only playing a game and so can afford to be philosophical. To the English not having their interest reciprocated is worse than having a tooth pulled. This aversion to rejection may explain why London women insist so strongly that the men make the moves and why the men are more than happy for the women to give it a try. The way they overcome rejection puts New Yorkers in a league of their own. Both the men and women of New York

have a coping mechanism that helps them deal with rejection, whether it's something practical, like physically moving places, or emotional, like seeking comfort from friends. They don't let rejection reduce them to a puddle on the floor. They get straight back out there and try out their charms on someone else. Here endeth the lesson.

FLIRT FILE

- Flirting is a numbers game. You can't win them all.
- Rejection is only bad, if your attitude towards it is bad.
- Flirt more = feel rejection less. Think of it as an effective weeding out mechanism. We don't want everyone to like us; who has that much time?
- Does rejection come from internal or external factors? If you think you caused your own rejection because you aren't good enough, than rejection will affect you negatively. If you believe the rejection was due to circumstances outside your control, then you won't be affected by rejection.
- Ask yourself, why do I flirt? For my own self-esteem? To test myself? If you're in it for your ego, you're going to take some knocks. However, do you do it for fun? To make the other person feel good? When you are thinking of the other person, and trying to make them feel good, thoughts about rejection can't get in the way. You are not asking anything from anyone, so what is there to 'reject'?
- Don't let others dictate your own self-worth. Why let a stranger judge our merits? The best case scenario is that you know who you are, and like it! If other people would like to get to know you, great! If they don't, then they are not a good fit for you anyway.

Chapter 28: Flirting – The Conclusion
THE LOW-DOWN

We've looked at what it is, why we do it, how we do it, when we do it, and who we do it with – this act, which may be innocent or sexual, sincere or manipulative, used to get what you want, or to help you find a partner. Part of the reason flirting might get a bad rap, is that its uses are far reaching, and it certainly is not a case of one-size fits all. So, what can we conclude?

A FUNDAMENTAL HUMAN NEED
Fundamentally, flirting fulfils a core need for humans to feel accepted and attractive. Everyone wants to feel they belong. However, a culture's attitude towards flirting varies. Some are wary of it, and have even changed the name of what they do, from flirting, so as not to be tainted by association. Other cultures think of it as just good fun. While you might not flirt with illicit intentions, it is the sexual undertones, which makes the interaction flirting. Without the undertone, then it's not flirting! It is being friendly, or charming. Ask the London lasses. Along with sexual undertones, what also separates flirting from other interactions is the emphasis on gender. Flirting is playing on the fact that 'I am a boy and she is a girl.' The flirting in Paris is sexually charged, because they play on their perspective genders. Conversely, this could also explain why the flirting is considered 'boring' in the egalitarian society of Stockholm.

SOCIETAL EXPECTATIONS AND INDIVIDUAL PREFERENCE
Flirting draws upon and highlights gender differences. Yet societal expectations and individual preference proved more of an influence on flirting behaviour than did biology. Men and women in the same cultures were more likely to have the same opinions on flirting, and engage in similar behaviours, than did the genders across the different cities studied. If biology were the main influencer of behaviour, than the women of Stockholm and Paris would share similar answers when, in fact, most of their attitudes towards flirting were polar opposites. Yet, however, the men and women of Stockholm shared very similar views.

As much as it was necessary to generalise in the conclusions, individual preference should not be discounted. For example, some men enjoyed women being the pursuers, just as some women preferred to make the moves - another indicator that men and women are much more similar than they are different. And, more examples of how individual preferences, rather than biology alone, influence behaviour.

GENDER EQUALITY AND STEREOTYPES
How much the people in a society are expected to adhere to gender roles is in direct proportion to that society's level of gender equality. Admittedly, the sample size for this comparison is low, because there are not many countries in the world where women have such a high level of equality. However, the parallel cannot be denied when comparing Stockholm, a culture which does not stick to gender roles and has high levels of equality (both gender and economic) and Paris, which sticks very firmly to gender roles and does not seem to have very high levels of equality. How does this affect the flirting? The tendency of a culture to adhere to gender roles, determines how the flirting is displayed. Therefore, in the cultures which stress gender differences, the flirting is more sexual, spicier, with added

frisson. In cultures which don't stress differences, well, there doesn't seem to be much flirting.

In the case of gender roles, specific rules of behaviour might make people feel comfortable, like such stringency often does, however it doesn't make for happy and healthy individuals. Men and women are both guilty of the collusion. Contrary to current belief, women are actually doing themselves a disservice by insisting the men stay in the traditional roles of doing the initiating, chasing, and proposing in the relationships. And, if you adhere to these rules, don't expect an equal partner out of it. If he does do things such as initiating, chasing, and proposing, it should be because he really likes you (and you like him too) but not because he is 'the man'.

Unfortunately for women, when these roles are adhered to, it's undoubtedly the women who lose out the most. When marking the boundaries of men being men and women being women, it's the men who are in the position of power and decision making. However, that's not to say they aren't repressed as well in this scenario. What if he really has a penchant for romantic comedies, and might even shed a tear at the end? If he is having to adopt strict gender roles, he's not allowed to do either, or at least not without ridicule or his manhood being called into question. Or, even worse, what if he would love nothing more than to be a stay-at-home dad, but instead must trudge off to work day after day because that's what expected of him. Or, what if his stay-at-home wife, looks at him every day with resentment because she would love for the chance to be out in the working world again - she loves her kids dearly, but they are really driving her crazy! Unlike the punishing slogan women had to adhere to in the 80's that she could 'have it all', women are slowly becoming used to the idea that you can't have it all - unless you don't mind losing your mind.

In the case of women, there seems to have been some progress in balancing the gender scale. And, as this study focused on the age group of 28-40, it will be interesting to see how these roles continue to flux for upcoming generations. Undoubtedly, Women's roles are becoming less rigid. It is becoming more accepted for them to take on high-powered jobs, and choose lifestyles different to traditional expectation, such as wanting to be single or deciding not to have children. The same does not seem to be true for men. If a man dares to be 'unmanly' by staying home with the kids, earning less money than the women, or admitting to liking romcoms, then his 'manhood' is challenged. Men don't seem to be allowed as much fluidity, from both women, and society in general, on the gender continuum.

Granted, it is much harder allowing people to be themselves than it is to label them. If a woman is head of a company and does her own carpentry on the weekends, than she isn't 'acting like a man'; she is just being herself. If a man stays home with the kids, admits to eating a pint of double chocolate ice-cream after his yoga class, he's not acting 'girly'; he is just being himself. It is only when both genders can be as they are, rather than playing at the gender roles expected of them, that people can be truly fulfilled and society enriched.

ABOUT THE AUTHOR

Since graduating with a masters in social anthropology from London's School of Oriental and African Studies, Jean Smith has dedicated her 15 year long career to the study of human attraction, making a name as one of Britain's leading experts in the field of flirting and attraction.

Originally from Iowa, USA, Jean first made her mark as the go-to flirting guru for numerous radio and television stations in the UK. Since then, she has become a spokesperson on broader social issues and has worked with prestigious brands (including Johnson & Johnson, Unilever and Stella Artois) as a corporate advisor into human behaviour, relationships and body language.

Having secured her status as relationships pro, Jean launched her brand Flirtology in 2004 to deliver light-hearted, savvy advice on the (social) science of attraction. Through personal coaching lessons and interactive seminars, Jean reveals her 'three methods of flirting attack' theory. However, it's her flirting and walking tours around London and Chicago which have really got singletons talking to strangers in a completely new way.

www.flirtology.co.uk
twitter.com/flirtology